OUTDOOR ADVENTURES

ACADIA NATIONAL PARK

YOUR GUIDE TO THE BEST
HIKING, BIKING, AND PADDLING

Jerry and Marcy Monkman

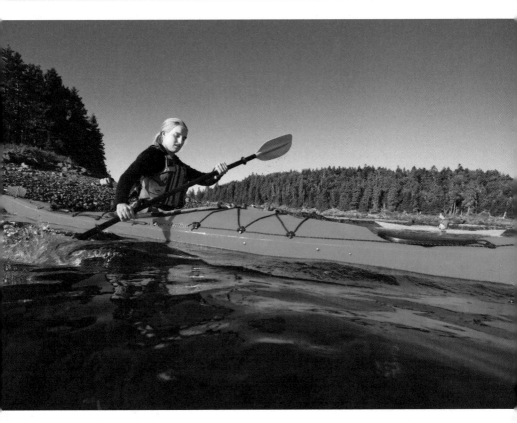

Appalachian Mountain Club Books
Boston, Massachusetts

AMC is a nonprofit organization, and sales of AMC Books fund our mission of protecting the North-east outdoors. If you appreciate our efforts and would like to become a member or make a donation to AMC, visit outdoors.org, call 800-372-1758, or contact us at Appalachian Mountain Club, 5 Joy Street, Boston, MA 02108.

outdoors.org/publications/books

Distributed by National Book Network.

Front cover photographs (from top, left to right) of sea kayaking near Sheep Porcupine Island, biking near Jordan Pond, and climbing the Beehive © Jerry and Marcy Monkman/EcoPhotography.
Back cover photographs (from top) of Schoodic Peninsula © Jerry and Marcy Monkman/EcoPhotography and of the beach at Acadia © Frank Crociata.
Interior photographs © Jerry and Marcy Monkman/EcoPhotography
Maps by Ken Dumas © Appalachian Mountain Club
Cover design by Kim Thornton
Interior design by Abigail Coyle

Library of Congress Cataloging-in-Publication Data
Names: Monkman, Jerry, author. | Monkman, Marcy, author.
Title: Outdoor adventures, Acadia National Park : your guide to the best hiking, biking, and paddling / by Jerry and Marcy Monkman.
Description: Boston, Massachusetts : Appalachian Mountain Club Books, 2017. | Includes index.
Identifiers: LCCN 2017000047 (print) | LCCN 2017012963 (ebook) | ISBN 9781628420586 (ePub) | ISBN 9781628420593 (Mobi) | ISBN 9781628420579 (pbk.)
Subjects: LCSH: Hiking--Maine--Acadia National Park--Guidebooks. |Cycling--Maine--Acadia National Park--Guidebooks. | Canoes and canoeing--Maine--Acadia National Park--Guidebooks. | Acadia National Park (Me.)--Guidebooks.
Classification: LCC GV199.42.M22 (ebook) | LCC GV199.42.M22 A3258 2017 (print) | DDC 796.510974145--dc23
LC record available at https://lccn.loc.gov/2017000047
The paper used in this publication meets the minimum requirements of the American National Standard for Information Sciences-Permanence of Paper for Printed Library Materials, ANSI Z39.48-1984. ∞

Interior pages contain 30 percent post-consumer recycled fiber.
Cover contains 10 percent post-consumer recycled fiber.
Printed in the United States of America, using vegetable-based inks.

MIX
Paper from
responsible sources
FSC
www.fsc.org
FSC® C005010

10 9 8 7 6 5 4 3 2 1   17 18 19 20 21

To all the photographers who devote their lives
to telling conservation stories with pictures

ACADIA NATIONAL PARK LOCATOR MAP

BAR HARBOR MAP

CONTENTS

3. QUIETWATER PADDLING IN ACADIA NATIONAL PARK   127

4. SEA KAYAKING THE WATERS OF MOUNT DESERT ISLAND   157

5. THE OTHER ACADIA: SCHOODIC PENINSULA AND ISLE AU HAUT   189

Essays

Appendices

AT-A-GLANCE TRIP PLANNER

	TRIP NUMBER	TRIP NAME	MAP	DIFFICULTY	DISTANCE AND ELEVATION GAIN	ESTIMA…
👣	**HIKING IN ACADIA NATIONAL PARK**					
	1	Conners Nubble	Eastern District	Easy	3.4 mi, 300 ft.	2 hrs
	2	Flying Mountain	Western District	Moderate	1.2 mi, 275 ft	45 min
	3	Great Head and Sand Beach	Eastern District	Moderate	1.8 mi, 200 ft	1 hr
	4	The Bubbles	Eastern District	Strenuous but short	1.6 mi, 550 ft	1.5 hrs
	5	Gorham Mountain and Ocean Path	Eastern District	Moderate then easy	3.5 mi, 500 ft	2 hrs
	6	The Beehive and the Bowl	Eastern District	Strenuous, with ladders	1.3 mi, 450 ft	1 hr
	7	Bar Harbor to Sand Beach	Eastern District	Moderate	4.7 mi, 100 ft	2 hrs
	8	Beech Mountain	Western District	Moderate	2 mi, 700 ft	1.5 hrs
	9	Norumbega Mountain	Eastern District	Strenuous	3.5 mi, 700 ft	2.5 hrs
	10	Huguenot Head and Champlain Mountain	Eastern District	Moderate, with one short, strenuous section	3.3 mi, 1,100 ft	2.5 hrs
	11	Pemetic Mountain and Bubble Pond	Eastern District	Strenuous then moderate then easy	4.1 mi, 950 ft	2.5 hrs
	12	Acadia and Saint Sauveur Mountains	Western District	Strenuous	3.7 mi, 1,050 ft	3 hrs
	13	Penobscot and Sargent Mountains	Eastern District	Strenuous	5.3 mi, 1,300 ft	3.5 hrs
	14	Western Mountains: Mansell and Bernard	Western District	Strenuous, with ladders on Perpendicular Trail	4.2 mi, 1,350 ft	3.5 hrs
	15	Peak Bagger's Delight: Bald Peak, Parkman Mountain, Gilmore Mountain, and Sargent Mountain	Eastern District	Strenuous	4 mi, 1,500 ft	3.5 hrs
	16	Dorr Mountain, the Gorge, and Sieur de Monts Spring	Eastern District	Strenuous, with a few ladders	4 mi, 1,500 ft	4 hrs
	17	Cadillac Mountain	Eastern District	Moderate	7 mi, 1,500 ft	4 hrs

TRIP HIGHLIGHTS	PUBLIC TRANSPORT	FAMILY	DOGS	X-C SKIING	SNOWSHOEING	SUP	PHOTO OPS	TRAIL RUNNING
A flat, easy carriage road walk followed by a short hike up to great views	✓	✓	✓			✓	✓	✓
A short hike to nice views of Somes Sound		✓	✓			✓	✓	
A beach walk followed by a wooded climb to the cliffs of Great Head	✓	✓					✓	
Great reward for a short hike	✓	✓	✓			✓	✓	
A moderate hike to a walk along a dramatic coastline	✓	✓	✓			✓	✓	✓
A challenging climb to spectacular views and a mountain pond	✓						✓	
A walk from Bar Harbor that includes mountain and ocean views	✓	✓	✓				✓	✓
An enjoyable hike over rocky ledges to the summit of Beech Mountain		✓	✓				✓	✓
A quick climb to views of Somes Sound	✓		✓					
A classic Acadia hike up steep pink granite to extraordinary mountain and ocean views			✓			✓	✓	✓
A strenuous hike to some of Mount Desert Island's most spectacular views	✓		✓			✓	✓	
A strenuous hike through a beautiful pitch-pine forest to the best views of Somes Sound	✓	✓	✓			✓	✓	
A strenuous hike with long periods of hiking on open ledges with magnificent views	✓					✓	✓	
A peaceful yet strenuous hike to the highest peaks on the western side of the island						✓		✓
A challenging hike over four peaks, including Sargent Mountain, Acadia's second highest peak	✓		✓			✓	✓	✓
A challenging hike to spectacular views and a narrow gorge	✓						✓	
A relatively long hike over open ledges with sustained great views	✓	✓	✓			✓	✓	✓

TRIP NUMBER	TRIP NAME	MAP	DIFFICULTY	DISTANCE AND ELEVATION GAIN	ESTIMA
18	Northeast Harbor to Eagle Lake via Sargent Mountain	Eastern District	Strenuous	8 mi, 1,800 ft	5 hrs
19	Bar Harbor to Jordan Pond via Dorr, Cadillac, and Pemetic Mountains	Eastern District	Strenuous	10 mi, 2,900 ft	6 hrs
20	Eastern Side Traverse: Sand Beach to Northeast Harbor	Eastern District	Strenuous, with ladders on Beehive Trail	11 mi, 2,500 ft	6.5 hrs

🚲 BIKING IN ACADIA NATIONAL PARK

21	Maple Spring–Hadlock Brook Loop	Eastern District	Easy	4 mi, 350 ft	1.25 hrs
22	Hio Fire Road	Western District	Easy	4 mi, 100 ft	1 hr
23	Witch Hole Pond and Paradise Hill	Eastern District	Easy	4.4 mi, 350 ft	1.25 hrs
24	Seal Cove Pond–Western Mountains Loop	Western District	Easy	5 mi, 150 ft	1.25 hrs
25	Long Pond Fire Road	Western District	Easy	5.5 mi, 250 ft	2 hrs
26	Amphitheater Loop	Eastern District	Moderate	5.5 mi, 350 ft	2 hrs
27	Echo Lake to Seal Cove Pond	Western District	Moderate	12 mi, 400 ft	2 hrs
28	Aunt Betty Pond Loop	Eastern District	Moderate	6 mi, 300 ft	1.5 hrs
29	Eagle Lake Loop	Eastern District	Moderate	6 mi, 350 ft	2 hrs
30	Bar Harbor to Ocean Drive Loop	Eastern District	Moderate	11.5 mi, 300 ft	2 hrs
31	Bar Harbor to Jordan Pond via Eagle Lake	Eastern District	Easy	8.3 mi, 200 ft	2 hrs
32	Day Mountain	Eastern District	Moderate	8 mi, 500 ft	2.5 hrs
33	Jordan Pond–Bubble Pond Loop	Eastern District	Moderate	9 mi, 500 ft	2.5 hrs
34	Giant Slide Loop	Eastern District	Difficult	8.5 mi, 600 ft	2.5 hrs
35	Around the Mountain Loop	Eastern District	Difficult	12 mi, 1,000 ft	4 hrs
36	Around the Mountain Loop II	Eastern District	Difficult	18.7 mi, 900 ft	5.5 hrs

TRIP HIGHLIGHTS	PUBLIC TRANSPORT	FAMILY	DOGS	X-C SKIING	SNOWSHOEING	SUP	PHOTO OPS	TRAIL RUNNING
Wide-open ridge hiking combined with scenic shoreline walks	✓		✓		✓		✓	✓
A strenuous hike starting with a walk from Bar Harbor to three of Acadia's four highest peaks	✓						✓	✓
A traverse of the eastern half of Mount Desert Island to some of Acadia's best known features	✓						✓	✓
A relatively easy ride to a 40-ft. waterfall and a visit to Upper Hadlock pond	✓	✓	✓	✓	✓		✓	✓
An easy ride for the family on a dirt road in prime bird-watching habitat		✓	✓					
An easy ride through beaver ponds and bogs to great views		✓	✓	✓	✓			✓
An easy ride through a boreal forest frequented by moose		✓						
An easy ride on a dirt road to a secluded cove on Long Pond		✓						
A ride through an evergreen forest past streams lined with pink-granite stones	✓	✓	✓	✓	✓			✓
A ride through spruce woods, from Echo Lake to Seal Cove Pond	✓	✓						
A ride with views of Sargent Mountain and Eagle Lake, with the chance to see beavers	✓	✓	✓	✓	✓			✓
A great ride for families through rich woodlands, with good views from Eagle Lake	✓	✓	✓	✓	✓		✓	✓
A road bike ride from Bar Harbor to scenic Ocean Drive	✓						✓	
A scenic bike ride from Bar Harbor to Jordan Pond	✓	✓					✓	✓
A ride up a mountain to great views of the ocean islands	✓	✓	✓	✓	✓		✓	✓
A moderate ride next to spectacular scenery	✓	✓	✓	✓	✓		✓	✓
A ride over rushing mountain streams to fantastic ocean and mountain views	✓		✓	✓	✓			✓
This ride has it all: waterfalls, mountain and ocean views, and 7 major bridge crossings	✓		✓		✓		✓	✓
A long ride through gorgeous forests and scenic ponds	✓		✓	✓				✓

QUIETWATER PADDLING IN ACADIA NATIONAL PARK

Trip Number	Trip Name	Map	Difficulty	Distance	Estimated
37	Little Long Pond	Eastern District	Easy	1.25 mi	1 hr
38	Echo Lake	Western District	Easy	1.5 mi	1 hr
39	Jordan Pond	Eastern District	Easy	2.5 mi	2 hrs
40	Long Pond: South End	Western District	Easy	3 mi	2 hrs
41	Seal Cove Pond	Western District	Easy	4.5 mi	2.5 hrs
42	Northeast Creek	Eastern District	Moderate	5 mi	2.5 hrs
43	Eagle Lake	Eastern District	Moderate	4 mi	3 hrs
44	Long Pond: North End	Western District	Strenuous	7.5 mi	4 hrs

SEA KAYAKING THE WATERS OF MOUNT DESERT ISLAND

Trip Number	Trip Name	Map	Difficulty	Distance	Estimated
45	Mount Desert Narrows	Ocean	Depends on weather conditions	6 mi	3 hrs
46	Frenchman Bay and the Porcupine Islands	Ocean	Depends on weather conditions	6.5 mi	3 hrs
47	Sutton and Bear Islands	Ocean	Depends on weather conditions	6 mi	3 hrs
48	Somes Sound	Ocean	Depends on weather conditions	7.5 mi	4 hrs
49	Seal Cove to Pretty Marsh	Ocean	Depends on weather conditions	10 mi	7 hrs
50	Cranberry Isles	Ocean	Advanced	12 mi	7 hrs

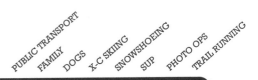

TRIP HIGHLIGHTS	PUBLIC TRANSPORT	FAMILY	DOGS	X-C SKIING	SNOWSHOEING	SUP	PHOTO OPS	TRAIL RUNNING
A short and easy paddle on a most picturesque pond		✓	✓				📷	
A short paddle beneath towering cliffs and a chance to see peregrine falcons		✓	✓			✓	📷	
A pleasant paddle on an incredibly scenic pond		✓	✓				📷	
A paddle beneath the steep cliffs of Beech and Mansell mountains		✓	✓					
A paddle on the westernmost pond, with good opportunities to see waterfowl and bald eagles		✓	✓			✓		
A quiet paddle on a narrow creek through extensive wetlands and prime wildlife habitat		✓	✓			✓		
A paddle on a beautiful lake with mountain views and wild shorelines		✓	✓				📷	
A long and popular paddle that explores wooded coves		✓	✓			✓		

TRIP HIGHLIGHTS	PUBLIC TRANSPORT	FAMILY	DOGS	X-C SKIING	SNOWSHOEING	SUP	PHOTO OPS	TRAIL RUNNING
A relatively sheltered paddle in shallow waters								
An exciting paddle around the beautiful and wild Porcupine Islands							📷	
A paddle past a remote lighthouse and a sea arch with great views of mountains							📷	
A paddle in the only fjord in the eastern United States							📷	
A paddle filled with wooded shoreline, beautiful islands, and bountiful wildlife								
An all-day paddle to historic islands with excellent views of mountains							📷	

PREFACE

Sweeping mountain views, rugged ocean scenery, and abundant wildlife all contribute to the splendor that is Acadia National Park. Acadia's 50,000 acres stretch from Isle au Haut in the southwest to the Schoodic Peninsula in the northeast. The heart and soul of Acadia, however, is Mount Desert Island, a place of scenic pink-granite mountains, deep glacial ponds, cobblestone beaches, and oceanside cliffs. Bald eagles, ospreys, and peregrine falcons patrol the skies while seals, porpoises, and seabirds fish the cold waters of Frenchman Bay and beyond. Mount Desert Island is the third-largest island in the continental United States and boasts such natural wonders as Somes Sound, the only fjord on the East Coast, and Cadillac Mountain, the highest point on the North Atlantic seaboard.

While it is the dramatic scenery that lures most visitors, it is the more intimate moments in Acadia that become a part of those who visit here: listening to the steady sound of the surf in Monument Cove on a quiet morning in June, inhaling the delicious smell of pitch pine along a rocky trail on a warm September day, or watching in surprise as a harbor porpoise surfaces next to your kayak on a calm August afternoon. Although your experiences in Acadia most likely will be different from ours, our hope is that this book will help you discover your own special moments in Acadia.

Formerly titled *Discover Acadia National Park,* this revised edition has incorporated dozens of changes in the park, including new hiking trails, the rerouting of some existing trails, new Island Explorer bus stops, and the new park service facilities recently opened in the Schoodic section of the park. This is the most complete and accurate multisport guide to Acadia National Park out there!

ACKNOWLEDGMENTS

We wrote the first edition of this book way back in 2000, and it has been a joy to keep going back year after to explore Acadia National Park and find the big and little changes that have found their way into each new edition. Over the course of those years, we have had conversations with probably dozens of individuals whose stories and insights about Acadia have no doubt influenced our work on this guide and other projects. We do want to specifically thank a few people who helped us out with *Outdoor Adventures: Acadia National Park*. As always, the personnel of the National Park Service were invaluable to us, and we extend a big thank you to Gary Stellpflug, Charlie Jacoby, Wanda Moran, and Karen Anderson. We also want to thank Glen Tucker at Coastal Kayaking and Chris Strout at Acadia Stand Up Paddleboarding for their help on the paddling sections of the book, and Wendy Lull and Dan DenDanto at the Seacoast Science Center who helped us update our interpretation of humpback whale science.

Of course, we could not have made this revision without the expert guidance of AMC Books, specifically Kevin Breunig, Jennifer Wehunt, Abigail Coyle, Emily Nason, and our excellent editor, Shannon Smith. As always, we want to thank both the Monkman and Wolin families for continuing to unconditionally support us in our careers as writers and "ecophotographers." Lastly, we would like to dedicate this book to our children, Quinn and Acadia, whose enthusiasm for the outdoors constantly reminds us of the wonders of Acadia National Park.

STEWARDSHIP AND CONSERVATION

Acadia National Park consistently ranks as one of the ten most visited national parks in the United States. With 2 million visitors entering the park every year, it sees the same amount of use as much bigger parks, such as Yellowstone and Yosemite.

ACADIA'S HISTORY AS A NATIONAL PARK

In 2016, Acadia celebrated is centennial, having been established in 1916 as Sieur de Monts National Monument by then president Woodrow Wilson. The new park consisted of 6,000 acres donated to the government by the Hancock County Trustees of Reservations, which had been established 15 years earlier to conserve land on Mount Desert Island. By 1919, the park had grown to 9,000 acres and was renamed Lafayette National Park. In 1929, the name was changed to Acadia National Park, which now protects more than 50,000 acres on Mount Desert Island, several smaller islands, and the Schoodic Peninsula.

LEAVE NO TRACE

With such a large number of people enjoying Acadia's limited and fragile resources, everyone must remember to help protect the park. It is imperative everyone learns and adheres to the seven Leave No Trace principles:

1. Plan Ahead and Prepare

When going into Acadia's backcountry (those parts accessible only by hiking trails,) plan an outing you know everyone in your group can finish. Be prepared for unexpected events by having extra food, water, and clothing. A well-planned day will prevent the need for an unnecessary night out in the woods, where you may be forced to build fires and trample delicate vegetation. Keep your group size to ten or fewer, splitting into smaller groups if necessary. Try to avoid travel in wet and muddy conditions, and use extra care when in Acadia's delicate subalpine zone.

2. Travel and Camp on Durable Surfaces

Camping in Acadia's backcountry is prohibited. When hiking, make every effort to stay on trails and rocks. When you are on a trail, look for blazes and cairns, and stay in the center of the trail, even when it is wet and muddy. That's what your boots are for! Trails are hardened sites where use should be concentrated. Avoid contributing to the widening and braiding of trails. Hiking off-trail into pristine areas is allowed, but it requires great understanding and diligence. First, consider if hiking off-trail is necessary. If you decide to hike off-trail, do it only on durable surfaces, such as rock, gravel, or grasses. Spread out your group, take different routes, and avoid places where unofficial "social" trails are beginning to develop.

3. Dispose of Waste Properly
Pack out everything you bring in. This includes any and all food you may drop while eating. Urinate at least 200 yards from any water source and pack out your used toilet paper in an odor-proof bag. To dispose of solid human waste in the backcountry, dig an individual "cat hole" at least 200 yards from a trail or water source. Organic topsoil is preferable to sandy mineral soil. Your hole should be 4 to 8 inches deep and about 6 inches in diameter. After use, mix some soil into the cat hole with a stick and cover it with the remainder of the soil. Disguise the hole by covering it with leaves or other brush. It is especially important in Acadia not to pollute near streams, rivers, lakes, and ponds, many of which lead to town water sources.

4. Leave What You Find
Leave all natural and historical items as you find them. Of particular concern to park naturalists is moving rocks, large and small, to build rock cairns or sculptures, which detract from the natural and scenic qualities of the landscape. Moving rocks wreaks havoc on the environment, causing soil erosion and destroying vital habitats for small plants and animals. Building unauthorized cairns is also a safety concern, as an improperly located cairn can cause hikers to get lost. There is much human history in and around Acadia in the form of American Indian shell heaps and arrowheads, as well as stone walls and old cellar holes from early European settlements. It is illegal to disturb any such cultural artifacts in the park. It is also illegal to move or take home natural features of the park, whether they are wildflowers, rocks, beach cobbles, or animal parts, such as feathers or antlers. The only exception is that you are allowed to pick fruit, nuts, and berries for personal consumption. Taking pine or spruce cones, mushrooms, fungi, and fiddlehead ferns is prohibited.

5. Minimize Campfire Impacts
Campfires are allowed only in designated fire pits in campgrounds and picnic areas.

6. Respect Wildlife
Remain quiet while in the backcountry and give animals enough space so they feel secure. If you notice wildlife changing their behavior, it is most likely because you are too close. In that case, back off and give the animals space. Avoid nesting or calving sites, and never attempt to feed any wildlife—not even seagulls or those cute little red squirrels. When kayaking, do not land on any island that has an active seabird colony or nesting bald eagles. To verify the location of any such islands, check with the National Park Service before your paddle. Remember that wildlife are residents of the intertidal zone, too. Do not remove starfish, sea urchins, or

other creatures from their natural habitat. For low-impact wildlife-watching tips, visit Watchable Wildlife's website, watchablewildlife.org.

7. Be Considerate of Other Visitors
Stay quiet. Refrain from using cell phones and radios. When hiking, take rests on the side of the trail (on a durable surface) so that other hikers do not have to walk around you. When paddling, remember that sound carries a long, long way. You must keep your dog on a leash while in the park. Dogs are not allowed on Sand Beach, Echo Lake Beach, or on trails with ladders.

You can learn more about the Leave No Trace Center for Outdoor Ethics by visiting the Leave No Trace website at lnt.org or by writing LNT Inc., P.O. Box 997, Boulder, CO 80306.

TRAIL MAINTENANCE
It takes a huge amount of work to keep hiking trails and carriage roads in good condition. Volunteering to help with trail maintenance is a great way to give back to the park. The Appalachian Mountain Club (AMC) offers several one-week Volunteer Vacations in Acadia National Park in the summer. See outdoors.org/volunteer for details. Friends of Acadia also runs a volunteer trail-maintenance program in conjunction with the national park. Currently, maintenance is scheduled for Tuesdays, Thursdays, and Saturdays from June through October. For more information, call Friends of Acadia at 207-288-3340 or the National Park Service at 207-288-3338. AMC's Echo Lake Camp (amcecholakecamp.org or 207-244-3747) also leads trail-maintenance trips twice a week in season.

MORE CONSERVATION OPPORTUNITIES
Get involved in trails and river stewardship, land protection, or conservation advocacy on a regional level by joining a conservation or recreation organization. Contributions to such organizations are key to the success of their missions. You can also get involved on the ground. AMC is a conservation and recreation organization that offers opportunities to:

- Maintain trails near you as part of a volunteer trail crew or as a Trail Adopter.
- Participate in hands-on air- and water-quality research through the Mountain Watch program at AMC backcountry destinations.
- Patrol White Mountain ridges in the summer as an Alpine Steward and help raise awareness of the public's impact on rare and fragile alpine environments.
- Support the Maine Woods Initiative, AMC's effort to promote conservation, recreation, sustainable forestry, and community partnerships in Maine's 100-Mile Wilderness region.

You can also join AMC's Conservation Action Network (CAN) and help increase public influence on critical conservation issues. Learn more at outdoors.org/can.

INTRODUCTION TO ACADIA NATIONAL PARK

It's hard to say exactly what draws so many people to Acadia, although the juxtaposition of granite-clad mountain peaks overlooking the deep blue waters of the Atlantic Ocean probably doesn't hurt. With mountains next to the ocean, Acadia gives visitors the chance to participate in almost any outdoor activity they can dream up, all with spectacularly scenic rewards. Of course, the mountains of Acadia are modest, even by New England standards, with the tallest peak, Cadillac Mountain, reaching a height of only 1,528 feet. Nonetheless, hiking is probably the most popular park activity, as most of the summits are treeless and provide spectacular views of the surrounding bays and islands. Trails vary from easy, ocean-side walks to steep, cliff-side climbs up iron ladders. Biking is also a popular activity in the park, particularly on the scenic system of crushed-gravel carriage roads built by John D. Rockefeller Jr. in the 1920s and 1930s. Thousands of years ago, glaciers left behind numerous deep lakes and ponds that now give visitors the opportunity to canoe, kayak, or stand-up paddleboard below the rocky scenery of the mountains. Over the past twenty years, sea kayaking has become one of the premier activities of more adventurous visitors to Acadia National Park. Sections 2 through 4 give detailed descriptions of hiking, biking, and paddling trips, from one-hour excursions to all-day adventures, with suggestions for winter activities included.

Other activities, such as rock climbing, birding, and whale watching, give the outdoor enthusiast plenty of alternative ways to experience Acadia. See the appendixes for information about participating in these other vacation adventures. The rest of this introductory chapter provides some basic information you can use to get started on your visit to Acadia National Park and Mount Desert Island.

GEOGRAPHY

Acadia National Park is located on the Maine coast, about 150 miles northeast of Portland, Maine's largest city. The park is composed of several different parcels that total more than 50,000 acres in size. The vast majority of the park is located on Mount Desert Island, a large island accessible by car via a causeway that connects it to the mainland in Trenton. About half of Mount Desert Island is part of the national park, with the remainder of the island home to several small fishing villages (Southwest Harbor, Northeast Harbor, Bass Harbor, and Bernard) and the town of Bar Harbor, which is where most of the tourism services on the island are located. A visit to Acadia usually involves travel through one or more of these villages on your way to exploring different areas of the park.

In addition to Mount Desert Island, Acadia protects approximately 2,000 acres of land on the Schoodic Peninsula (about a 45-minute drive northeast from Bar Harbor) and several thousand acres on numerous offshore islands. The largest of these offshore islands (and the only one with park services) is Isle au Haut, which is a 35-minute boat ride from the village of Stonington (itself a 1.5-hour drive west from Bar Harbor).

CLIMATE

Acadia has a typical New England coastal climate. Cold, wet conditions are common, but so are sunny and warm days. In general, Acadia's climate is no problem for the outdoor adventurer who comes prepared for unexpected weather. Spring is often foggy, with daytime temperatures ranging between 30 and 70 degrees Fahrenheit, and nighttime lows in the upper 20s to low 50s. Summer is mild, with daytime temperatures usually in the 70s and 80s. Summer evenings are cool, especially when there is a sea breeze, and with ocean temperatures in the 50s, any activity on the water requires an extra layer of clothing. Fall in Acadia varies from subfreezing temperatures at night to warm days in the 70s. Rain and fog are common, but so are perfect, clear leaf-peeping days. Winter is cold, with daytime temperatures usually in the 30s, though colder days are certainly possible, and lows ranging to below zero. Acadia averages 61 inches of snow per year.

GETTING THERE

Bar Harbor and Acadia National Park are located 45 miles southeast of Bangor, Maine, the closest city to the park with commercial air service. From Bangor, drive east on Alternate Route 1 to Route 3 in Ellsworth. Following Route 3 south will take you to Mount Desert Island, the landmass on which most of Acadia National Park is located. The entrance to Acadia National Park is off Route 3 in Hulls Cove, just north of the town of Bar Harbor. Several airlines and bus lines provide regular service to Bangor, and during the summer months, Down East Transportation (downeasttrans.org) provides bus service from Bangor and Ellsworth to Bar Harbor. Once you are on the island, you can take advantage of the park's free bus system, Island Explorer, from late June through early October.

ISLAND EXPLORER BUS SYSTEM

One of the best things to happen to Acadia since the release of the first edition of this guidebook in 1999 is the introduction of the Island Explorer bus system. Using the Island Explorer opens up a whole new array of hiking and biking opportunities that lets you explore the park without having to spot a car (or to use a car at all), and it's a great way to leave no trace. This system of propane-powered buses can help you to avoid spending your vacation hunting for parking spots at crowded trailheads. Six of the routes can be boarded at the Village Green in Bar Harbor. These routes go to Blackwoods and Seawall campgrounds, Sand Beach and Otter Cliffs, Jordan

Pond, Eagle Lake, the villages of Northeast Harbor, Southwest Harbor, Bass Harbor, and Tremont, private campgrounds, and many places in between. There is also a bus around the Schoodic Peninsula. Best of all, the buses are free! The system runs only during the busy summer months and into early fall, and the schedule changes from year to year based on current funding levels, so check with the National Park Service or Downeast Transportation before planning your trip. For a schedule, contact Downeast Transportation at 207-667-5796 or visit exploreacadia.com.

LODGING

There are three National Park Service campgrounds in the national park: Blackwoods, Seawall, and Schoodic Woods. Blackwoods is open year-round, while Seawall is open from late May through September, and Schoodic Woods is open from late May until Columbus Day. Reservations for all three campgrounds can be made online at recreation.gov or by calling 207-288-1300. The towns of Bar Harbor, Northeast Harbor, and Southwest Harbor are full of inns, hotels, bed-and-breakfasts, and private campgrounds. A complete listing of these can be attained by calling the local areas' chambers of commerce; see barharborinfo.com, acadiachamber.com, and mountdesertchamber.org for more information. AMC's Echo Lake Camp offers tent-based lodging, group meals, and daily activities led by volunteers. A weeklong stay is usually required. Visit amcecholakecamp.org or see the sidebar following Trip 38 for details.

FOOD

Restaurants are located throughout the island, with the biggest selection in Bar Harbor. The Hannaford on Cottage Street in Bar Harbor is the island's largest grocery store. A and B Naturals, on Cottage Street in Bar Harbor, has a good selection of health foods. In Southwest Harbor, you can buy groceries at the Southwest Food Mart IGA on Main Street.

NATIONAL PARK SERVICE INFORMATION

First-time visitors to Acadia National Park should begin their visit by stopping in at the Hulls Cove Visitor Center on Route 3, 3 miles north of the Village Green in Bar Harbor. Here you can pick up a schedule of ranger-led events, talk to a park ranger about your visit, and pick up fliers and books about Acadia. The Hulls Cove Visitor Center is open daily from April 15 through October 31, from 8:30 A.M. to 4:30 P.M., with extended hours (8 A.M. to 6 P.M.) from mid-June through Labor Day. During the winter months, visitors should check in at the park headquarters on Route 233, west of Bar Harbor. For preplanning, visit nps.gov/acad. You can also request information about the park before your visit by writing to the National Park Service at Acadia National Park, P.O. Box 177, Bar Harbor, ME 04609, or by calling 207-288-3338.

HOURS AND FEES

There are fees for accessing Park Loop Road, which runs within the National Park boundaries, as well as fees for using the park campgrounds. All park visitors are required to pay an entrance fee from May through October. In 2016, a one-week pass for entrance to the park for a private vehicle and its passengers was $25. Individuals visiting on foot or by bicycle can buy a one-week pass for $12. An Acadia annual pass is $50 and is valid for 12 months from the date of purchase. These fees can change and there are usually several days each year where entrance to the park is free. An up-to-date listing of current fees and fee-free days can be found at nps.gov/acad/planyourvisit/fees.htm. Camping fees at Blackwoods, Seawall, and Schoodic Woods range from $15 to $40 per site, per night. Always call ahead for the latest hours and fees.

ACCESSIBILITY

Throughout this book, we use the word "accessible" to indicate that a trip or a trail accommodates wheelchairs and other mobility aids. Most park facilities, including the visitor center and campgrounds, are accessible to those who use mobility aids. When exploring the backcountry, the park's carriage roads are the best option since these roads, which are closed to motorized vehicles, tend to have level, firm surfaces. The two most level sections of the carriage roads can be reached from Eagle Lake and Bubble Pond. (Note: There is no parking at Bubble Pond during the summer months, but it can be accessed via the Island Explorer bus.) Wildwood Stables, near Jordan Pond, also has accessible horse-drawn carriage rides. For more information, the park service offers an accessibility guide at nps.gov/acad/planyourvisit/accessibility.htm. You can request to receive the accessibility guide via mail by calling the park at 207-288-3338.

WINTER ACCESS

Acadia is a beautiful place to visit in winter, and while the park is open, most park facilities like bathrooms, changing rooms, and picnic areas are closed. A limited number of campsites at Blackwoods Campground remain open for primitive camping from December through March; campers must obtain a permit from park headquarters on Route 233. Park Loop Road is typically closed from December 1 through April 14, with two exceptions that remain open year-round: the Ocean Drive section between Schooner Head Road and Otter Cliff Road, and the section from Route 3 in Seal Harbor to Jordan Pond. A limited number of hotels and restaurants on the island remain open during the winter months. Cross-country skiing is popular on the park's carriage roads, and carriage roads are groomed for skiing in some sections when snowfall exceeds 4 inches. Snowshoeing can be done on many of the hiking trips in this guide, and we have noted those trips best suited to winter hiking. Trail conditions are often icy and dangerous, though, so be prepared to turn around if you do not have sufficient gear (crampons are often needed) or winter trail experience. Fat-tire biking is not allowed on groomed portions of the carriage roads in winter, but it is permitted on those portions of the carriage roads with snowmobile access, as well as on Hio Road and the Long Pond fire road. Since many trailheads in the park are located on state highways and village roads, they remain accessible by car during the winter months. However, those along Park Loop Road are not, except for those near Jordan Pond and along Ocean Drive.

EMERGENCIES
All injuries that happen in the park should be reported to a ranger. In the event of an emergency, immediately dial 911. Other important phone numbers include the following:

- Bar Harbor Police (nonemergency calls): 207-288-3391
- Mount Desert Police (nonemergency calls): 207-276-5111
- Southwest Harbor Police (nonemergency calls): 207-244-7911
- Maine State Police, Orono Barracks: 800-432-7381
- Acadia National Park (nonemergency calls): 207-288-3338
- U.S. Coast Guard Emergency: 207-244-5121

CHOOSING YOUR TRIP
The dozens of hiking, biking, and paddling trips included here provide a variety of outdoor experiences. For the purposes of this book, we use the word "trip" to mean a specific outing or adventure; for example, hiking Conners Nubble (Trip 1). Our hope is that you combine and enjoy many such trips during your greater visit to Acadia National Park. Before heading out on the trail or on the water for a specific trip, decide what you're looking for: beachcombing, mountain views, wild-life-watching, etc. You should also decide how strenuous a trip you and your group are willing and able to complete. The At-a-Glance Trip Planner that follows the table of contents offers an easy-to-digest listing of all the trips in this book, including difficulty, length, and highlights. Once you narrow down your choices, read the detailed trip descriptions in the individual chapters to get a better idea of what a given trip entails and what you might encounter. Hikers interested in trails other than those detailed in the Hiking chapter can read through a complete listing of trails in Appendix A.

HIKING

HIKING IN ACADIA NATIONAL PARK

Hiking through Acadia's forests to its storied rocky coasts or its bare mountain summits has been a popular activity since the mid-1800s. With more than 100 miles of maintained trails providing access to almost every corner of the park, it is possible to explore ocean cliffs, rocky gorges, quiet mountain ponds, and wide-open granite mountaintops with spectacular views of both forest and ocean. During a hike in Acadia, you may spot bald eagles and peregrine falcons flying overhead, deer and beaver feeding in and around ponds, or loons and harbor seals swimming in the Atlantic. While most of Acadia's trails are short, creative trip planning can make for some enjoyable extended hiking. This chapter suggests twenty hikes that are, in our opinion, some of the most scenic in the park. For some trips, we have combined several trails into one hike. For others, we have included walks on the park's carriage roads and dirt fire roads, as well as on Park Loop Road. A complete listing of trails can be found in Appendix A.

HIKING TIMES AND TRAIL RATINGS

Our hiking times are estimates based on our experiences as average hikers carrying 15 to 30 pounds of gear. Obviously, these times can vary according to the weather, the physical-fitness level of your group, and how much gear you stuff into your pack. While we think these times are useful for planning a trip, your hiking times undoubtedly will differ from ours. Distances listed are the round-trip mileage, and elevation gains are calculated using data from AMC's Acadia National Park Map, which can be found in the pocket on the inside of the back cover of this guide. We have adopted the National Park Service's system for rating trails, which uses a scale of easy, moderate, strenuous, and ladder. Easy trails are suitable for families with kids of any age. Moderate and strenuous trails can be fun for older children who have experience hiking steep and rocky trails. Expect a strenuous trail in Acadia to be similar to climbing a very steep staircase with large and uneven steps. Trails with ladders have at least one section of climbing iron rungs that are driven into granite cliffs, which is exactly what it sounds like: climbing a ladder on the side of a mountain. These can be challenging and fun trails, but they are also frightening for small children or people with a fear of heights. It is illegal to bring a dog on a ladder trail, and you should consider your dog's fitness level before bringing him or her along on any hike.

Facing page: A hiker on Cadillac Mountain.

SAFETY AND ETIQUETTE

Its mild summer climate makes Acadia an enjoyable and relatively safe hiking destination. Of course, bad weather or poor planning can spoil any hiking adventure. Before heading into Acadia's backcountry, consider the following tips:

- Leave your plans with a friend or, if you are on vacation, with a staff person at the lodge or campground where you are staying.

- Select a trip that is appropriate for everyone in the group. Match the hike to the abilities of the least capable person in the group.

- Plan to be back at the trailhead before dark. It's always OK to end a hike without reaching your destination, but it's never OK to push the group too far. Determine a turnaround time and stick to it—even if you have not reached your goal for the day.

- Check the weather. Wet weather can make Acadia's granite very slick, and high winds and pelting rain can make the summits an uncomfortable place to be. Avoid trails with iron rungs and ladders in the rain, as they become very slippery and dangerous when wet. You can get a current weather forecast from the local radio station WDEA's weather line: 207-667-8910.

- Bring a pack with the following items:

    ✓ Water: Two quarts per person is adequate, depending on the weather and length of the trip. Be sure to bring a water purification method for longer trips.

    ✓ Food: Even for a short hike, it is a good idea to bring some high-energy snacks, such as nuts, dried fruit, or snack bars. Bring a lunch for longer trips.

    ✓ Map and compass: Be sure you know how to use them!

    ✓ Headlamp or flashlight with spare batteries and light bulb.

    ✓ Extra clothing: Rain gear, a wool or fleece sweater, a hat, and mittens.

    ✓ First-aid kit, with adhesive bandages, gauze, and nonprescription painkiller.

    ✓ Sunscreen.

    ✓ Pocketknife.

    ✓ Waterproof matches and a lighter.

    ✓ Insect repellent: Mosquitoes are always present in Acadia during the warm weather months. Be aware that blackflies can be a significant nuisance in July and August.

    ✓ A trash bag.

- ✓ Toilet paper.
- ✓ Binoculars for wildlife viewing.

- Wear appropriate footwear and clothing. Wear wool hiking socks and comfortable, sturdy hiking boots that are waterproof and give you good traction and ankle support. Bring rain gear even in sunny weather, since unexpected rain, fog, or wind is possible at any time in Acadia National Park. Avoid wearing cotton clothing, which absorbs sweat and rain, making for cold, damp hiking. Polypropylene, fleece, silk, and wool are all good materials for wicking moisture away from your body and keeping you warm in wet or cold conditions.

- In addition to practicing the no-impact, Leave No Trace techniques described in this book's introduction, it is also a good idea to keep the following things in mind while hiking:

  - ✓ Try not to disturb other hikers. While you may often feel alone in the wilderness, wild yelling or cell phone usage undoubtedly will upset another person's quiet backcountry experience.

  - ✓ When you are in front of the rest of your hiking group, wait at all trail junctions. This avoids confusion and keeps people in your group from getting lost or separated.

  - ✓ If you see downed wood that appears to be purposely covering a trail, it probably means the trail is closed due to overuse or hazardous conditions.

  - ✓ If a trail is muddy, walk through the mud or on rocks, never on tree roots or plants. Wearing waterproof boots will keep your feet comfortable, and by staying in the center of the trail you will keep the trail from eroding into a wide "hiking highway."

For the most part, Acadia is not a frightening place to be. Cool, quiet forests and tranquil ocean views are the norm. When hiking, expect an enjoyable time and keep your senses tuned to your surroundings. Every one of the trips in this chapter passes through two or more different natural habitats, adding variety to every outing. Don't expect to see eagles and bears and moose on every hike. But by paying attention to details such as a rare alpine flower on Saint Sauveur, the jack pines on Cadillac, or the salamanders in a forested wetland, you can finish a hike with a satisfying sense of wonder.

The following hikes will take you from the shores of Sand Beach to the summit of Cadillac Mountain. You will encounter forests shaped by fire, people, and nature. You will hike through valleys and over hills created deep within Earth before being pushed up by earthquakes and scoured by glaciers. Eagles, falcons, and hawks will soar overhead, and warblers will fill the forest with birdsong. If you have visited Acadia before, you may find some new and interesting hikes you have yet to try.

If you are new to the park, you should find the trips described in this book to be a great way to explore this special place.

FLAT AND EASY WALKS

While many of Acadia's trails consist of steep hikes with rough footing, a few are flat and easy but still worthwhile destinations. In midsummer, these trails do attract the crowds; however, early mornings and evenings tend to be less busy than the middle of the day.

Shore Path

This 1.5-mile path conveniently starts in downtown Bar Harbor. It begins on the shoreline at the pier of the Bar Harbor Inn, next to the parking lot at the municipal pier. From the path, you can look out over the harbor toward Bar Island, the Porcupine Islands, and Schoodic Peninsula. You will also get a good view of the most impressive homes in Bar Harbor. The path ends at Hancock Street, which will lead you back to Main Street.

Dorr Point

This small parcel of Acadia in Bar Harbor, adjacent to Compass Harbor, was once the property of the first superintendent of Acadia National Park, George Dorr. From the parking lot on the east side of Route 3, a mile south of the Bar Harbor Village Green, follow the hiking path into the woods. Turn left at either of the first two trail junctions for a short walk (0.5 mile) to the coast and views of Frenchman Bay and nearby Bald Porcupine Island.

Ocean Path

This trail (which is also part of the Gorham Mountain hike, Trip 5) is an easy walk from Sand Beach to Otter Point. It provides an up-close experience with the shoreline of Acadia over the course of about 2 miles. There are cobble beaches and tide pools to explore, as well as Thunder Hole and Otter Cliffs. The soothing sounds, smells, and sights of the Atlantic Ocean are so captivating, you hardly notice nearby Park Loop Road.

Jordan Pond Path

This trail's 1.5 miles on the east side of Jordan Pond are flat with relatively good footing. Look for mergansers and loons on the pond as well as peregrine falcons on the cliffs of Penobscot Mountain. This is an especially good destination for children. Please note the portion of this trail on the west side of Jordan Pond has extremely difficult footing and is rated as a moderate hike.

Jesup Path

Close to Bar Harbor, this easy, nearly 1-mile-long walk passes the beaver ponds of the Great Meadow and through hemlock and mixed hardwood forests. It also passes by Sieur de Monts Spring, home of the Abbe Museum, specializing in American Indian history; the Wild Gardens of Acadia; and the Acadia National Park Nature Center.

Wonderland
Located between Seawall Campground and the Ship Harbor Nature Trail on Route 102A, the Wonderland area can be explored via a gravel fire road that takes you to a cobble beach in about 0.5 mile. From the beach, you can see the Duck Islands to the southeast and Great Cranberry to the northeast. This is a good place to bring kids for beach and tide-pool exploration.

Ship Harbor Nature Trail
This trail leaves Seawall Road 1.5 miles from Seawall Campground and provides ocean views from the western side of Mount Desert Island, including the tidal currents at work as Ship Harbor empties into the Atlantic only to be filled back in a few hours later. It is flat, 1.3 miles long, and the first 0.3 mile is wheelchair accessible.

TRIP 1

CONNERS NUBBLE

NPS Rating ➤ Easy

Distance ➤ 3.4 miles

Elevation Gain ➤ 300 feet

Estimated Time ➤ 2 hours

Map ➤ AMC's Acadia National Park Map: D6

This easy carriage-road walk leads into a short hike up to 360-degree views of Eagle Lake and Cadillac Mountain.

DIRECTIONS

From the intersection of Route 3 and Route 233 in Bar Harbor, take Route 233 west toward Cadillac Mountain. After 2.1 miles, you will see two parking areas for the carriage road, one on the right and one on the left. The parking area is stop B on the Island Explorer Brown Mountain route (route 6). *GPS coordinates: 44° 22.648′ N, 68° 15.141′ W.*

TRIP DESCRIPTION

Conners Nubble provides excellent views for little effort, with much of the hike following a carriage road next to Eagle Lake. From the carriage road, a short ascent into the woods is relatively easy but makes a great adventure for young children. The summit is typical Acadia: a pink-granite dome, devoid of trees and providing views in all directions.

If you parked on the north side of Route 233, turn left on the carriage road, which soon passes under Route 233. Go straight at post 6. If you parked on the south side of Route 233, go right on the carriage road and turn left at post 6. About 100 yards past post 6, stay to the left at post 9. The carriage road rises gradually through tall spruce trees on its way to views of Eagle Lake and Cadillac Mountain about 0.5 mile from the parking area. Soon afterward, the forest transitions to a mosaic forest (see "Acadia's Mosaic Forest" on page 14). At 1.3 miles from the parking area, you will see Eagle Lake Trail on the left. Turn here and follow the trail about 100 yards then turn right on Bubbles Trail.

Bubbles Trail makes for a moderate 0.4-mile hike up to the summit of Conners Nubble, which rises above a stand of short, shrub-sized paper birch trees to reveal a dome of pink, lichen-encrusted Cadillac granite. Low-bush blueberries grow wherever enough soil has collected in the cracks in the granite. There are excellent views of nearby Cadillac and Pemetic mountains, as well as the waters of Frenchman Bay and Mount Desert Narrows to the east and north. To the west looms Sargent Mountain, and directly below the summit is the sparkling blue water of 3-mile-long Eagle Lake.

Eagle Lake was the site of some of the first efforts to conserve land on Mount Desert Island in the early twentieth century. The deep, clean lake serves as a public water supply for the town of Bar Harbor. When a wealthy summer resident began plans to build a home on the lake, island residents became concerned that the development could compromise the water supply. By 1913, George Dorr had acquired most of the land around Eagle Lake and nearby Jordan Pond for the Hancock County Trustees of Public Reservations, and the land subsequently became part of the park when it was established in 1916.

Since this is an out-and-back trip, retrace your steps to the parking area after enjoying the views from the summit. If you like what you've seen so far and want to make a longer day out of it, consider the strenuous hike from Northeast Harbor to Eagle Lake described in Trip 18.

Eagle Lake, as seen from Conners Nubble, is the largest freshwater lake in Acadia National Park.

TRIP 2

👪 🐕 🔖 📷

FLYING MOUNTAIN

NPS Rating ➤ Moderate

Distance ➤ 1.2 miles

Elevation Gain ➤ 275 feet

Estimated Time ➤ 45 minutes

Map ➤ AMC's Acadia National Park Map: F4

This short hike leads to good views of the water surrounding the entrance of Somes Sound.

DIRECTIONS

From the intersection of Routes 102 and 198 in Somesville, follow Route 102 south for 5.4 miles to Fernald Point Road. Turn left (west) onto Fernald Point Road. The Fernald Cove parking area is on the left, 0.9 mile from Route 102. There is no direct access to this trailhead via the Island Explorer. The closest stop is Smugglers Den (stop F, about 2 miles from the trailhead) on the Southwest Harbor route (route 7). *GPS coordinates: 44° 17.936' N, 68° 18.871' W.*

TRIP DESCRIPTION

Flying Mountain stands as a sentinel at the southern end of Somes Sound, jutting out into the water at a point that almost closes off the entrance to the sound. At 284 feet tall, Flying Mountain is more a hill than a mountain, but it provides good views for a small amount of effort. This hike loops over the mountain to Valley Cove, a protected tongue of water that laps up against 500 vertical feet of rock known as Eagle Cliff. For only 45 minutes of work, this hike has a lot to offer.

Start this hike on Flying Mountain Trail, which begins on the west side of the Fernald Cove parking area. The trail, marked with blue blazes, climbs moderately through a pure spruce forest. Recent trail work has shored up the eroded path here with a series of rock and wooden steps. You will reach the summit fairly quickly, 0.3 mile from the parking lot. There are views of the south end of Somes Sound and out to Greening, Sutton, and Bear islands as well as the Cranberries. Cadillac and Norumbega mountains are also visible across the sound.

About 0.3 mile beyond the summit, a side path leads to the right, toward an overlook with more views of the sound and the large houses of Northeast Harbor. Flying Mountain Trail leads to the left then descends steeply to Valley Cove. This is a place where you can explore tide pools and gaze up at the steep walls of Eagle Cliff. The cove is one of the safest places on Mount Desert Island for boats to drop anchor in big storms, as Flying Mountain extends into Somes Sound far enough to prevent large storm swells from making their way into the cove.

As you follow the shoreline, look for a path on the left, just after climbing a set of wood-and-gravel steps. Valley Cove Trail leads right, toward Acadia Mountain, but to complete this hike, turn left then left again when the Flying Mountain Trail reaches a gravel fire road in a few yards. Follow the fire road through a mature forest of spruce and cedar. The parking area is 0.6 mile from Valley Cove.

Though one of the lowest peaks in the park, Flying Mountain offers excellent views of Somes Sound.

TRIP 3

🚌 🚶 📷

GREAT HEAD AND SAND BEACH

NPS Rating ➤	Moderate
Distance ➤	1.8 miles
Elevation Gain ➤	200 feet
Estimated Time ➤	1 hour
Map ➤	AMC's Acadia National Park Map: E8

This beach walk segues into a wooded climb to the 145-foot cliffs of Great Head, overlooking the Atlantic Ocean.

DIRECTIONS

From downtown Bar Harbor, drive south on Route 3 for 2.1 miles and turn right at the Sieur de Monts entrance to Park Loop Road. Follow the signs for Sand Beach. The Sand Beach parking area is on the left, 3.25 miles south of the Sieur de Monts entrance. The parking area is stop C on the Island Explorer Sand Beach route (route 3) and stop D on the Loop Road route (route 4). *GPS coordinates:* 44° 19.783′ N, 68° 11.058′ W.

TRAIL DESCRIPTION

This hike starts at Sand Beach and climbs east to the cliff outlooks along Great Head: a peninsula of granite, basalt, and sedimentary rock. The cliffs are as high as 145 feet and provide a dramatic perspective for watching the wildlife plying the waters below. This loop hike returns to Sand Beach, which is composed of small grains of quartz and pieces of clamshells, blue mussel shells, and green sea urchins.

From the Sand Beach parking area, walk down the stairway that leads to Sand Beach. Walk east across the beach, which is about 300 yards long, to the beginning of Great Head Trail. A stream cuts through the beach just before the trail. Depending on the tide and the season, the stream can be completely dry or a couple of feet deep. Be prepared to ford the stream, as there is no bridge. The current is not strong, so the crossing is easy, but you will want to wear waterproof boots or sport sandals because the bottom is rocky. The stream can be an interesting place to study the rocks that exist beneath the beach, as the water tends to carry the sand here to the ocean. Pink granite, dark basalt, and brownish sedimentary rocks give the stream a multicolored appearance.

Great Head Trail begins by climbing a short stretch of granite steps, at the top of which is an old millstone. Turn right here and start a moderate climb over granite slabs. Keep an eye out for blue blazes painted on the rocks, as the footpath is not always obvious. The trail levels out and reaches a "T"-shaped trail junction about 0.2 mile above the beach. It can be a little confusing because all three trails are part of the Great Head Trail. For this hike, turn right (south), descending to the right, into the woods, and on to an overlook with views of Sand Beach, Gorham Mountain, and the Beehive.

From this overlook, the trail follows the coast to the left (northeast) and gradually climbs over rocky cliffs before reaching the high point of Great Head, marked by the stone foundation of an old teahouse. The small gazebo-like structure was part of the estate of Louisa Satterlee, who in 1910 received Great Head and Sand Beach as a present from her father, the financier J.P. Morgan. The teahouse was destroyed in the great fire of 1947, and the Morgan property was donated to the park two years later. Great Head is the highest point on the coast of Mount Desert Island. The entire walk over these cliffs is out in the open, with the sights and sounds of the ocean on the right. Open ocean is due south, while the mouth of Frenchman Bay and Schoodic Peninsula are to the east. To the west are Otter Cliffs, probably named for the otterlike sea minks seen here until they became extinct in the

With lifeguards on staff, south-facing Sand Beach is perfect for families.

mid-nineteenth century. The rocky shoal between Great Head and Otter Cliffs is called Old Soaker and is a favorite hangout for seabirds. The cliffs are a good place to sit and watch for porpoises, seals, gulls, terns, guillemots, and common eider ducks. In the fall and winter, common loons can be seen here as well.

From the top of Great Head, follow the trail north, then northwest, as it descends back into a forest of spruce. At the next trail junction, continue straight as the forest changes into a mix of white birch, aspen, and balsam fir. About 0.5 mile from Great Head, the trail reaches a junction with a narrow dirt service road. Turn left onto the service road, which seems much more like a woodland path than a road. In 0.3 mile, the road completes the Great Head loop at the millstone you passed at the beginning of the hike. To finish your hike, go down the stairs to Sand Beach and walk back to the west end of the beach.

TRIP 4

THE BUBBLES

NPS Rating ➤	Strenuous but short
Distance ➤	1.6 miles
Elevation Gain ➤	550 feet
Estimated Time ➤	1.5 hours
Map ➤	AMC's Acadia National Park Map: E6

This short but irresistible climb summits Jordan Pond's distinctive mountains.

DIRECTIONS

From the Hulls Cove Visitor Center, drive south on Park Loop Road for 6.3 miles. Be sure to continue straight at the intersections marked "Sand Beach" and "Cadillac Mountain." The Bubble Rock parking area will be on your right. The parking area is a by-request-only stop between stops C and D on the Island Explorer Jordan Pond route (route 5). *GPS coordinates:* 44° 20.461′ N, 68° 15.023′ W.

TRIP DESCRIPTION

The Bubbles are two well-rounded granite hills standing at the northern end of Jordan Pond, home to loons and mergansers. Their shape and location are so distinctive, it is hard to imagine Jordan Pond without them. At 766 feet and 872 feet, they are far from the tallest mountains in the park, but they do provide good views of Jordan Pond and the taller surrounding peaks. South Bubble also is home to perhaps the best-known rock in the state of Maine: Bubble Rock.

This hike starts at the Bubble Rock parking lot, about 1.1 miles south of Bubble Pond on Park Loop Road. From the parking lot, follow Bubbles Divide Trail west for a short distance; continue straight where it passes the Jordan Pond Carry. The footpath is wide and level as it passes through one of the few true northern hardwood forests on the island. Birch and American beech dominate. Search the forest floor for beechnuts, a favorite food of bears, turkeys, and other animals. With the demise of the American chestnut, which was decimated by a fungus early in the twentieth century, beechnuts became an even more important food source for the animals of eastern North America. Now the American beech is under attack by the combination of a fungus and a scale (a sucking insect) introduced by imported European beech trees. Without the natural defenses

Look for granite scored by glaciers on South Bubble's summit.

necessary to fight off this threat, it is possible the American beech could go the way of the American chestnut.

The trail turns left and climbs up a set of stairs to a junction with Bubbles Trail, where you should turn right, climbing steeply over granite ledges toward North Bubble. Scree, or small rock, walls built by the park's trail crew line the trail in an attempt to keep hikers on the footpath. Like most trails in Acadia, this one is heavily used. It is very important to stay on the trail in order to keep the surrounding vegetation healthy.

Views begin to open up as thick forest gives way to pitch pines and blueberry bushes. You'll reach the summit of North Bubble 0.6 mile from the parking lot. The view takes in Jordan Pond and the surrounding group of Mount Desert Island's highest peaks: Cadillac, Pemetic, Penobscot, and Sargent.

For South Bubble, head back down the Bubbles Trail toward the parking lot. At the junction with Bubbles Divide Trail, turn right. The trail is fairly level for 0.1 mile, until you reach a junction where continuing straight will take you down to the northern end of Jordan Pond. Turn left on Bubbles Trail for a moderate 0.2-mile ascent to the summit of South Bubble. Although lower than North Bubble, this summit has better views of Jordan Pond.

Bubble Rock, which lies just east of South Bubble's summit, is the most conspicuous example of a glacial erratic on Mount Desert Island. Glacial erratics are rocks carried by glaciers and dropped far from their places of origin. They are easily identifiable by the fact that they are made of a different type of rock than that found in their general surroundings. Bubble Rock is made of coarse-grained white granite that contrasts markedly with the pink granite of the Bubbles and the other peaks on Mount Desert Island. Bubble Rock most likely came from Lucerne, 40 miles to the northwest. (Another erratic from Lucerne, Balance Rock, is visible from Shore Path in Bar Harbor.) Estimated to weigh between 8 and 12 tons, Bubble Rock is often described as being about the size of a living room.

For the return, retrace your steps to Bubbles Divide Trail and the parking area.

FAMILY ADVENTURES IN ACADIA NATIONAL PARK

One big change for us since we first wrote this guidebook seventeen years ago is that we now have two children to share the Acadia experience with us. It is rewarding and refreshing to see the park through their eyes, and many of the adventures in the park are well-suited to kids. It is no surprise Acadia is a popular family destination for those with kids of all ages.

Acadia contains a multitude of trails kids will love, including this hike on South Bubble.

It's easy to introduce kids to hiking on the park's trails. Except on ladder trails, ambitious parents can carry babies and toddlers in child-carrier backpacks without too much trouble. We found that when our kids were younger, they loved napping while being carried on the trail and were wide-eyed when awake. Once kids are scrambling around on their own, good first "mountain climbs" include Conners Nubble (Trip 1), Great Head (Trip 3), the Bubbles (Trip 4), and Gorham Mountain (Trip 5).

A key for parents hiking with young kids is to be patient. Your pace will be slow, as everything in nature is interesting to young kids, and they will want to stop and explore often. You will need to have snack and water breaks more often and to play games to keep kids moving at times; hide and seek works well. By the time kids are 8 or 9 years old, they will be capable of all but the longest trips in this book, and they can usually handle 4 or 5 miles with elevation gain. Hiking with kids often goes smoother if you can bring a young friend or two along. With their peers alongside them, engaged in their own conversations, kids are less likely to complain about fatigue.

All of the paddling trips in Section 3 of this book are appropriate for families, and the carriage roads offer bike rides for any level of cycling ability. Appendix D has suggestions for places that rent canoes and bikes, as well as all of the kid gear that goes with them. Sea kayaking is another great activity for families with older kids, but it has inherent dangers that parents must take into consideration. None of the sea-kayaking trips in Section 4 are suggested for inexperienced paddlers, let alone kids without significant kayaking experience. For experienced sea-kayaking families, the Mount Desert Narrows paddle (Trip 45) is a good first choice in nice weather and calm seas, as it is more sheltered than other trips in this guide. For inexperienced sea-kayakers who want to get their kids into the sport, we suggest taking a guided trip with one of the sea-kayaking outfitters listed in Appendix D. Some offer trips appropriate for kids as young as 8; on these trips, kids are always in a tandem kayak with a parent or another adult.

Friends of Acadia and park officials are actively working to provide more opportunities for families. This includes Acadia Quest, a competition in which teams complete a series of six events and activities in the park between April and November. To qualify, all a team needs is one member over 18 and one under 18. The teams that meet all of the Acadia Quest requirements are entered into a grand-prize drawing at November's annual Take Pride in Acadia Day.

TRIP 5

GORHAM MOUNTAIN AND OCEAN PATH

NPS Rating >	Moderate then easy
Distance >	3.5 miles
Elevation Gain >	500 feet
Estimated Time >	2 hours
Map >	AMC's Acadia National Park Map: E8

A moderate hike up to wide-open views of the ocean leads into a walk along the dramatic coastline between Sand Beach and Otter Cliffs.

DIRECTIONS

From downtown Bar Harbor, drive south on Route 3 for 2.1 miles and turn right at the Sieur de Monts entrance to Park Loop Road. Follow the signs for Sand Beach. The Gorham Mountain parking area is on the right, 4.4 miles south of the Sieur de Monts entrance. The parking area is an unscheduled stop between Thunder Hole (stop D) and the Fabbri Picnic Area (stop E) on the Island Explorer Sand Beach route (route 3). *GPS coordinates:* 44° 19.024' N, 68° 11.471' W.

TRIP DESCRIPTION

This hike makes the climb up Gorham Mountain from a parking area opposite Monument Cove along Park Loop Road. A short detour explores the caves on Cadillac Cliffs before reaching the Gorham summit, with views over the Ocean Drive section of Park Loop Road. After descending the north ridge of Gorham Mountain, the hike follows an easy footpath along Ocean Drive and passes Thunder Hole. Moderate grades and relatively accessible views make this a good trip for families with young children.

From the parking area, Gorham Mountain Trail enters a forest of paper birch and red spruce that soon transitions into a forest of pitch pine spread among ledges of pink Cadillac granite. At 0.3 mile, Cadillac Cliffs Path heads to the right. If you'd rather avoid rough footing and a short but steep ascent, continue straight on Gorham Mountain Trail. Otherwise, turn right and follow the 0.5-mile side trail along Cadillac Cliffs. The two trails reconnect just below the summit.

This cobblestone beach and adjacent Otter Cliffs are two of the many highlights to be found along Ocean Path.

The trail meanders around and under modest, fern-covered cliffs and caves that were once at sea level. Huge boulders have broken off the cliffs and created a jumbled trail of tunnels and "lemon squeezers," or places where the trail narrows to pass between large pieces of granite. In addition to challenging hiking, the cliffs also create a cool, moist microclimate where ferns and mosses grow thick.

After the last big set of boulders, the trail turns left and climbs quickly to rejoin Gorham Mountain Trail. Turn right to hike over open ledges to the summit of Gorham Mountain in 0.4 mile. While only 522 feet above sea level, Gorham Mountain is less than 0.5 mile from the Atlantic Ocean. The views of Ocean Drive, Otter Cliffs, and Sand Beach are excellent, as are the views of Champlain, Dorr, and Cadillac mountains.

To resume this trip, continue north on Gorham Mountain Trail as it descends gently into a forest of mixed hardwoods. The hardwoods here grew up out of the ashes of the great fire of 1947. It is now difficult to imagine this area as the charred, treeless plain it was 70 years ago, but the fire here burned so hot that the ground was sterilized in some places, and many years passed before trees recolonized the area. The trail descends and in 0.1 mile reaches a trail that leads right (northeast), toward Bowl Trail. Turn right then right again in another 0.1 mile onto Bowl Trail. Follow Bowl Trail 0.4 mile to Park Loop Road. Cross Park Loop Road and turn right onto Ocean Path.

Ocean Path follows the Ocean Drive section of Park Loop Road for the entire mile from here to the Monument Cove parking area. Ocean Path provides the park's best access to Mount Desert Island's famed pink-granite coastline. During this walk, you can scramble over smooth granite ledges and explore the cobble beaches of Newport and Monument coves, all while watching and listening to the surf make landfall. Herring and great black-backed gulls are common. Unfortunately, they are often fed by tourists, even though the practice is prohibited in Acadia. Feeding wildlife is never a good idea, as it endangers the health of the animals and people. Eider ducks and double-crested cormorants cruise the waters, feeding on fish, crustaceans, and mollusks.

The biggest attraction along Ocean Path is Thunder Hole, a narrow cleft in the granite shoreline. When the waters of the rising tide hit this hole in the rock just right, a giant splash of water hurtles skyward, emitting a thunderous crash and soaking any visitor who happens to be standing in the wrong spot. While it is rather tame most of the time, chances are good Thunder Hole will be booming if you visit near high tide on a windy day. Be sure not to go beyond the barriers. Tide times are listed in the local newspaper, *Mount Desert Islander* (mdislander.com). You can also buy official tide charts at local bookstores.

Monument Cove is just beyond where Ocean Path reaches the parking area. Take a few minutes to hike down to this cove filled with melon-sized cobbles of granite. These fascinating globe- and egg-shaped rocks have been smoothed and sanded over time by constantly rolling and grinding against one another as the waves wash over them. As time goes on, these cobbles will become smaller and smaller, eventually becoming a pebble beach. For more than 300 years, cobbles from Maine's beaches were harvested and used for ships' ballast, building materials, and cobblestone streets. We now know, however, that cobbles are an important part of the environment and should be left on the beach. The Gorham Mountain parking area is directly across Park Loop Road from Monument Cove.

TRIP 6

🚌 📷

THE BEEHIVE AND THE BOWL

NPS Rating ➤ Strenuous, with ladders

Distance ➤ 1.3 miles

Elevation Gain ➤ 450 feet

Estimated Time ➤ 1 hour

Map ➤ AMC's Acadia National Park Map: E8

Take a challenging climb up iron rungs to spectacular views and a visit to a quiet and beautiful mountain pond.

DIRECTIONS

From downtown Bar Harbor, drive south on Route 3 for 2.1 miles and turn right at the Sieur de Monts entrance to Park Loop Road. Follow the signs for Sand Beach. The Sand Beach parking area is on the left, 3.25 miles south of the Sieur de Monts entrance. Bowl Trail is across the road from the parking area. The parking area is stop C on the Island Explorer Sand Beach route (route 3), and stop D on the Loop Road route (route 4). *GPS coordinates:* 44° 19.783′ N, 68° 11.058′ W.

TRIP DESCRIPTION

The challenging nature of ascending the mountain known as the Beehive makes this one of the more popular hikes in the park. The fact that it is just across the road from Sand Beach and has good views probably adds to its popularity as well. The Bowl is a beautiful pond nestled between the Beehive and Champlain Mountain and, along with Sargent Pond, is one of two ponds in the park accessible only by foot.

Caution: This hike is very steep and uses iron rungs and ladders to scale the cliffs of the Beehive The hike is very dangerous in wet weather. People who have a fear of heights should consider climbing the Beehive from the Bowl instead of via Beehive Trail. It is not a recommended hike for small children, and parents of older children should consider hiking it without kids first to determine if it is appropriate for their family.

Begin this hike on Bowl Trail, at the trailhead across Park Loop Road from the Sand Beach parking area. Beehive Trail is the first trail junction, 0.2 mile from the road. Turn right to follow Beehive Trail toward the 350-foot cliffs of the Beehive. Like most of the mountains on Mount Desert Island, as well as on many of the is-

Breathtaking views from atop the Beehive make this strenuous hike worth the effort.

lands surrounding it, the Beehive has a gradual-sloping north face and steep cliffs on its south face. Glaciers during the last ice age created this landscape feature, when the pressure of the ice caused water to fill the cracks on the south face of the peaks. The rock weakened as the water went through repeated cycles of freezing and thawing. As the glacier moved forward, it sheared off these weakened pieces of granite, creating the cliffs.

Designed and built by Rudolph Brunnow, the man who built Precipice Trail on Champlain Mountain, Beehive Trail quickly rises to meet the cliff wall and begins to climb almost straight up. The iron rungs and ladders alternate with stretches of granite ledges. Views of the Atlantic Ocean, Sand Beach, and Champlain Mountain get better and better as you climb, but be sure of your footing before you look back over your shoulder! While strenuous, the climb up the Beehive is relatively short, and most hikers can finish the 0.5-mile hike to the summit in about 30 minutes. The views of the ocean are good, but the view toward the interior of the island is one of the prettiest mountain views in the park. While looking over the Bowl toward Dorr and Cadillac mountains, you see no sign of man: no Park Loop Road, no carriage roads, no power lines.

To hike down to the Bowl, a small 9.5-acre pond, follow Beehive Trail northwest, away from the cliffs. A side trail leads left back to Bowl Trail but bypasses the Bowl. Continue straight on Beehive Trail to reach the Bowl, a good example of a glacial tarn, which is a deep, typically circular lake that forms when an alpine glacier melts. The Bowl is a quiet place with a unique, southern view of Champlain Mountain. To finish the hike, follow the trail to the left, along the southern end of the pond. In the middle of a set of wooden puncheons, or split logs, built to protect the boggy shoreline, Bowl Trail comes in from the left. Turn left on Bowl Trail and follow it 0.6 mile back to Park Loop Road.

TRIP 7

🚌 🚶 🐕 📷 🏃

BAR HARBOR TO SAND BEACH

NPS Rating ➤ Moderate

Distance ➤ 4.7 miles

Elevation Gain ➤ 100 feet

Estimated Time ➤ 2 hours

Map ➤ AMC's Acadia National Park Map: C8, D8, E8

Walk to the beach from downtown Bar Harbor and enjoy both mountain and ocean views.

DIRECTIONS

Park anywhere in Bar Harbor, such as at the public lots on Rodick Street and at the municipal pier at the end of Main Street. This hike begins at the corner of Main Street and Mount Desert Street at the Village Green. (See Bar Harbor map at the back of this book.)

TRIP DESCRIPTION

Since 1986, Friends of Acadia has been working with the National Park Service to create several village connector trails that allow residents and visitors to walk into the park while leaving their cars behind. In 2009, trail crews completed the restoration of Schooner Head Path, a historic but previously abandoned trail that once connected Bar Harbor to Schooner Head and nearby Sand Beach. This trip describes the route from Bar Harbor to Sand Beach using this trail, sidewalks, a short stretch of park road, and a section of Great Head Trail. The hike follows the road for most of its length, but there's something special about being able to walk from your home or hotel to enjoy the beauty of Sand Beach and views of Champlain Mountain and the Beehive. It is a flat 5.1 miles one way, and you can either walk back to town or pick up the free Island Explorer shuttle bus at Sand Beach for your return trip.

This trip starts at the Bar Harbor Village Green, on the corner of Main and Mount Desert streets. Follow Main Street south (away from the water and toward the mountains), taking the sidewalks past restaurants and motels. After about 1 mile, you will reach a National Park Service parking area on the left, where there are trails that lead 0.5 mile through the woods to the water at Dorr Point (worth a look if you have the time). Follow the path into the woods at the parking area, keeping to the right at two trail junctions within the first few hundred yards. The trail soon crosses Old Farm Road then meanders through the woods for 0.5 mile before crossing Schooner Head Road near Jackson Laboratory.

From here, the path is basically a gravel sidewalk in the woods. It crosses the road a few times and is never far from the pavement, but the road is quiet and there are few interruptions. About 2.3 miles from Main Street, you will pass Orange and Black Path on the right, which leads to the trails at the north end of Champlain Mountain. In another 0.5 mile, you pass another trail on the right, Murphy Lane, which leads to Precipice Trail. Continuing on Schooner Head Path, you soon pass through a beautiful forest of paper birch trees and get great views of Champlain Mountain over a large beaver pond.

After crossing the outlet of the pond, the trail crosses the road one last time and leads 0.1 mile through the woods to the Schooner Head parking area. There are great ocean views here, as well as a 0.25-mile side trail that leads down to the cliffs overlooking Schooner Head. At low tide, you can crawl into Anemone Cave, a popular destination since the heyday of Bar Harbor tourism in the nineteenth century. If you do wish to explore the cave, be aware that the trail to the cave is poorly marked, steep, and follows the ledges at the water's edge. To continue to Sand Beach, follow the road from the parking area back toward Schooner Head Road for 0.1 mile. Turn left here and follow the road for 0.4 mile through the woods to the parking area for Great Head Trail.

Hikers make it to Sand Beach, the culmination of this moderate day hike.

Great Head Trail makes a figure-eight that leads to both Great Head and Sand Beach. From the parking area, follow the trail into the woods then follow the right fork for a 0.4-mile walk through the woods down to the beach, taking a second right at a fork in about 0.3 mile. You will reach the beach via a dune above a tidal creek, with views of the Beehive to the right and the open ocean to the left. Cross the creek and you are on a beautiful sandy beach, surrounded by high cliffs on either end. Feeling brave? Take a dip in the Gulf of Maine, with a water temperature that rarely rises above the mid-50s, even on the hottest days of summer.

If you are hiking between late June and Columbus Day, you can grab a shuttle bus back to Bar Harbor. To do so, walk up the stairs at the far (west) end of the beach to the Sand Beach parking area and wait for Island Explorer bus 3.

THE GREAT FIRE OF 1947

In 1947 an event occurred that still has an effect on Acadia today. Maine received only 50 percent of its usual rainfall that summer, and by October, Mount Desert Island was as dry as it has ever been. On October 17 the fire department received a call that smoke was rising from a cranberry bog near a dump on Crooked Road, west of Hulls Cove. It was a modest blaze at the time and burned only 167 acres during the next three days. But on October 21, strong winds took control, and soon another 2,000 acres were burning. The fire continued to intensify as firefighters proved no match for the gale-force winds, which blew the fire south and east. At one point, the fire moved 6 miles in less than three hours and burned 67 summer cottages in the section of Bar Harbor known as Millionaires' Row. Downtown Bar Harbor itself was spared, although the fire came close enough that 400 people fled by sea to Winter Harbor, across Frenchman Bay.

After burning more than 17,000 acres, 10,000 of them within Acadia National Park, the fire burned itself out in a massive fireball over the Atlantic Ocean, near Ocean Drive. For such an intense fire, casualties were low: One person died while trying to rescue a cat from his burning home, and two people died in a car accident while fleeing the island. Park rangers believed that most animals were able to outrun the fire and take refuge in lakes and ponds. The ecology of the park, however, was altered dramatically. Before the fire, spruce and fir dominated the landscape, but with the spruce-fir canopy gone, sun-loving species, such as birch and aspen, were able to grow. Today, a mosaic forest has reclaimed the burned areas of the park. This forest—a mix of spruce, fir, white pine, hemlock, beech, maple, birch, and aspen—supports a variety of wildlife, including beaver, white-tailed deer, and ruffed grouse. On the exposed, rocky ledges of the mountains that burned, fire-resistant pitch pine flourishes. All in all, the park now contains a more diverse mix of flora and fauna than it did before the fire.

A mosaic forest flourished after the great fire of 1947 burned much of the existing plant life. Without the canopy of spruce and fir, sun-loving species, such as birch and aspen, were able to thrive.

The fire of 1947 brought about the end of the era of huge summer cottages, most of which burned, although the lavish lifestyle surrounding these coastal vacation mansions had already begun to decline due to such factors as the introduction of the income tax, the Great Depression, and World War II. Even so, tourism remains the largest economic driver for Mount Desert Island, and more than 2 million people a year visit Acadia to walk its wooded paths, breathe in the salty scent of the Atlantic, and watch the wildlife of Maine's wild coast. Acadia National Park has healed its fire scars and is now a vibrant and healthy ecosystem.

TRIP 8
BEECH MOUNTAIN

NPS Rating ➤	Moderate
Distance ➤	2 miles
Elevation Gain ➤	700 feet
Estimated Time ➤	1.5 hours
Map ➤	AMC's Acadia National Park Map: F3

This enjoyable hike over rocky ledges leads to the summit of Beech Mountain, with excellent views.

DIRECTIONS

From the center of Southwest Harbor, go west on Seal Cove Road. Take the first paved road on the right, Long Pond Road. Follow Long Pond Road through a residential area until it ends at the south shore of Long Pond. There is a small parking area to the right of the water-pumping station. There is no Island Explorer stop at this parking area. The closest stop (2 miles away) is Echo Lake (stop E) on the Southwest Harbor route (route 7). *GPS coordinates:* 44° 18.898′ N, 68° 21.210′ W.

TRIP DESCRIPTION

This hike begins at the southern end of Long Pond and makes its way up 700 feet of granite ledges to the fire tower atop Beech Mountain. Due to its relatively easy access and good views, this is the most popular summit on the western side of Mount Desert Island. A longer walk down the open south ridge of Beech Mountain makes for a less-steep return trip filled with good views.

From the parking area, follow Beech West Ridge Trail along the eastern shore of Long Pond. The trail stays near the shore of the pond for 0.3 mile and passes two private homes along the way. Please respect the residents' privacy. After passing the second house, the trail turns right and begins climbing the relatively steep west ridge of Beech Mountain. The trail quickly reaches open granite ledges populated by white pine and scrub oak. Views begin to open up across Long Pond to Mansell Mountain.

You will reach Beech Mountain Trail 0.9 mile from the parking area. Turn right on this trail for a 0.1-mile trek to the summit. Beech Mountain's summit is only 841 feet above sea level, but like most peaks on Mount Desert Island, it is treeless, making for excellent views in all directions. The fire tower is not cur-

Beech West Ridge Trail leads to the summit of Beech Mountain and excellent 360-degree views.

rently staffed, as small planes are now used to patrol for fires. While you can't climb the tower at present, the summit has excellent views of Somes Sound, Cadillac Mountain, Sutton and Greening islands, the Cranberry Isles, Isle au Haut, and all of the western mountains.

To return to your car, look for a trail that heads south. This is Beech South Ridge Trail. The trail descends moderately through a forest of spruce that regularly opens up for more good views past Southwest Harbor and out to the Atlantic Ocean. The views finally end as the trail enters a thick forest of tall spruce. The trail descends steeply here, with switchbacks and stone steps easing the hiking. You will reach a trail junction 0.6 mile from the summit, marking the end of Beech South Ridge Trail. Turn right on Valley Trail for a 0.4-mile forested walk back to the parking area at Long Pond.

TRIP 9

NORUMBEGA MOUNTAIN

NPS Rating ➤	Strenuous
Distance ➤	3.5 miles
Elevation Gain ➤	700 feet
Estimated Time ➤	2.5 hours
Map ➤	AMC's Acadia National Park Map: E5

Take a quick climb to good views of Somes Sound followed by a visit to the quiet waters of scenic Lower Hadlock Pond.

DIRECTIONS

Follow Routes 198/3 for 1.4 miles north from Northeast Harbor. The Norumbega parking area will be on the left (west) side of the road. The parking area is an unscheduled stop between Gate House (stop E) and Parkman Mountain (stop D) on the Island Explorer Brown Mountain route (route 6). *GPS coordinates:* 44° 19.558' N, 68° 17.489' W.

TRIP DESCRIPTION

At 850 feet tall, Norumbega Mountain is not one of the highest peaks in the park, but it is an important geological feature because it forms the eastern wall of Maine's only fjord, Somes Sound. This loop hike has the typical Acadia features: great views, tranquil forests, and welcome moments of solitude. It makes a quick ascent to the summit before following a leisurely return route along the shores of Lower Hadlock Pond, which is home to tall spruce and calling loons.

From the Norumbega parking lot on Route 198, hike up Goat Trail, which seems to follow the steepest route possible to the summit. Besides its steep grade, the trail is rough—filled with roots and boulders as it gains 600 feet in the first 0.3 mile. A heavy backpack will work against you here, but once you complete that first 0.3 mile, you will face easy walking along a ridge sparsely populated by short pitch pines and lowbush blueberries. Views open up in all directions as you near the summit, only 0.6 mile from the parking area. Scattered pine trees obscure the view from the top, but there are excellent views from a ledge 150 yards beyond the summit.

Hadlock Brook cascades over granite as it flows into Lower Hadlock Pond.

Follow the trail, now called Norumbega Mountain Trail, beyond the summit, as it continues along a semiopen granite ridge, providing occasional views of the mountains to the east and west, Southwest Harbor, and the Cranberry Isles. At 1.3 miles, the trail reenters the forest and reaches a junction with Golf Course Trail, where you should turn left, heading toward Lower Hadlock Pond. The descent along the south ridge of Norumbega is much gentler than the ascent you made earlier; you can allow your mind to drift away from total concentration on the trail and take in the beautiful spruce forest that surrounds you.

At 1.8 miles, you'll reach the southern end of Lower Hadlock Pond, a small, quiet pond ringed with spruce trees; the mile or so of shoreline appears to be an impenetrable wall of green. When you reach the pond, turn left on Hadlock Ponds Trail and follow the western shore for about 0.5 mile to the northern end. Here you will find a series of small cascades where Hadlock Brook tumbles into the pond. The trail follows the west side of the brook away from the pond, passing two other paths within about 200 yards. Stay left at both intersections, following a sign at the second intersection that reads, "To Goat Trail Parking." This is Lower Norumbega Trail.

After leaving the brook, the Lower Norumbega Trail rolls over uneven terrain through more spruce woods, paralleling Route 198 for 1.3 miles on its way to the Norumbega parking area, completing the loop.

TRIP 10

HUGUENOT HEAD AND CHAMPLAIN MOUNTAIN

NPS Rating ➤	Moderate, with one short, strenuous section
Distance ➤	3.3 miles
Elevation Gain ➤	1,100 feet
Estimated Time ➤	2.5 hours
Map ➤	AMC's Acadia National Park Map: D8, E8

This classic Acadia hike climbs steep, pink granite for spectacular mountain and ocean views.

DIRECTIONS

This hike begins at the Tarn parking area, 2.2 miles south of Bar Harbor on Route 3. Across Route 3 from the parking area, look for a granite staircase marking the trailhead of Beachcroft Trail. The closest Island Explorer stop is at Sieur de Monts (stop B, about 0.25 mile from the Tarn) on Sand Beach route (route 3). *GPS coordinates: 44° 21.508′ N, 68° 12.344′ W.*

TRIP DESCRIPTION

Champlain Mountain is a popular wildlife-viewing spot due to its pair of nesting peregrine falcons. It's also one of the best places to view Frenchman Bay from Mount Desert Island. Beachcroft Trail makes a moderate ascent of Champlain from the west and offers distinctive views of the Tarn, a glacial pond nestled below the cliffs of Dorr Mountain, as well as of Dorr Mountain itself from Huguenot Head. This trail is a good alternative to the east face's Precipice Trail, a steep climb up iron rungs. Precipice Trail is usually closed for much of the summer to avoid disturbing the nesting falcons. By combining Beachcroft Trail with Champlain North Ridge Trail and Park Loop Road, it is possible to have a varied hike above treeline, to watch for eagles and falcons, and to visit an active beaver pond.

This hike starts on the east side of Route 3, across the road from the north end of the Tarn. Look for a set of granite stairs and a wooden sign marking Beachcroft Trail. George Dorr had Beachcroft Trail built in 1915, using stones from the base of the mountain as the material for the 1,482 steps that ease the climb. The first few hundred yards of the trail follow a sidewalklike stretch of skillfully laid granite through a deciduous forest. The trail then rises quickly above the trees

A young hiker takes in the autumn view from Huguenot Head. Photo: Kirk Betts.

on switchbacks built into the steep face of Huguenot Head. At 0.4 mile, the trail reaches the southwestern shoulder of Huguenot Head, passing within 150 yards of Champlain's summit. This open granite ledge provides views of Dorr Mountain, the Tarn, and the Atlantic Ocean.

The trail drops back below the trees for 0.1 mile before beginning the climb to Champlain's summit. The next section of the hike is the most difficult. A short, steep climb over rocks and through the trees brings you to a prime example of a pitch-pine forest. Due to its open nature, a pitch-pine forest looks like few others in New England. The widely spaced trees grow on exposed granite ledges, accompanied only occasionally by prostrate shrubs, such as lowbush blueberry and mountain cranberry. The trees themselves seldom grow to more than 20 feet in height and are gnarled and twisted by constant exposure to high winds. The open aspect of the forest makes it possible to see the summit of Cadillac Mountain, now visible directly behind Dorr Mountain.

The climb through the pines to the summit of Champlain is over smooth but steep granite. This part of the hike can be very slippery when wet, so exercise caution in rainy and foggy conditions. Beachcroft Trail ends at the summit, 0.8 mile from Route 3. Champlain's open, rocky peak is a good place to watch for wildlife and follow the boat traffic in Frenchman Bay. During the summer, peregrine falcons are often conspicuous, with the chicks loudly announcing the return of either parent to the nest. In addition to the falcons, bald eagles and other raptors frequent the thermals of warmed air around Champlain Mountain. With a good pair of binoculars, it is possible to spot harbor porpoises, harbor seals, and minke whales plying the waters of Frenchman Bay. The views of the bay are breathtaking, as you sit 1,058 feet above sea level and less than 1 mile from the water. From here, you can see the Porcupine Islands and Bar Harbor to the north, Egg Rock and Schoodic Peninsula to the northeast, the Cranberry Isles to the south, and the other mountains of Mount Desert Island to the west.

To begin your descent, look for Champlain North Ridge Trail at the summit cairn. Follow the trail north, toward Bar Harbor and the Porcupine Islands. This trail has good views to the east and north as it descends moderately over smooth granite ledge. It stays on open ledge for most of its mile-long traverse of Champlain Mountain's north ridge and enters the forest shortly before ending at Park Loop Road.

At this intersection, turn left and follow Park Loop Road. You will soon come to an active beaver pond with views of both Huguenot Head and Champlain Mountain. The beaver are most active at night, but you can often see them from the road at dawn and dusk. This is also a good spot to look for warblers, phoebes, and flycatchers and to photograph the abundant waterlilies.

At 0.75 mile from Champlain North Ridge Trail, turn left toward Sieur de Monts Spring. Turn left again in about 200 yards. In 300 more yards, turn right on Route 3 for a short walk to the parking area.

IMPRESSIVE SPEED: THE PEREGRINE FALCON

The peregrine falcon is about the size of a crow, but it has the speed of a Corvette. A peregrine regularly attains speeds in excess of 100 miles per hour while diving to catch and kill its prey in flight. Even in regular flight, this awesome predator reaches speeds of 60 miles per hour. In the air, a peregrine looks like a typical falcon, with long, pointed wings and a long tail. The bird has a white or buff-colored breast, a slate-gray back, a small head made distinctive by long gray "sideburns," and yellow legs.

By the mid-1960s, the peregrine was considered virtually extinct in the eastern United States. Hunting contributed to its dwindling numbers, but the ingestion of chemical pesticides accelerated extinction by making it nearly impossible for the falcon to reproduce successfully. The peregrine was declared an endangered species in 1973. Acadia National Park began participating in a peregrine-reintroduction program in 1984 and released 22 hand-raised chicks into the park between 1984 and 1986. In 1987 adult peregrines began returning to the park, and in 1991 peregrines successfully fledged chicks in Acadia for the first time since 1956.

The program has been such a success that, depending on the year, two or three pairs of peregrines now nest in the park, where they seek out small ledges on high cliffs. The nest sites are consistently located on Champlain Mountain, the Valley Cove Cliffs, Jordan Cliffs on Penobscot Mountain, and privately owned Ironbound Island in Frenchman Bay. The park usually closes any hiking trails in nest areas when the nests are active.

The best opportunity to observe peregrines is on Champlain Mountain during spring and summer. From the parking area for Precipice Trail, it is possible to view the birds on the cliffs above with a spotting scope or a good pair of binoculars. (Both Precipice Trail and the nearby Orange and Black Path are closed while the birds are nesting.) The National Park Service often stations a volunteer in the parking area to answer questions and to help visitors locate the birds. It is also possible to see the birds soaring above the cliffs from the summit of Champlain Mountain.

To protect the peregrine falcon, Acadia National Park asks visitors to:

- Learn the characteristic field marks and behaviors of peregrines so you can make a positive identification when you see one in the park.

- Report any peregrine sightings to a park information station.

- Keep away from areas where peregrines are nesting. Avoid observing the birds from a location higher than the nest. Adult peregrines generally won't tolerate people above them and may dive at intruders.

TRIP 11

🚌 🐕 📍 📷

PEMETIC MOUNTAIN AND BUBBLE POND

NPS Rating >	**Strenuous then moderate and easy**
Distance >	**4.1 miles**
Elevation Gain >	**950 feet**
Estimated Time >	**2.5 hours**
Map >	**AMC's Acadia National Park Map: E6**

This hike takes initial effort but leads to some of Mount Desert Island's most spectacular views.

DIRECTIONS

From the Hulls Cove Visitor Center, drive south on Park Loop Road for 5.2 miles. Be sure to continue straight at the intersections marked "Sand Beach" and "Cadillac Mountain." The Bubble Pond parking area will be on your left. The parking area is stop C on the Island Explorer Jordan Pond route (route 5). *GPS coordinates:* 44° 21.006′ N, 68° 14.456′ W. This parking area is closed during the summer months, but is accessible via the Island Explorer.

TRIP DESCRIPTION

At 1,247 feet, Pemetic Mountain is the fourth highest on Mount Desert Island and affords excellent views of Cadillac Mountain, Jordan Pond, and the Atlantic Ocean. Beginning and ending at Bubble Pond, a picturesque glacial pool nestled between Pemetic and Cadillac mountains, this hike climbs the northeast face of Pemetic via Pemetic North Ridge Trail. The long hike above treeline on the south ridge of Pemetic is nicely complemented by an easy walk along the carriage road on the western shore of Bubble Pond.

Pemetic North Ridge Trail starts at the south end of the Bubble Pond parking area. After crossing the carriage road, follow Pemetic North Ridge Trail to the right. (The trail to the left is Cadillac West Face Trail.) Pemetic North Ridge Trail quickly crosses back over the carriage road before starting its climb to the summit.

The trail climbs moderately through a forest of mixed hardwoods and conifers before transitioning into a steep climb through pure hemlock. Due to the thick hemlock canopy, the forest floor here is devoid of undergrowth except for spruce saplings and the occasional striped maple. The climb stays steep, and the footing gets rougher as the elevation increases.

The trail crosses a few open ledges with views of Cadillac Mountain. Lowbush blueberry and sheep laurel are common here. After going in and out of the trees several times, the trail leaves the forest for good at its junction with Pemetic Northwest Trail, 1.1 miles from the trailhead. (Pemetic Northwest Trail proceeds to the right and leads to the Bubble Rock parking area.) Avoid it and continue to follow Pemetic North Ridge Trail, which turns left, climbs over open ledge, and reaches the summit of Pemetic Mountain in another 0.1 mile.

From the summit of Pemetic (*pemetic* is the Wabanaki word for "gently sloping land"), there are views in all directions. To the northeast are Bubble Pond and Cadillac Mountain. To the south are the Atlantic Ocean and the Cranberry Isles. Jordan Pond is directly below the mountain to the west, and the summits of Penobscot and Sargent mountains rise up directly behind the pond. Eagle Lake is to the north.

When you're finished taking in the view, go south from the summit on Pemetic South Ridge Trail, which is marked by cairns and blue blazes on the bare rock. The south ridge of Pemetic is gently sloping exposed granite, making for an extended walk with views in all directions. The views end at 1.9 miles, where Pemetic South Ridge Trail forks to the right. Follow Pemetic East Cliff Trail left into the trees. The trail makes a short, steep descent before becoming a moderate footpath through a northern hardwood forest.

A carriage road follows one side of Bubble Pond just beyond the tree line, making for a pleasant hike.

At 2.2 miles, the trail intersects Bubble and Jordan Ponds Path. Turn left onto this path, which makes an easy descent for 0.3 mile to a carriage road. Follow the carriage road left for 1.6 miles back to the Bubble Pond parking area. Along the way, the carriage road follows the western shore of Bubble Pond. You'll have a view across the pond of the steep west slope of Cadillac Mountain, including a large boulder field that rises from the southeast corner of the pond. While on the carriage road, remember you are now sharing the trail with horses and bikes.

TRIP 12

🚌 🚶 🐕 📍 📷

ACADIA AND SAINT SAUVEUR MOUNTAINS

NPS Rating ➤	Strenuous
Distance ➤	3.7 miles
Elevation Gain ➤	1,050 feet
Estimated Time ➤	3 hours
Map ➤	AMC's Acadia National Park Map: E4, F4

Don't miss the only fjord on the East Coast of the United States.

DIRECTIONS

Parking for Acadia Mountain Trail is on the west side of Route 102, 3.3 miles from the intersection of Routes 102 and 198 in Somesville. The parking area is an unscheduled stop on the Island Explorer Southwest Harbor route (route 7), between Somesville (stop D) and Echo Lake (stop E). *GPS coordinates:* 44° 19.319′ N, 68° 19.972′ W.

TRIP DESCRIPTION

Acadia and Saint Sauveur mountains form the western wall of Somes Sound, providing a symmetrical counterpart to Norumbega Mountain on the east side of the sound. Although Acadia and Saint Sauveur are both under 700 feet in height, this is a strenuous hike that starts at around 150 feet and drops nearly back to sea level between the two peaks. Both the summit of Acadia Mountain and the ledges of Eagle Cliff offer excellent views of the sound.

Acadia Mountain Trail begins at a set of stone steps directly across the road from the parking area. At 0.1 mile, Saint Sauveur Trail leads to the right. You will return via this trail in a few hours. Instead, turn left to continue on Acadia Mountain Trail, which meanders through a forest of pine and spruce with an understory of blueberries and sheep laurel. At 0.2 mile, the trail crosses a dirt fire road then begins climbing steeply over granite ledges and stone stairs.

The trail quickly reaches its first reward, an area of open ledges with views to the south and west of Echo Lake, Beech Mountain, and Saint Sauveur Mountain. At 0.8 mile from the parking area, the trail reaches Acadia Mountain's summit, a beautiful, flat area of pitch pine, blueberry, and prostrate juniper. The trail continues east over granite, in and out of the pine, to a point where the mountain drops almost straight down to Somes Sound. From here, you get excellent views of the eastern mountains and the whole of Somes Sound—its deep waters bordered by steep mountains, making it the only fjord on the East Coast of the United States. The sound was carved by the Wisconsin Glacier between 15,000 and 25,000 years ago, and the water in the sound reaches depths of almost 200 feet.

To continue on, follow Acadia Mountain Trail to the right as it descends very quickly through beautiful pitch-pine forest. At 1.5 miles, the trail levels out at Man o' War Brook. A side trail leads left, to where the brook cascades over rock directly into Somes Sound. During the seventeenth and early eighteenth centuries, when Down East Maine was hotly contested territory between the French and British, Mount Desert Island was a dangerous place to visit for ships of either side. According to legend, this made Somes Sound a haven for pirates, who would sail up to the cascade at Man o' War Brook and fill up with freshwater.

Soon after the brook you'll reach a trail junction. Take the right fork, heading toward the Man o' War Brook Road and Saint Sauveur Mountain. In another 100 yards, the road leaves the trail to the right, and Valley Cove Trail leads left to Valley Cove. Continue straight on what is now called Valley Peak Trail. From here, the trail climbs steeply through a mixed conifer forest of white pine, red pine, cedar, spruce, and fir before reaching the open ledges of Eagle Cliff. Eagle Cliff rises 500 feet straight up from Valley Cove, a very protected part of the sound where boats often drop anchor to wait out bad storms. From here, you get a good view of Flying Mountain and the estates of Northeast Harbor across Somes Sound.

Acadia Mountain is known for its views of Somes Sound.

At a trail junction on the cliff, turn right on the Saint Sauveur Mountain Trail to head toward the summit of Saint Sauveur. In another 0.1 mile, you will reach a second trail junction. Turn right again for a 50-yard walk to the wooded summit of Saint Sauveur, which was known as Dog Mountain before becoming part of the national park. The forest here is a fairly thick stand of pitch pine, while blueberry bushes fill in the understory and turn a spectacular fire-engine red in late fall.

From the summit, it's 1.3 miles back to the parking area on Route 102. The rest of the hike is a moderate descent of the north ridge of Saint Sauveur. Just 0.3 mile below the summit, Ledge Trail enters from the left. Continue straight both here and at the next trail junction as Saint Sauveur Mountain Trail makes its way through a rocky forest of pine, cedar, and spruce. As the trail flattens out, it reaches a junction with Acadia Mountain Trail. From here, the parking area is 0.1 mile to the left.

TRIP 13

🚌 📍 📷

PENOBSCOT AND SARGENT MOUNTAINS

NPS Rating ➤	Strenuous
Distance ➤	5.3 miles
Elevation Gain ➤	1,300 feet
Estimated Time ➤	3.5 hours
Map ➤	AMC's Acadia National Park Map: E5, E6

A challenging hike leads to two of Acadia's highest peaks, with long stretches on open ledges offering spectacular views.

DIRECTIONS

From the Hulls Cove Visitor Center, drive south on Park Loop Road for 7.3 miles. Be sure to continue straight at the intersections marked "Sand Beach" and "Cadillac Mountain." The Jordan Pond parking area will be on your right. The parking area is stop D on the Island Explorer Jordan Pond route (route 5) and stop F on the Loop Road route (route 4). *GPS coordinates:* 44° 19.332′ N, 68° 15.121′ W.

TRIP DESCRIPTION

The cliffs of Penobscot Mountain rise steeply from the western shore of Jordan Pond, providing a habitat for one of Acadia's nesting pairs of peregrine falcons. This hike provides an alternative to Jordan Cliffs Trail, which is often closed due to the nesting falcons. Sargent Mountain is the second-highest peak on Mount Desert Island, and its flat, wide-open, subalpine summit provides some of the island's best views of Somes Sound, the Cranberry Isles, and the western mountains.

This hike starts on Spring Trail, located behind and to the left of Jordan Pond House. The trail crosses a carriage road after about 50 yards. Cross the stream on the other side of the carriage road, where there is a trail junction. The trail to the left is the Asticou and Jordan Pond Path. This hike continues straight on Spring Trail.

The trail rises and falls gently through the mixed hardwood and conifer forest to the west of Jordan Pond. After crossing another brook, the trail begins a steep ascent up a well-built set of rock steps. These steps are a good example of how proper trail maintenance can prevent severe erosion on a trail that receives a lot of

The hike to the summits of Sargent and Penobscot Mountains includes long stretches above treeline.

use. Just before crossing another carriage road, Spring Trail turns left at a junction with Jordan Cliffs Trail. After crossing the carriage road, Spring Trail begins a very steep ascent up the cliffs of Penobscot Mountain. There are a few iron rungs on this section of the hike as the trail squeezes through narrow cracks in the granite cliff face. About 0.5 mile from Jordan Pond House, Spring Trail ends at Penobscot Mountain Trail, where you should turn right.

Penobscot Mountain Trail soon emerges from the trees as it makes a moderate ascent of the south ridge of Penobscot Mountain. The walk up the south ridge crosses open granite ledges with good views of most of the mountains in the park, as well as of the Atlantic Ocean. The environment is subalpine, populated by prostrate trees and plants from the heath family, including sheep laurel and rhodora. Lowbush blueberries are very common along this trail.

Looking north from the summit of Penobscot (1.6 miles from Jordan Pond), you will see Sargent Pond and the summit of Sargent Mountain. Both summits are a good place to watch for ravens and hawks riding the thermals of air warmed by the sunbaked granite peaks. You may be able to spot the peregrines if they are nesting on Jordan Cliffs. The small but swift-flying sharp-shinned hawk can also be seen here. Hawk-watching in Acadia is particularly good in the fall on a sunny day that follows several days of storms. After hunkering down in the wet weather, the hawks are eager to find thermals and ride the winds out of the northeast.

Continuing north from the summit, Penobscot Mountain Trail descends quickly to the col between Penobscot and Sargent mountains. At this col, Deer Brook Trail enters from the right. Stay to the left on Penobscot Mountain Trail, and you will soon reach Sargent Pond. This pond is fairly typical of those in the spruce-fir forests of Maine: a bowl of water surrounded by spruce forests, with blueberry bushes and rhodora clinging to its banks. From the pond, the trail rises moderately to a junction with Sargent South Ridge Trail.

Turn right on Sargent South Ridge Trail. From here, the trail ascends very gradually for 0.8 mile to the summit of Sargent Mountain. This part of the hike is reminiscent of the Table Land plateau on northern Maine's Katahdin, though at a much lower elevation. Sargent's summit is surrounded by an extensive area of relatively flat, open terrain filled with sedges, wildflowers, and stunted versions of spruce, cedar, and birch. On the way to the summit, two more trails come in from the left. Continue straight on Sargent South Ridge Trail at these junctions to keep on track for the summit cairn. The views from the summit are excellent.

To return to Jordan Pond House, you have two choices. If the weather is dry and you don't mind very steep descents, follow Sargent East Cliff Trail southeast for a steep 0.7-mile descent to Deer Brook Trail, where you should turn left. In wet weather, you can avoid Sargent East Cliff Trail by walking back down Sargent South Ridge Trail to Penobscot Mountain Trail and turning left toward Sargent Pond. After passing by Sargent Pond again, the trail rises to meet Deer Brook Trail. Turn left on Deer Brook Trail, which goes down toward Jordan Pond. This trail descends steadily and has very rough footing over wet rocks and tree roots. The trail follows a stream, which overflows onto the trail after heavy rains.

At 0.6 mile from Penobscot Mountain Trail (or 0.1 mile from Sargent East Cliff Trail), Deer Brook Trail reaches a carriage road. Turn right on the carriage road for an easy 1.5-mile walk back to Jordan Pond House. Shortly after leaving Deer Brook Trail, the carriage road passes through a boulder field below Jordan Cliffs. There are good views of the pond and the Bubbles from here. The rest of the walk is through northern hardwood forest. At the only intersection, stay to the left.

TRIP 14

WESTERN MOUNTAINS: MANSELL AND BERNARD

NPS Rating ➤ Strenuous, with ladders on Perpendicular Trail

Distance ➤ 4.2 miles

Elevation Gain ➤ 1,350 feet

Estimated Time ➤ 3.5 hours

Map ➤ AMC's Acadia National Park Map: F2, F3

The views are limited, but the climb to the highest peaks on the western side of Mount Desert Island is physically rewarding.

DIRECTIONS

From the center of Southwest Harbor, go west on Seal Cove Road. Take the first paved road on the right, Long Pond Road. Follow Long Pond Road through a residential area until it ends at the south end of Long Pond. There is a small parking area to the right of the pumping station. There is no Island Explorer stop at this parking area. The closest stop (2 miles away) is Echo Lake (stop E) on the Southwest Harbor route (route 7). *GPS coordinates:* 44° 18.898' N, 68° 21.210' W.

TRIP DESCRIPTION

This is a hard hike with few views. It is, however, a great chance to enjoy a seldom-used trail through a mature spruce forest that was untouched by the 1947 fire that burned several thousand acres on the eastern side of Mount Desert Island (see "The Great Fire of 1947" on page 25). This hike starts at the southern end of Long Pond and climbs Mansell Mountain via Perpendicular Trail, which features an amazing stretch of stone staircases. Unlike the rest of the higher peaks on Mount Desert, the summits of both Mansell (938 feet) and Bernard Mountain (1,071 feet) are wooded, obscuring the view.

From the parking area at the southern end of Long Pond, follow the western shore of Long Pond on Long Pond Trail, which starts behind the pumping station. After 0.2 mile, turn left on Perpendicular Trail. This trail rises quickly, angling over a boulder field on the east face of Mansell.

The 704 stone steps built by the Civilian Conservation Corps in 1933 and 1934 give the trail a spiral-staircase look. The craftsmanship of this stretch of trail is excellent, rivaling that of Ladder Trail on Dorr Mountain (Trip 16). From the boulder field, views open up of Long Pond, Southwest Harbor, and the Cranberry Isles.

Perpendicular Trail levels off for a while as it works its way through a mixed forest dominated by spruce and cedar. The trail resumes its steep climb and, shortly before the summit of Mansell, reaches an overlook with perhaps the best views of the hike. A sign marks the short path on the right that will take you to a granite ledge high above Long Pond. From here, there are good views of Beech Mountain; Cadillac Mountain; the towns of Southwest Harbor, Bass Harbor, and Bernard; the Cranberry Isles; and the Atlantic Ocean.

Soon, you'll reach the wooded summit of Mansell after 0.1 mile of gradual climbing. The trail goes west, through a spruce forest that tops the west ridge of Mansell. At junctions with Mansell Mountain Trail and Razorback Trail, continue hiking straight on Perpendicular Trail. The trail crosses a granite ledge that affords views across Great Notch to Bernard Mountain, as well as views west and north of Blue Hill Bay, Pretty Marsh, and Bartlett Island. After the junction with Razorback Trail, Perpendicular Trail descends steeply for 0.3 mile into Great Notch, a narrow passage between the summits of Bernard and Mansell. From here, Great Notch Trail leaves to the left and descends quickly to Cold Brook Trail and eventually the south end of Long Pond. Long Pond Trail leaves to the right and makes a gradual and lengthy descent to the western shore of Long Pond.

Because of their heavily wooded summits, Bernard Mountain and Mansell Mountain have restricted views but offer rewarding scenic landscapes such as Bass Harbor Marsh, pictured here.

To continue this hike, go straight (west) on Perpendicular Trail and begin the steep climb to the summit of Bernard, 0.6 mile from Great Notch. After the steepest part of the climb, an overlook on the left has limited eastern and southern views of Mansell Mountain, Southwest Harbor, and the Atlantic Ocean. Shortly after this overlook, the trail crosses the wooded Knight Nubble before descending 0.1 mile to Little Notch and a junction with Sluiceway Trail. Continue straight on what is now called Bernard Mountain Trail and make a short but steep climb to the Bernard overlook, which has limited views north and west to Bartlett Island and over Blue Hill Bay to Blue Hill.

Like that of Mansell, the summit of Bernard Mountain is a viewless spruce forest, thick and mossy but also quiet and secluded. Bernard Mountain Trail makes a gradual descent through this forest, which is one of the highest spruce forests on the coast of Maine. From the summit to the Western Mountain fire road, it is 1.7 miles. At the only trail junction (with West Ledge Trail), turn left to stay on Bernard Mountain Trail. As the trail descends, the forest becomes increasingly diverse, with hardwoods and pines filling the spaces not occupied by spruce. At times the trail is steep, but the footing is good. After crossing a stream, the trail ends at a parking area on Western Mountain Road.

Hike up the road for a short distance to where another road leads to the left. Take this left, and you will soon find yourself in a cul-de-sac. On the right side of the cul-de-sac, look for a sign pointing you toward Cold Brook Trail, which leads east toward the southern end of Long Pond. This trail is relatively flat, through mixed forest. Continue straight at intersections with Razorback and Mansell Mountain trails. Cold Brook Trail ends at Long Pond Trail on the southern shore of Long Pond, completing the loop you started several hours ago. From here, the parking area is 0.1 mile to the right.

TRIP 15

🚌 🐕 📍 📷 🏃

PEAK BAGGER'S DELIGHT:

BALD PEAK, PARKMAN MOUNTAIN, GILMORE MOUNTAIN, AND SARGENT MOUNTAIN

NPS Rating ➤	Strenuous
Distance ➤	4 miles
Elevation Gain ➤	1,500 feet total
Estimated Time ➤	3.5 hours
Map ➤	AMC's Acadia National Park Map: E5

This difficult hike traverses four peaks, including Sargent Mountain, Acadia's second-highest point.

DIRECTIONS

For this hike, park at the Norumbega parking area on Routes 198/3, 1.5 miles north of Northeast Harbor. Hadlock Brook Trail is directly across the street. The parking area is an unscheduled stop between Gate House (stop E) and Parkman Mountain (stop D) on the Island Explorer Brown Mountain route (route 6). *GPS coordinates: 44° 19.558′ N, 68° 17.489′ W.*

TRIP DESCRIPTION

With the potential to summit four peaks in less than four hours, this hike can be tiring but enjoyable. Starting on Route 198 north of Northeast Harbor, this hike loops up and over Bald Peak and Parkman, Gilmore, and Sargent mountains. Sargent, at 1,379 feet, is the second-highest peak on Mount Desert Island and has one of the more interesting summits, with a large plateaulike area full of subalpine vegetation, including mountain sandwort, mountain cranberry, and alpine club moss. While lower than Sargent, the other three peaks on this hike all have open summits with good views. The return trip from the summits follows the cool waters of Maple Spring as it courses down the southeast flank of Sargent Mountain, through a forest with large trees and a small gorge.

Begin this hike on Hadlock Brook Trail, which starts on the eastern side of Route 198, directly across the road from the Norumbega parking lot. Hike past the junction with Parkman Mountain Trail then turn left onto Bald Peak Trail, 0.3 mile from the road. Bald Peak Trail crosses a carriage road and ascends moderately through a forest of cedar and spruce. After crossing a second carriage road, Bald Peak Trail climbs more steeply, breaking out of the trees and providing views of Norumbega Mountain, Upper Hadlock Pond, and the islands at the mouth of Somes Sound.

More steep hiking brings you to the summit of Bald Peak, 0.8 mile from the parking area. The great views here are similar to those you will have on Parkman and Gilmore mountains. The other peaks on this hike are visible to the north and east, while Penobscot and Cedar Swamp mountains lie to the east and south. The views do not end with the surrounding peaks, however, as on a clear day you can see beyond Mount Desert Island and its environs to Isle au Haut, Blue Hill, and the Camden Hills to the west.

After you enjoy the views, Parkman Mountain is up next. Follow Bald Peak Trail northwest and down into the col between Bald Peak and Parkman Mountain. The descent is steep but only 0.1 mile long. At 0.2 mile from Bald Peak, turn right on Parkman Mountain Trail for the short hike to the summit of Parkman. From here, turn right on Grandgent Trail and head east toward Sargent Mountain. The trail descends first moderately, then steeply, through a forest of spruce and birch, reaching the low point between Parkman and Gilmore in 0.3 mile. Here the trail crosses Giant Slide Trail before making a short but steep climb to the summit of Gilmore Mountain. You can soak up more of the same great views on Gilmore before continuing toward Sargent Mountain. Follow Grandgent Trail, which heads north from the summit for a short distance before turning east and descending

Bald Peak is the first of four summits conquered on this hike.

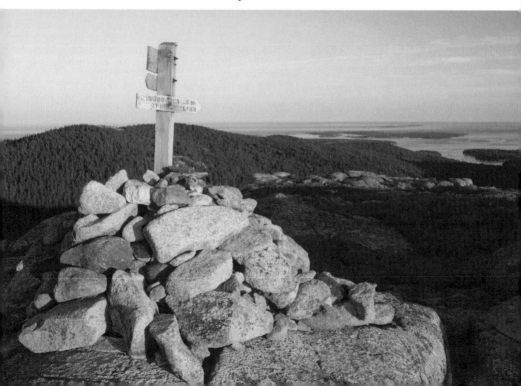

moderately into a mixed forest of spruce, cedar, birch, and maple. You soon come to the col between Gilmore and Sargent. After crossing a brook, the blue-blazed Grandgent Trail reaches an intersection with Maple Spring Trail. Continue left on Grandgent Trail.

The climb up Sargent on Grandgent Trail is steep, and the footing is rough in places, but the forest here is an interesting mixture of spruce, fir, cedar, and hardwoods. The entire hike from Gilmore to Sargent feels wilder than other hikes on Mount Desert Island because the area is relatively difficult to reach by Acadia National Park standards. As Grandgent Trail emerges from the trees, more views of Somes Sound and beyond appear. You'll reach the summit of Sargent Mountain 0.7 mile from Gilmore Mountain.

Sargent's summit is surrounded by an extensive area of relatively flat terrain filled with sedges, wildflowers, and stunted versions of spruce, cedar, and birch. The views from the summit are excellent. Beyond the Bubbles and Jordan Pond is Cadillac Mountain to the east. Somes Sound and the western mountains are to the west. Somes Sound, with mountains on both sides and a "V"-shaped, 200-feet-deep bottom, is the only fjord on the entire East Coast of the United States. On clear days you can see as far as Isle au Haut, 20 miles to the southwest, and the Camden Hills.

For the return trip, turn right (south) on Sargent South Ridge Trail. It is an almost flat walk above treeline for 0.3 mile to a trail junction, where you turn right onto Maple Spring Trail. Maple Spring Trail descends moderately over open granite ledges for the first 0.3 mile before entering the forest for the rest of the hike. Rocks and tree roots make the footing on this trail rough for most of its length, creating a longer hike than you would expect. This trail is one of the few in the park that follows a stream, often crossing it during the descent. At 0.5 mile below Sargent South Ridge Trail, turn left to stay on Maple Spring Trail at its intersection with Grandgent Trail. Maple Spring Trail passes Giant Slide Trail in another 0.5 mile. Continue straight on Maple Spring Trail as it enters a small but beautiful gorge before crossing under an attractive stone carriage-road bridge. In this area, the trail is lined with large white pines, hemlocks, and cedars.

Maple Spring Trail dead-ends into Hadlock Brook Trail. Turn right onto Hadlock Brook Trail for the final 0.4 mile to the parking area on Route 198.

TRIP 16

🚌 📷

DORR MOUNTAIN, THE GORGE, AND SIEUR DE MONTS SPRING

NPS Rating ➤	Strenuous, with a few ladders
Distance ➤	4 miles
Elevation Gain ➤	1,500 feet
Estimated Time ➤	4 hours
Map ➤	AMC's Acadia National Park Map: D7

Take in spectacular views, a narrow gorge, and quiet forests on this difficult hike.

DIRECTIONS

This hike starts at the parking area on the west side of Route 3, just past Sieur de Monts Spring at the north end of the Tarn, 2.2 miles south of Bar Harbor. The closest Island Explorer stop is at Sieur de Monts (stop B, about 0.25 mile from the Tarn) on Sand Beach route (route 3). *GPS coordinates:* 44° 21.508′ N, 68° 12.344′ W.

TRIP DESCRIPTION

The first leg of this hike is very steep, gaining 1,100 feet in about 1 mile. The Ladder Trail's continuous series of stone steps makes much of the climb relatively straight-forward, though strenuous. After reaching the summit of Dorr Mountain, this hike loops around the north ridge of Dorr, descending through a picturesque gorge that separates Dorr from Cadillac. The hike meanders through the forest near historic Sieur de Monts Spring before returning to the parking area near the Tarn.

From the south end of the Tarn parking lot, begin your hike by following the trail that skirts the north end of the Tarn, a pond gouged out by glaciers during the last ice age. After crossing the outlet of the Tarn, turn left onto Kane Path, which follows the west side of the pond. The trail traverses the bottom of a large field of granite boulders plucked off the east face of Dorr Mountain by glaciers. Luckily for hikers, the builders of this trail managed to create an almost side-walklike trail through the boulder field using granite they found among the rubble. Shortly after Kane Path leaves the shore of the pond, turn right onto Ladder Trail. From here, it is 0.9 mile to the summit of Dorr. Ladder Trail is so named for the three sets of iron ladders used to scale particularly steep sections of the trail; however, the trail just as easily could have been named the "Hike of 1,000 Stairs."

This small waterfall can be found along the Gorge Path which explores the notch between Dorr Mountain and Cadillac Mountain.

While the ladder sections of this trail are very short, there is a seemingly endless proliferation of impressive stone steps, which were built in 1893 and restored by the Civilian Conservation Corps in the 1930s.

Kane Path rises quickly through a mixed forest of paper birch, yellow birch, beech, oak, white pine, big-tooth aspen, and maple. After squeezing through a very narrow passage between a large boulder and the cliff face, the trail continues over iron ladders and stairs into a forest of pitch pine and scrubby red oak. The stairs end for good once the trail meets up with Schiff Path, where you will turn left. The trail climbs up steep granite slabs (be extremely cautious on these in wet weather) during the next 0.3 mile, and the views really start to open up, with Frenchman Bay visible over Huguenot Head and Champlain Mountain.

Just below Dorr's true summit, the trail reaches a junction with Cadillac-Dorr Connector and Dorr North Ridge Trail. Turn left on Dorr North Ridge Trail to walk the final few hundred yards to the summit. Cadillac Mountain looms directly to the west and seems almost close enough to touch. Otter Creek and the Cranberry Isles are now visible, as is all of Frenchman Bay and Schoodic Peninsula. At 1,265 feet, Dorr Mountain is the third-highest peak on Mount Desert Island.

For the next part of the hike, return to the trail junction just north of the summit. Turn left onto Cadillac-Dorr Connector. The trail descends steeply 0.2 mile over Cadillac pink-granite boulders to the gorge between Cadillac and Dorr mountains. Once the trail levels off, A. Murray Young Path goes south, while Gorge Path goes north to Park Loop Road. Turn right onto Gorge Path.

Gorge Path takes an interesting route through the narrow, rocky gorge separating Dorr and Cadillac mountains. The trail passes under steep cliff walls, descending moderately along a stream and past small cascades. The footing can be rough, but much of the trail features flat rocks strategically placed to improve the hiking. The trail crosses the stream often, and sometimes trail and stream coincide. Waterproof your boots before this hike! While the forest here consists mostly of mixed hardwoods, several impressive hemlocks somehow survived a 1947 fire that burned much of the surrounding forest (see "The Great Fire of 1947" on page 25).

About a mile from its intersection with Cadillac-Dorr Connector, Gorge Path levels off and Hemlock Trail enters from the east. Turn right onto Hemlock Trail, which will lead you to Sieur de Monts Spring. After briefly rising to meet Dorr North Ridge Trail, Hemlock Trail runs into an old dirt service road, known as Hemlock Road, which is now used as a hiking trail from Sieur de Monts Spring. Turn right on the road and then right again 0.3 mile later onto Jesup Path. (If you reach the Sieur de Monts parking area, you have gone too far.) Just before the Park Service nature center building, the trail forks. Stay to the right on Jesup Path. After crossing Emery Path, as well as a road and a sidewalk that both lead to the Abbe Museum, Jesup Path continues through the woods to the Tarn. When you reach the Tarn, you have completed the loop. Turn left on Beachcroft Path and head up the trail to return to the Tarn parking area.

A FOREST AND A WETLAND IN ONE?

Wetlands and forests both have received considerable attention in recent years as vital habitats for sustaining the health of our planet, increasing species diversity, and providing a natural filtering system for drinking-water supplies. But there's also the forested wetland, a combination habitat often overlooked by scientists and amateur naturalists alike. Forested wetlands are usually small areas of forest, an acre or two in size, that have standing water for only part of the year. In Acadia National Park, trees—such as the northern white cedar—grow in these wetlands, and the ground is often covered with sphagnum moss.

While it can look like the rest of the forest on the surface, a forested wetland is a bonanza of biodiversity that provides habitat for a disproportionate number of threatened and endangered plants and animals. Forested wetlands are a good place to look for unusual wildflowers, such as orchids, in spring and summer, and they are the most likely ecozone in Acadia for spotting uncommon amphibians, such as the four-toed salamander. Common plants include skunk cabbage, starflower, and partridgeberry. Common birds include the cedar waxwing, hermit thrush, and northern saw-whet owl. Like other wetlands, forested wetlands are important for regulating water flow and helping to recharge groundwater supplies.

Forested wetlands can be found throughout Acadia, especially on the western side of Mount Desert Island. They are common along the Long Pond, Western Mountain, and Hio fire roads.

With their rich array of vegetation, forested wetlands are home to a diverse array of animals, from amphibians to birds to mammals, such as the white-tailed deer.

TRIP 17

🚌 🧑‍🦯 🐕 📍 📷 🏃

CADILLAC MOUNTAIN

NPS Rating ➤ Moderate

Distance ➤ 7 miles

Elevation Gain ➤ 1,500 feet

Estimated Time ➤ 4 hours

Map ➤ AMC's Acadia National Park Map: E7, D7

Take a relatively long hike over open ledges to the summit of Mount Desert Island's highest mountain, with consistently great views.

DIRECTIONS

The trailhead for Cadillac South Ridge Trail is just west of the entrance to Blackwoods Campground on Route 3, 5.6 miles south of Bar Harbor. The parking area is stop F on the Island Explorer Sand Beach route (route 3). *GPS coordinates: 44° 18.810′ N, 68° 12.854′ W.*

TRIP DESCRIPTION

Although this hike is not a loop, the south ridge of Cadillac Mountain, with its open forests of pitch and jack pine, is worth experiencing twice in one day. This hike starts on Route 3 near the entrance to Blackwoods Campground and makes a moderate, enjoyable climb to Cadillac's busy summit over a leisurely 3.5 miles. While the summit may not be the wildest spot in the park, with its gift shop and parking lot rife with tourists, the south ridge of Cadillac is relatively quiet and full of excellent views.

Cadillac South Ridge Trail starts on the north side of Route 3, about 50 yards west of the entrance to Blackwoods Campground. It is legal to park on the shoulder of the highway. The first mile of this hike rises gently, then moderately, through a forest dominated by white pine and spruce. At the 1-mile mark, a spur path on the right leads 0.1 mile to an overlook called Eagle Crag, which has good views of Otter Creek and the Atlantic Ocean. This is a worthwhile destination for families staying at the campground who are not up for the full hike to the summit. The spur path loops around to reconnect with the main trail after a total of about 0.2 mile. Turn right on Cadillac South Ridge Trail to head toward the summit. Almost immediately, the hike enters a forest of pitch pine spread over granite ledge, taking on an open, airy feeling. The occasional boulder among the gnarled and twisted trees contributes to the forest's look of a grown-up Japanese bonsai garden. Of course, this is a real forest, and wind and water are the gardeners. From here to the summit, there are good views of the island and the surrounding waters.

Next the trail passes though one of the few pockets of jack pine on the island just before making a short descent to the Featherbed, a boggy area 2.3 miles from the trailhead. This is one of the highest wetlands in the park. The trail crosses Canon Brook Trail, which leads east to Dorr Mountain and west to Jordan Pond. Continuing straight on Cadillac South Ridge Trail, this hike soon reaches its steepest climb. A trail junction 0.5 mile below the summit marks the Cadillac West Face Trail, which leads west to Bubble Pond. Stay on Cadillac South Ridge Trail, which nears the summit road before making its final ascent.

For much of the year, the summit of Cadillac Mountain is the first place to see the sunrise in the United States.

Shortly before reaching the summit, the trail descends into a thick spruce-fir forest, which stands in marked contrast to the open pine forest of the previous 2.5 miles. This forest grows in an area protected from the strong summit winds, and it collects just enough soil and water to allow the spruce-fir forest to thrive. The trail crosses a fire road and reaches the summit parking area just below the actual summit, which is marked by a set of interpretive signs describing the views, extending in all directions, of Frenchman Bay, Schoodic Peninsula, the islands to the west, and even Katahdin 115 miles to the north.

Sixteen species of hawks, eagles, and falcons live in or migrate through Acadia. In the fall, Cadillac Mountain's location and elevation make it an excellent spot to watch for migrating raptors, especially when the wind is out of the north. Check with the park visitor center for information about hawk-watching programs run by park naturalists throughout September and early October. To complete the hike, retrace your steps to your car.

TWISTED PINES

While hiking on Cadillac Mountain and most of the other rocky summits in Acadia, you will encounter beautiful stands of pitch and jack pine. Although these pines can grow to be as tall as 70 feet in ideal conditions, they usually top out at 20 or 30 feet in the exposed environment of Acadia's mountains. Harsh winds twist the trunks into gnarled, stunted, surreal shapes that make for a fascinating forest to hike through. The lack of fertile soil also creates an "open" forest, making it quite common to have good views out past the trees, even those 30 feet tall. It is relatively easy to tell these pines apart by studying their needles. A pitch pine has 4-inch needles in bundles of three, while the jack pine's 1-inch needles come in bundles of two.

In Acadia, pitch is the more common of the two pines, but it is most often associated with the sandy pine barrens of southern New England and New Jersey. Jack pine is less common in Acadia, as it is a more northerly species that grows primarily in Canada. Both species are highly resistant to fire, and jack pine actually depends on fire

In Acadia, pitch and jack pines colonize granite ledges.

to heat open its cones and release its seeds. Without fire, both species would gradually be replaced by hardwoods. In Acadia, pitch and jack pines colonize granite ledges where there is little soil and where they are usually joined by an understory of blueberries, sheep laurel, and sometimes scrubby oaks.

TRIP 18

NORTHEAST HARBOR TO EAGLE LAKE VIA SARGENT MOUNTAIN

NPS Rating >	Strenuous
Distance >	8 miles
Elevation Gain >	1,800 feet
Estimated Time >	5 hours
Map >	AMC's Acadia National Park Map: E5, E6, D5, D6

Along this scenic route, you will find both wide-open ridge hiking and shoreline walks.

DIRECTIONS

To the Brown Mountain gatehouse. Follow Routes 198/3 for 0.5 mile north from Northeast Harbor. The parking area is stop E on the Island Explorer Brown Mountain route (route 6). *GPS coordinates:* 44° 18.681′ N, 68° 17.131′ W.

To Eagle Lake. From the intersection of Route 3 and Route 233 in Bar Harbor, take Route 233 west toward Cadillac Mountain. There are two parking areas for the carriage road in 2.1 miles, one on the right and one on the left. The parking area is stop B on the Island Explorer Brown Mountain route (route 6). *GPS coordinates:* 44° 22.648′ N, 68° 15.141′ W.

TRIP DESCRIPTION

This is a great one-way trip that spends about half the time on open ridges populated with pockets of pitch pines. It offers great views, particularly from Sargent Mountain and North Bubble, although it requires spotting a car (that is, leaving a second car) or riding the Island Explorer bus at either end of the trip. In addition to climbing Sargent Mountain and North Bubble, this hike crosses the summits of Cedar Swamp Mountain and Conners Nubble, passes the north shore of Jordan Pond, and parallels most of the western shore of Eagle Lake. Starting at the Brown Mountain gatehouse in Northeast Harbor, you will use the carriage-road system and the following trails: Sargent South Ridge Trail, Jordan Cliffs Trail, Deer Brook Trail, Jordan Pond Path, Bubbles Divide Trail, and Bubbles Trail. This description follows the hike from south to north, but the hike just as easily can be hiked from north to south.

This strenuous hike combines wide-open ridge walking on Sargent Mountain and scenic lake shore walks.

From the Brown Mountain parking area, follow the carriage road 0.1 mile to post 18 and turn right. Turn right again at post 19 (0.3 mile) then turn left onto Sargent South Ridge Trail at 0.8 mile. The trail climbs moderately through spruce forest and open areas populated with lowbush blueberry and sheep laurel; enjoy the views to the south and west. At 1.7 miles, you'll reach ledges with big views to the east. Good views continue for the next 0.2 mile, at which point you'll reach the summit of Cedar Swamp Mountain. (To reach the true summit, take the 75-yard side trail to the summit cairn.)

After Cedar Swamp Mountain, Sargent South Ridge Trail descends back into the forest and crosses Amphitheatre Trail next to Birch Spring. Continue straight and begin the moderate climb to an intersection with Penobscot Mountain Trail. From here it is an easy climb over open ridge, past Hadlock Brook Trail and Maple Spring Trail (both enter from the left) to the summit of Sargent Mountain, about 3.5 miles from the Brown Mountain parking area. Sargent's summit (1,379 feet) is a broad, windswept plateau with spectacular views in all directions and flora matching the alpine world of New England's much higher summits: three-toothed cinquefoil; mountain sandwort; and rock-hugging, heart-shaped paper birch.

From the summit, turn right onto Jordan Cliffs Trail and make the steep descent to Deer Brook Trail, 0.4 mile below. Turn left onto Deer Brook Trail and continue descending a rough trail filled with rocks and tree roots for 0.2 mile. You'll cross a carriage road then, in another 0.2 mile, you'll reach the northern shore of Jordan Pond; turn left on Jordan Pond Path. A flat, 0.2-mile shore walk brings you to Bubbles Divide Trail, where you will turn left and make a steep climb over a pink-granite boulder field. At 0.3 mile above the pond, Bubbles Trail leads right to the summit of South Bubble. (If you feel like a detour, take the short side trip to the summits of South Bubble and Bubble Rock.) Continue straight on Bubbles Divide Trail for 0.1 mile then turn left onto the northern section of Bubbles Trail.

A short but steep climb brings you to the summit of North Bubble, where there are good views of Sargent and Penobscot mountains. Continuing beyond the summit, you'll be rewarded with extensive easterly views of Cadillac Mountain and Eagle Lake before descending into the trees and reaching a carriage road, 0.6 mile below the summit. Bubbles Trail crosses the road and makes another quick climb to the top of Conners Nubble, which has good views in all directions.

Conners Nubble is only a stone's throw from Eagle Lake; it is common to hear loon calls and see circling osprey while sitting on the summit. The trail continues over the summit and down to the lake, reaching Eagle Lake Trail in 0.4 mile. Turn right for a 100-yard walk to a carriage road then turn right again on the carriage road for an easy walk through spruce woods next to the lake. Stay straight at post 9 and you will reach the Eagle Lake parking lot 1.3 miles from Bubbles Trail and 8 miles from the Brown Mountain parking area. It is an eleven-minute ride on an Island Explorer bus (route 6) back to Brown Mountain or a five-minute ride to Bar Harbor.

TRIP 19

🚌 📷 🏃

BAR HARBOR TO JORDAN POND VIA DORR, CADILLAC, AND PEMETIC MOUNTAINS

NPS Rating ➤ Strenuous

Distance ➤ 10 miles

Elevation Gain ➤ 2,900 feet

Estimated Time ➤ 6 hours

Map ➤ AMC's Acadia National Park Map: C7, D7, E6, E7

This lengthy hike starts with an easy walk from downtown Bar Harbor before bagging three of Acadia's four highest peaks.

DIRECTIONS

Park anywhere in Bar Harbor. There are public lots on Rodick Street and at the municipal pier at the end of Main Street. This hike will start at the corner of Main Street and Mount Desert Street at the Village Green. (See Bar Harbor map at the back of this book.)

Jordan Pond parking area. From the Hulls Cove Visitor Center, drive south on Park Loop Road for 7.3 miles. Be sure to continue straight at the intersections marked "Sand Beach" and "Cadillac Mountain." The Jordan Pond parking area will be on your right. The parking area is stop D on the Island Explorer Jordan Pond route (route 5) and stop F on the Loop Road route (route 4). *GPS coordinates:* 44° 19.332′ N, 68° 15.121′ W.

TRIP DESCRIPTION

This is a great trip no matter where you are staying on the island, but it's particularly enjoyable if you are staying in Bar Harbor and can begin your hike right from your hotel door. By following Great Meadow Loop Trail, you can go from town sidewalks to the park's trail system in just a few minutes. The trip then ascends Dorr, Cadillac, and Pemetic mountains before ending at Jordan Pond. This hike is strenuous and includes a very steep descent on the west side of Cadillac that can be dangerous in wet weather. Keep your pack light (but well stocked with safety gear; see the list at the beginning of this chapter) and keep an eye on the weather. Over the course of this hike, you will use the following trails: Great Meadow Loop Trail, Hemlock Road, Jesup Path, Homans Path, Schiff Path, Emery Path, Cadillac-Dorr Connector, Cadillac South Ridge Trail, Cadillac West Face Trail, Pemetic North Ridge Trail, Pemetic South Ridge Trail, Bubble and Jordan Ponds Path, and Jordan Pond Path. You will need to spot a car (that is, to leave a car at your destination before beginning the hike) or use the Island Explorer bus system (route 5) to complete this trip.

To start this hike, find the beginning of Great Meadow Loop Trail on Cromwell Harbor Road. The easiest way to do this is by walking up Ledgelawn Avenue from Mount Desert Street (three streets west of the Village Green). About 0.6 mile from Mount Desert Street, turn right onto Cromwell Harbor Road. The trail will be on the left side of the road in a few hundred yards, just east of a large cemetery. Great Meadow Loop Trail parallels the cemetery in the woods for 0.2 mile before it crosses a stream and reaches a road. Turn right onto the road; after about 100 yards the trail reenters the woods across the street. Great Meadow Loop Trail crosses the road again in another 0.4 mile then parallels Park Loop Road and a golf course for about 0.3 mile, where you should turn left, crossing Park Loop Road and following Hemlock Road, an abandoned woods road now used as a hiking trail. Hemlock Road skirts the edge of Great Meadow, a marshy wetland popular with birders. At 0.2 mile from Park Loop Road, turn left at a trail junction onto Jesup Path.

After a 0.4-mile walk through a beautiful grove of maples and paper birch, you'll reach another junction with Hemlock Road, a few hundred yards from the parking

Cadillac Mountain is one of Acadia's iconic hikes and offers stunning views to the south.

area at Sieur de Monts Spring. Turn right onto the dirt road then make a quick left onto Homans Path. Up until this point, the hike has consisted of about 2 miles of leisurely, flat walking, but that's all about to change, as you will now climb Dorr Mountain. The steep ascent of Homans Path, a recently restored historic trail, is made a little easier by switchbacks lined with beautiful pink-granite steps. The new trail work here is impressive. You quickly rise to views of Great Meadow and Frenchman Bay, reaching Emery Path 0.3 mile above Hemlock Road and 2.3 miles from Bar Harbor.

Emery Path continues the steep climb over switchbacks, passing Kurt Diederich's Climb in 0.2 mile, where you should continue straight (taking the right fork) on what is now called Schiff Path. In another 0.6 mile, turn right to stay on Schiff Path at its intersection with Ladder Trail. The trees get sparser and the views bigger as you climb, eventually topping out at a trail junction on the north ridge of Dorr Mountain, 1.3 miles from Homans Path. Turn left and walk 150 yards to the 1,270-foot summit of Dorr Mountain, which has excellent views in all directions. To continue the hike, return to the trail intersection below the summit and turn left toward Cadillac Mountain on Cadillac-Dorr Connector.

Cadillac-Dorr Connector makes a short, steep descent to the notch between Dorr and Cadillac, where A. Murray Young Trail leads left and Gorge Path leads right. Continue straight on Gorge Path and make the steep, 0.5-mile, 500-foot climb to the summit of Cadillac Mountain. Cadillac Mountain is the tallest in Acadia, and the views are superb. Expect to share your experience with a few hundred others, though, as there is an auto road to the summit. There's also a gift shop, where you can refill your water bottle or buy a sports drink and a candy bar.

Two summits down, one to go. From Cadillac Mountain, this trip next heads to Bubble Pond, a picturesque glacial tarn nestled between Cadillac and Pemetic mountains. From Cadillac's summit, look for Cadillac South Ridge Trail, just east of the gift shop. Follow this trail through the spruce forest near the summit then down 0.5 mile to Cadillac West Face Trail, where you will turn right. The next 0.7 mile is a very steep descent over granite ledges and boulders. Caution: It can be dangerous in wet weather and uncomfortable with a heavy pack; however, the views of Bubble Pond and Pemetic Mountain are spectacular. When you reach Bubble Pond, turn left onto a path and follow the north shore of the pond until you reach Pemetic North Ridge Trail. Turn right on Pemetic North Ridge Trail, cross the carriage road, and begin your climb up Pemetic Mountain.

The trail makes a steep climb (600 feet in 0.5 mile) through conifers to a good view of Bubble Pond and the cliffs of Cadillac's west face towering above the water. After the initial climb, the hiking gets easier, going gently up (and sometimes down) in and out of the woods. At 1.1 miles above the pond, you'll reach a junction with Pemetic Northwest Trail, which leads right to the Bubbles; continue straight on Pemetic North Ridge Trail for an easy 0.1-mile walk over bald granite to the

1,234-foot summit of Pemetic Mountain, where there are good views in all directions, especially out toward the Cranberry Isles.

From the summit, continue hiking on what is now called Pemetic South Ridge Trail as it traverses the wide-open granite ridge south of the mountain's peak. At 0.8 mile from the summit, turn right to stay on Pemetic South Ridge Trail, which makes a moderate descent into spruce forest, reaching Bubble and Jordan Ponds Path 1.4 miles below the summit. Turn right onto Bubble and Jordan Ponds Path and follow it across Park Loop Road, reaching the shores of Jordan Pond in about 0.5 mile. Turn left onto Jordan Pond Path for a scenic walk next to the pond en route to Jordan Pond House and the end of your hike.

CAIRNS

Cairns are traditionally conical-shaped piles of rocks used to mark hiking trails above treeline. Many of the cairns in Acadia are slightly different in shape, consisting of two stones on the bottom, a middle "pointer" stone, and one smaller stone on top. Known as Bates cairns, they are named after one of the premier early trail builders on Mount Desert Island, Waldron Bates. Given Acadia's mostly open summits, cairns are numerous and play an important role in keeping hiking traffic confined to the intended trails. This in turn helps to prevent erosion of what little soil exists above treeline and to prevent the destruction of important plants and animals that need the rocks for shelter. Cairns are also an important safety feature on trails, as they help keep hikers from getting lost, particularly in bad weather.

The cairns in Acadia seem to take on a life of their own, growing over time—and even reproducing. Many park visitors aren't able to resist adding a rock to a cairn or building their own. This is a problem for two reasons: First, trail maintainers build cairns to direct hiking traffic along specific routes. Adding a cairn interrupts these im-

For plant and hiker safety, leave cairns alone.

portant route landmarks, increases trail erosion, and gets hikers lost. Second, moving rocks above treeline disturbs delicate microhabitats. The flora and fauna that survive in these microhabitats usually perish when rocks are removed.

Park naturalists ask that you admire the cairns during your visit to Acadia—but please leave them as you find them.

TRIP 20

EASTERN SIDE TRAVERSE: SAND BEACH TO NORTHEAST HARBOR

NPS Rating ➤	Strenuous, with ladders on Beehive Trail
Distance ➤	11 miles
Elevation Gain ➤	2,500 feet
Estimated Time ➤	6.5 hours
Map ➤	AMC's Acadia National Park Map: E5, E6, E7, E8, F5, F6

This traverse of the eastern half of Mount Desert Island visits some of Acadia's best-known features and follows some of the park's quietest trails.

DIRECTIONS

To Sand Beach. From downtown Bar Harbor, drive south on Route 3 for 2.1 miles and turn right at the Sieur de Monts entrance to Park Loop Road. Follow the signs for Sand Beach. The Sand Beach parking area is on the left, 3.25 miles south of the Sieur de Monts entrance. Bowl Trail is across the road from the parking area. The parking area is stop C on the Island Explorer Sand Beach route (route 3) and stop D on the Loop Road route (route 4). *GPS coordinates:* 44° 19.783′ N, 68° 11.058′ W.

To the Brown Mountain gatehouse. Follow Routes 198/3 for 0.5 mile north from Northeast Harbor. The parking area is stop E on the Island Explorer Brown Mountain route (route 6). *GPS coordinates:* 44° 18.681′ N, 68° 17.131′ W.

TRIP DESCRIPTION

Sand Beach, Champlain Mountain, and Jordan Pond are some of our favorite places in Acadia, and this hike takes you to all of them and more. You will need to spot a car or use the Island Explorer bus system to avoid turning this trip into a 22-mile out-and-back epic, but it's definitely worth the extra logistical effort. Focus your eyes on the eastern side of your Acadia National Park Map and look for the parking area at Sand Beach in grid E8. From this starting point, the hike works its way over the Beehive, Champlain Mountain, and the south ridge of Cadillac then down to Jordan Pond and over to the Brown Mountain gatehouse, just west of Northeast Harbor. It uses the following trails: Bowl Trail, Beehive Trail, Champlain South Ridge Trail, Beachcroft Trail, Kane Path, Canon Brook Trail, Bubble and Jordan Ponds Path, and Asticou and Jordan Pond Path.

If you get an early start from the Sand Beach parking lot, you can take a prehike dip in the cold waters of the Gulf of Maine by running down the steps at the southeast end of the parking lot to the beach. To reach your start on Bowl Trail, walk to Park Loop Road and follow it to the right for about 40 yards, where the trail begins across the road. After 0.2 mile on Bowl Trail, turn right onto Beehive Trail and make the short, steep climb up iron rungs to Beehive's summit and its views of the beach, Frenchman Bay, and the island's interior mountains.

Caution: This hike traverses the cliffs of the Beehive via iron rungs and ladders and is very dangerous in wet or icy weather. It is not recommended for people with a fear of heights or those hiking with small children. As an alternative, follow Bowl Trail around to the backside of the Beehive.

From the summit, follow Beehive Trail northwest down to the Bowl (a beautiful, sheltered glacial tarn), continuing straight at an intersection with Bowl Trail, 0.1 mile from the summit. After reaching the Bowl, the trail follows the shore to the left and soon reaches Champlain South Ridge Trail, which continues to hug the shoreline before beginning a moderate climb up the pink-granite south ridge of Champlain Mountain. This ridge hike goes in and out of open pitch-pine forest with an understory of blueberries and sheep laurel. There are good views much of the way to Champlain's summit, which, at 1,058 feet has spectacular views of Frenchman Bay and its islands. At this point, you have tackled about half of your elevation gain for the day but only about a quarter of your mileage.

From Champlain's summit, turn left onto Beachcroft Trail and follow it around the summit of Huguenot Head. Descend via a series of switchbacks sporting some very impressive stone trail work that continues most of the way down to Route 3, ending up across from the Tarn (0.8 mile below the summit of Champlain). Cross the street and follow Beachcroft Trail along the north edge of the Tarn to a trail intersection. Here, turn left onto Kane Path. This trail leads south over boulders that lie practically in the Tarn, offering dramatic views of the cliffs across the pond as well as a look at the pickerelweed, small fish, and bullfrog tadpoles living in the pond. At 0.5 mile from its beginning at the north end of the pond, Kane Path passes Ladder Trail, which leads right to the summit of Dorr Mountain. Bypass Ladder Trail and, in another 0.2 mile, watch for Canon Brook Trail entering from the left. Continue straight on what is now Canon Brook Trail (not signed).

Canon Brook Trail continues in a southerly direction through hardwoods and past beaver ponds before turning right and beginning its climb up to the south ridge of Cadillac Mountain. The trail soon passes Dorr South Ridge Trail on the right then reaches an intersection with A. Murray Young Path, 0.8 mile from Kane Path. At this intersection, take the left fork to stay on Cannon Brook Trail, crossing the brook and following a sign that points to Eagles Crag. Here the trail begins a steep climb, paralleling and sometimes crossing the brook, which tumbles over

The lawn at Jordan Pond House overlooks the pond and the Bubbles, in the background.

ledges of pink Cadillac granite. This is a little-used trail that is enjoyably quiet but sometimes a little tricky to follow. About 2.3 miles from Kane Path and 4.5 miles from Sand Beach, Canon Brook Trail reaches the Featherbed, a small wetland on the south ridge of Cadillac Mountain.

If you are feeling strong and of a peak-bagging mind, take a right here on Cadillac Mountain South Ridge Trail for a 2.5-mile round-trip side hike to the summit and its heavy dose of civilization. Otherwise, from the Featherbed, continue hiking west on what soon becomes Bubble and Jordan Ponds Path. You are treated almost immediately to spectacular views of Pemetic Mountain and the Cranberry Isles from atop steep cliffs. The next 0.5 mile is a very steep and rocky descent to a stream crossing. After this crossing, it is an easy 1.5 miles of hiking to Jordan Pond. Along the way, you will cross a carriage road, Pemetic East Cliff Trail, Pemetic South Ridge Trail, and Park Loop Road, hiking through beautiful groves of spruce, pine, and cedar. Continue straight on Bubble and Jordan Ponds Path through all of these intersections. When you reach Jordan Pond, turn left on Jordan Pond Path for a short walk to Jordan Pond House.

At Jordan Pond House, you will find restrooms and refreshments upstairs in the gift shop. You can also ask for a table and enjoy a meal, or tea and popovers. This is a regular stop on Island Explorer route 5, so if you're feeling tired or daylight is waning, you can end your hike here. Otherwise, look for a path that leads into the woods directly behind the restrooms. This path crosses a carriage road and Jordan Stream before reaching Asticou and Jordan Pond Path, where you should turn left. Asticou and Jordan Pond Path has no drama or views, but provides crowd-free, mostly easy hiking through some of the most beautiful spruce woods on the island. Some of the older spruce are more than 20 inches in diameter—a great example of what many of the trees in Acadia must have looked like before the 1947 forest fire (see "The Great Fire of 1947" on page 25).

About 1 mile from Jordan Pond House, Asticou and Jordan Pond Path crosses the carriage road (twice) and Penobscot Mountain Trail. Soon it crosses Harbor Brook and Harbor Brook Trail; continue straight. In another 0.4 mile, follow the right fork, where Eliot Mountain Trail leads left for Eliot Mountain. In another 0.3 mile, turn right onto Sargent South Ridge Trail and make the 150-yard climb to a carriage road. Turn left onto the carriage road for a 0.8-mile walk to the Brown Mountain gatehouse, taking care to turn left at posts 19 and 18. From this parking lot, you can catch an Island Explorer bus (route 6) for a five-minute ride into Northeast Harbor, where you'll find fine dining and shopping, or you can catch a 20-minute ride into Bar Harbor and switch to a bus bound for Sand Beach (route 3) and the beginning of this hike.

TOURISM AND THE CREATION
OF ACADIA NATIONAL PARK

During the first half of the nineteenth century, Mount Desert Island was a quiet place, home to subsistence farmers and fishermen. Things started to change in the 1850s, as visiting artists and journalists began to tell the world about the beauty of Mount Desert Island. The most prominent of these early visitors were painters of the Hudson River School, such as Thomas Cole and Frederic Church. Their dramatically lit renditions of landscapes—Eagle Lake, the Beehive, and the Porcupine Islands—lured visitors from the big cities on the East Coast. These early visitors, known as "rusticators," rented rooms from local farmers and fishermen and ate simple meals with their hosts.

Of course, as word got out about Mount Desert Island's simple life, salty spruce-scented air, and mild summer climate, tourism grew substantially. By 1870, steamers began landing in Southwest Harbor, and tourists made their way to Bar Harbor. By 1871, Bar Harbor had eleven hotels and was visited by four steamers a week. Daniel Rodick built the largest of the hotels, the Rodick House, which by 1882 could hold more than 600 guests. Magazines, such as *Harper's*, began calling Bar Harbor a "fashionable spa," and before long tourists from around the world were spending their summers on Mount Desert Island.

The 1880s saw the beginning of the building of summer "cottages" by America's wealthy elite. These estates of 50 or more rooms, complete with ten to fifteen servants, were the summer residences of families such as the Rockefellers, Astors, Fords, Morgans, and Carnegies. At one point, there were as many as 90 of these estates. Wealthy families also bought up huge tracts of desirable Mount Desert Island real estate. For example, J.P. Morgan owned Great Head and Sand Beach, which he gave to his daughter in 1910. The wealthy summer residents also contributed to the towns on the island, greatly improving sanitation and building libraries and hospitals. It was this spirit of philanthropy that would lead to the establishment of Acadia National Park.

In 1901 Charles Eliot, the president of Harvard and a summer resident of Northeast Harbor, grew concerned that the invention of the portable sawmill would bring about the demise of Mount Desert Island's tranquil beauty. He asked George Dorr, a wealthy Bostonian and a fellow summer visitor to Mount Desert Island, to help him preserve the best of the island. Dorr convinced other summer residents, such as John S. Kennedy and George Vanderbilt, to help him start a nonprofit organization whose sole purpose was "to acquire by devise, gift, or purchase, and to own, arrange, hold, maintain, or improve for public use lands in Hancock County, Maine, which by reason of scenic beauty, historical interest, sanitary advantage or other like reasons may become available for such purpose." So began the Hancock County Trustees of Public Reservations.

Quaint shops line Main Street in downtown Bar Harbor.

With George Dorr at the helm, the trustees acquired substantial pieces of Mount Desert Island, including the summit of Cadillac Mountain and Otter Cliffs. Dorr worked tirelessly for years to persuade landowners to donate land to the group. By 1913 the trustees had acquired 6,000 acres, and in 1916 they gave the land to the federal government for the creation of Sieur de Monts National Monument. Dorr continued to acquire land for the park, and in 1919 the national monument became Lafayette National Park, the first national park east of the Mississippi River. Dorr was hired as the park's first superintendent and is generally thought of as the father of Acadia National Park, which became the park's official name in 1929. Acadia now protects more than 50,000 acres on Mount Desert Island, Schoodic Peninsula, and Isle au Haut, and is the only national park in the United States for which all of the land was donated to the government.

BIKING

BIKING IN ACADIA NATIONAL PARK

During much of the twentieth century, the Rockefeller family donated large amounts of time, money, and land in an effort to make Acadia and Mount Desert Island a nature paradise for future generations to enjoy. Perhaps the greatest Rockefeller legacy is the network of carriage roads John D. Rockefeller Jr. had built during the 1920s and 1930s. These roads were built originally so that walkers and horse-drawn carriages could enjoy the island's backcountry without the disturbing noise and pollution of automobiles.

Horses and walkers still use the carriage roads, but today these roads get most of their traffic from bicycle riders. The roads follow easy grades and blend into the contours of the hills in a way that makes them seem a natural part of the landscape, and their crushed-gravel surface makes an excellent base for cycling. Built by local craftsmen, the roads traverse a series of intricate stone bridges that cross streams, gorges, and Park Loop Road while providing visitors with the greatest viewing pleasure. With no singletrack mountain-bike trails to speak of (bikes are not allowed on hiking trails), Acadia is not a place for hardcore mountain biking. The carriage roads, however, as well as the dirt fire roads on the western side of the island and the new bike paths on Schoodic Peninsula, provide an excellent way to experience the park on two wheels. Trips range from flat one-hour rides through mature spruce forest to steep half-day climbs with spectacular views of the surrounding peaks, lakes, and bays.

Biking the carriage roads is a wonderful way to explore the natural beauty of Mount Desert Island's eastern district. Forty-five miles of these roads take you to the scenic splendor of places like Jordan Pond, Eagle Lake, and Day Mountain. Passing through a variety of natural habitats, they create the opportunity for extensive nature study and wildlife-watching. Magnificent bridges provide views of waterfalls and mountain vistas, and the roads make occasional climbs to reveal stunning views of the Atlantic Ocean and the rest of Maine. The carriage roads also make great winter trails for snowshoeing and cross-country skiing. That said, because most of Park Loop Road is closed in winter, winter access to the carriage roads is available only at the Jordan Pond, Eagle Lake, Brown Mountain gatehouse, and Parkman Mountain parking areas.

You can explore the western part of the island—with its cool, quiet boreal forests—on a series of dirt fire roads. These fire roads are as great a way to see the natural habitats of Mount Desert Island as they were before the great fire of 1947. Plus, as of 2015, 9 miles of new bike paths on Schoodic Peninsula explore the forests around Schoodic Campground and provide access to Winter Harbor, Frazer Point, and Schoodic Park Loop Road.

TRIP TIMES AND RATINGS

While we think the bike trip times we list are useful for planning, your times undoubtedly will differ from ours. Our times are based on our experience as average cyclists. Obviously, the times can vary based on the weather, the physical fitness level of your group, and how much gear you bring with you. The times we list do not include breaks, so if you plan to stop often and take in the scenery, your trips will last longer.

Trip ratings vary, based on the length of the trip and the elevation gain. Most trips in Acadia are fairly short and easy from a road-biking standpoint, but the elevation gains can make a trip seem much longer.

SAFETY AND ETIQUETTE

Its mild summer climate makes Acadia an enjoyable and relatively safe biking destination. Of course, bad weather or poor planning can spoil any biking adventure. Before heading into Acadia's backcountry, consider the following:

- Select a trip that is appropriate for everyone in your group. Match the ride to the abilities of the least capable person in the group.

- Plan to be back at the trailhead before dark. It's always OK to end a ride without reaching your destination, but it's never OK to push the group too far. Determine a turnaround time and stick to it—even if you have not reached your goal for the day.

- Check the weather. Acadia's carriage and fire roads are safe places to be during wet weather, but riding can be less enjoyable in a steady rain or when there are strong winds. Give yourself more time to stop in the rain, as wet brakes do not work as well as dry ones.

- Bring a pack with the following items:
    - ✓ Water: Bring 1 or 2 quarts per person, depending on the weather and the length of the trip.
    - ✓ Food: Even for a short trip, it is a good idea to bring some high-energy snacks, such as nuts, dried fruit, or snack bars. Bring a lunch for longer trips.
    - ✓ Map.
    - ✓ Extra clothing: Rain gear, sweater, hat, gloves.
    - ✓ Headlamp or flashlight, with spare batteries and light bulb.
    - ✓ Sunscreen.
    - ✓ First-aid kit.
    - ✓ Pocketknife.
    - ✓ Basic bike-maintenance tools and a spare inner tube.

- Wear appropriate footwear and clothing. Legwear should be tight-fitting, as loose pants can get stuck on pedals and in the gears of a bike, causing nasty accidents. Bring rain gear, even in sunny weather, since unexpected rain, fog, or wind is possible at any time in Acadia. Avoid wearing cotton clothing, which absorbs sweat and rain, making for cold, damp riding. Polypropylene, nylon, fleece, silk, and wool are all good materials for keeping moisture away from your body and keeping you warm in wet or cold conditions.

- The best bikes to use on the carriage paths in Acadia National Park are hybrid-style bikes (which combine the best aspects of road bikes, touring bikes, and mountain bikes) with tires that are 35mm wide. Fat-tire bikes will also work well.

In addition to practicing the no-impact Leave No Trace techniques described in this book's introduction, it is a good idea to keep the following things in mind:

- Call the National Park Service to confirm that carriage roads are open. In the spring, the roads are often closed, when they are too wet to handle traffic of any kind. It can cost thousands of dollars to repair one tire rut, so if the roads are closed, please stay off them.

- Bikes are not permitted on hiking trails or on the carriage roads to the south of Jordan Pond and to the east of Stanley Brook Road.

- Always wear a helmet.

- When on paved roads or dirt fire roads where cars are allowed, wear bright colors and follow the same rules of the road as when driving a car.

- Ride slowly and in control, and try to avoid stopping quickly. Gravel surfaces are loose, and quick stops are dangerous.

- Do not obstruct the road by riding (or resting) three or four cyclists abreast.

- Yield to hikers.

- Yield to horses and walk your bike past them. A horse can get spooked by a bicycle speeding past.

- When passing, politely inform the person you are passing by saying, "On your left," or "On your right."

- Try not to disturb other cyclists and hikers. While you may feel alone in the wilderness, wild yelling or cell phone usage will undoubtedly upset another person's quiet backcountry experience.

- When you are ahead of the rest of your group, stop and wait at all road junctions. This avoids confusion and keeps people in your group from getting lost or separated.

TRIP 21

🚌 🚶 🐕 🎿 📍 📷 🏃

MAPLE SPRING– HADLOCK BROOK LOOP

NPS Rating ➤ Easy

Distance ➤ 4 miles

Elevation Gain ➤ 350 feet

Estimated Time ➤ 1.25 hours

Map ➤ AMC's Acadia National Park Map: E5, F5

Sights along this relatively easy ride include a 40-foot waterfall and Upper Hadlock Pond.

DIRECTIONS

Park at the Parkman Mountain parking area on Routes 198/3, 1.8 miles north of Northeast Harbor. The parking area is stop D on the Island Explorer Brown Mountain route (route 6). *GPS coordinates:* 44° 19.898' N, 68° 17.653' W.

TRIP DESCRIPTION

This trip may be short, but it packs in views of the Cranberry Isles, rides through sweet-smelling spruce forests, and visits one of Acadia's biggest waterfalls. The carriage roads on this ride pass over Maple Spring and Hadlock Brook on two of the magnificent granite bridges that are synonymous with Acadia's carriage-road system. Except for one short and steep section, the grades are reasonable and the pedaling easy. The trip finishes with a ride along the afternoon-sun-soaked eastern shore of Upper Hadlock Pond, which provides a good habitat for a variety of waterfowl.

From the Parkman Mountain parking area, follow the sign that points toward post 13. At post 13, turn left for a steep climb through a beautiful spruce forest. To the south, Upper Hadlock Pond and the Cranberry Isles come into view shortly before you reach post 12, at 0.4 mile from the parking area. This is the steepest part of this trip. At post 12, turn right. At 0.8 mile, you come to Hemlock Bridge, which rises high above Maple Spring, a beautiful pine- and hemlock-lined stream that tumbles down to Upper Hadlock Pond from just below the summit of Sargent Mountain. Only 100 yards or so beyond Hemlock Bridge is Waterfall Bridge, with its single arch spanning Hadlock Brook. Like many of the bridges on the carriage roads, viewing turrets entice you to stop and soak in the sights and sounds of nature. To the left of the bridge, Hadlock Brook tumbles

Young cyclists pass one of the largest falls in the park, Hadlock Brook Waterfall.

40 feet over Cadillac granite, carrying the soothing sounds of rushing water past the bridge to the valley below.

Beyond Waterfall Bridge, the carriage road parallels the south ridge of Cedar Swamp Mountain, making a long, gradual descent that will have you wishing all biking was this easy. As you coast through the dark green of a spruce forest, the calls of chickadees and nuthatches fill the air, and a pungent woodsy smell wafts over you. Just before reaching post 19, at 2.2 miles, you'll pass through a grove of northern white cedar. This cedar variety's scientific name is *arborvitae*, Latin for "tree of life," and its bark and foliage are high in vitamin C. It tends to grow in wet, acidic soils covered with a thick layer of sphagnum moss, creating a forested wetland that is the ideal habitat for rare orchids. Birds that live in cedar stands include northern saw-whet owls, alder flycatchers, hermit thrushes, cedar waxwings, Canada warblers, and black-throated green warblers.

At post 19, turn right then turn right again at post 18. A fairly level ride brings you to Upper Hadlock Pond at 3 miles. In the afternoon, the sun shines on the eastern shore of the pond, which is only a few yards to the west of the carriage road. It is a peaceful spot to take a break and watch for the ducks that live on the pond. Norumbega Mountain rises steeply beyond the west side of the pond, its thick spruce-fir forest looking like an impenetrable covering. As the road makes its way around the northern end of the pond, it crosses a small stream over a modest bridge made of large granite blocks. While not as large or dramatic as the taller and longer bridges of the carriage-road system, this small bridge and others like it display the same intricate craftsmanship. After the bridge, the road begins a 150-foot climb back to post 13. Turn left at this intersection to complete your journey.

TRIP 22

HIO FIRE ROAD

NPS Rating ➤ Easy

Distance ➤ 4 miles

Elevation Gain ➤ 100 feet

Estimated Time ➤ 1 hour

Map ➤ AMC's Acadia National Park Map: G4

This easy, family-friendly ride follows a dirt road through prime bird-watching habitat.

DIRECTIONS

From Southwest Harbor, follow Route 102 south. At the intersection with 102A, bear right to stay on 102. In another 1.4 miles, the Hio fire road will be on your left, just before crossing the Bass Harbor Marsh. The closest Island Explorer stop (about 1 mile) is the Tremont School stop (stop M) on the Southwest Harbor route (route 7). *GPS coordinates:* 44° 15.227′ N, 68° 20.363′ W.

TRIP DESCRIPTION

Hio Road is an unused dirt fire road near Seawall Campground that traverses a spruce-fir forest near a large bog called the Big Heath. Birds more common to Canada than coastal Maine inhabit the woods along this road, which is relatively flat and has a good riding surface for most of its length. Although there are a few very brief rough spots, kids will enjoy this trip. Since it is short, you can take your time, watching and listening for birds, exploring vernal pools for frogs and salamanders, and enjoying flora such as rhodora, bog laurel, and skunk cabbage. You can also add a short ride to the Atlantic Ocean at Seawall.

This is an out-and-back trip that you can start either from Route 102 or from the group camping area in Seawall Campground. This description assumes you will start from Route 102.

From the east side of Route 102, Hio Road begins near Bass Harbor Marsh, which has excellent views of Bernard, Mansell, Beech, and Acadia mountains. The road immediately enters the spruce-fir forest that will be the dominant feature of this ride. The forest attracts northern bird species, such as boreal chickadees, gray jays, black-backed woodpeckers, and spruce grouse. At 0.8 mile, you cross a small stream that flows through a northern white cedar swamp toward the Big Heath. In

The Atlantic Ocean at Seawall is a short ride from Hio Road.

April skunk cabbage is the first herbaceous, or nonwoody, plant to appear in large quantities, sprouting through a layer of fuzzy green sphagnum moss.

The Big Heath is one of Acadia's largest bogs. Bogs usually form in glacial depressions that were once lakes or ponds. Over time, the lake fills with accumulated plant material that decays slowly. What results is a layer of peat that can be as deep as 40 feet and often floats on top of the water. For this reason, bogs are a less-than-pleasant place to walk through. If you attempt to pass through a bog on foot, consider yourself lucky if all you lose is a boot or two. This slowly decaying plant material creates a highly acidic and nutrient-poor environment that makes it difficult for plants to grow. Insectivorous plants, such as sundew and pitcher plants, survive there by trapping insects and consuming the bugs' nutrients. Other plants that tend to grow in bogs are evergreen shrubs, such as Labrador tea, sheep laurel, bog laurel, and orchids. As for trees, black spruce, larch, and white cedars usually manage to survive in the acidic soil of a bog. Birds you might find in the Big Heath include Lincoln's sparrow, northern waterthrush, and palm warblers.

Two miles from Route 102, you reach the end of Hio Road. Through the gate is the group camping area at Seawall Campground. From this end of the campground, it's about a 0.4-mile ride over pavement to the Atlantic Ocean, where there's a picnic area on a natural seawall overlooking the sea. The 10-foot-high cobblestone seawall is impressive, winding its way along the coast for about a mile.

TRIP 23

WITCH HOLE POND AND PARADISE HILL

NPS Rating >	Easy
Distance >	4.4 miles
Elevation Gain >	350 feet
Estimated Time >	1.25 hours
Map >	AMC's Acadia National Park Map: C6

This great trip for families passes beaver ponds and bogs en route to excellent views of Hulls Cove and Frenchman Bay.

DIRECTIONS

From the intersection of Routes 3 and 233 in Bar Harbor, head west on Route 233 for 2 miles then turn right on a road (Duck Harbor Road) unmarked except for a sign that reads, "Entering Acadia National Park." The road ends at the parking area in another 1 mile. There is no Island Explorer stop for this parking area. *GPS coordinates: 44° 23.499′ N, 68° 14.130′ W.*

Note: Duck Harbor Road was previously accessible via West Street in Bar Harbor, but a landslide closed that portion of road, and it is no longer open to vehicles. Cyclists may still use the closed portion of Duck Harbor Road for access to the carriage roads.

TRIP DESCRIPTION

Witch Hole Pond is a beautiful, remote lake surrounded by colorful bogs and filled with beaver lodges. This bike ride takes you past more beaver activity than any other trip in this book. We saw numerous dams and lodges, as well as recent tree cuttings. A great view from Paradise Hill reminds you the ocean is only a few thousand feet away. This is an easy trip with only a few short gradual climbs, making it a perfect choice for families with small children. It is also very convenient to downtown Bar Harbor, as you can ride your bike to the carriage road from town. Of course, this easy access draws crowds in midsummer, so you may want to get an early-morning start in order to enjoy the peacefulness of Witch Hole Pond.

Begin your trip by crossing Duck Brook Bridge, an impressive triple-arch structure built in 1929. The views of Duck Brook and Acadia's mountains from the bridge

This ride starts with a great overhead view: Duck Brook, as seen from Duck Brook Bridge.

are especially spectacular in the fall. Stone steps lead down from the bridge to Duck Brook, where the sound of the rushing stream can make it seem as though you are miles from civilization. Once you cross the bridge, turn right at post 5 to make your way toward Witch Hole Pond. After 0.7 mile and a short but gradual uphill section, you will come to a beaver pond with a small dam and lodge. Beavers are most active at night, but you can sometimes catch a glimpse of them in the early morning.

In the spring, this is a good place to listen for the drumming of ruffed grouses. The 17-inch-long ruffed grouse is the most common member of the partridge family in New England and is well suited to Acadia's mixed woodlands. To attract females, a male will perch on a favorite "drumming log" and beat its wings in an accelerating drum roll. The noise sounds like a distant helicopter or a tractor engine starting up. The beaver pond is also an ideal breeding ground for insects, which in turn attracts all kinds of small songbirds, such as swamp sparrows and flycatchers. This seemingly small and insignificant pond bustles with activity on a warm, sunny day.

About 1 mile after Duck Brook Bridge, Witch Hole Pond appears on your left, with views of Youngs and McFarland mountains providing a backdrop. You will see beavers have dammed the inlet to the pond, creating an extensive marshy area to the right. Witch Hole Pond itself has at least three large beaver lodges, which are up to 6 feet tall. With both the marsh and pond surrounded by bogs and mixed woodlands, this is a good place to look for the large variety of ducks that can be seen in Acadia, such as mallards, black ducks, wood ducks, and blue-winged teals. Witch Hole Pond is big enough to support a good population of fish, which draws both ospreys and human fly-fishers.

After passing between Witch Hole Pond and the marsh, the carriage road comes to post 3. Turn right to head up Paradise Hill. At this point, it is possible to turn left to avoid the extra mile required to summit Paradise Hill, but the views of Hulls Cove and Frenchman Bay are well worth the extra effort. The climb up to the summit is gradual and relatively short, about 0.4 mile from post 3. From the summit, you can see beyond the deep blue waters of Frenchman Bay toward the hills of Schoodic Peninsula and the rest of eastern Maine. As you loop back toward Witch Hill Pond, continue straight at post 1. (Turning to the right would take you to the park visitor center.) You'll return to Witch Hole Pond at post 2; turn right to explore the bogs surrounding the southern end of the pond. Stunted spruce and white pine attempt to grow in the acidic soil, which is held together by sphagnum moss.

A long but very gradual uphill section brings you through more mixed wood-lands peppered with beaver activity. Just before reaching post 4, you come upon Halfmoon Pond on your right, which has a small beaver lodge in its center. There are good views here of Youngs Mountain. At post 4, bear to the left for the final mile of this trip. Sheep laurel and rhodora are common on the roadside here. Both plants have beautiful pink blossoms in late May and early June. At post 5, turn right to cross over Duck Brook Bridge and return to your car.

TRIP 24

SEAL COVE POND– WESTERN MOUNTAINS LOOP

NPS Rating ➤ Easy

Distance ➤ 5 miles

Elevation Gain ➤ 150 feet

Estimated Time ➤ 1.25 hours

Map ➤ AMC's Acadia National Park Map: F2, G2

This easy ride passes through a boreal forest frequented by moose.

DIRECTIONS

From Route 102 in Southwest Harbor, drive east on Seal Cove Road. After 3.3 miles, turn right on a dirt National Park Service road. After 0.4 mile, there will be a sign for Western Mountain Road. Turn right. After another 0.3 mile, there will be a sign for Seal Cove Pond. Follow this sign to the left. You are now on Western Mountain Road. The road ends at Seal Cove Pond in another 0.7 mile. There is no nearby Island Explorer stop for this parking area, which is about 4 miles from Southwest Harbor. *GPS coordinates:* 44° 17.513′ N, 68° 23.536′ W.

TRIP DESCRIPTION

The system of fire roads around Acadia's western mountains provides about 10 miles of bike riding. The roads are all similar in character: dirt and gravel auto roads that pass through a dark yet enchanting boreal forest. Views are nonexistent, but that only adds to the feeling of wilderness in what could pass for Maine's North Woods. This trip begins and ends at Seal Cove Pond, which is home to herons, loons, and bald eagles. The rest of the trip loops through tall spruce and past biologically interesting cedar bogs. This is an easy route that leaves plenty of time for a paddle on Seal Cove Pond (Trip 41) or a hike up the West Ledge Trail (page 239), the latter of which provides almost instant views of Blue Hill Bay and the Atlantic Ocean. Cars are allowed on this road, and while traffic is light, you still need to observe the rules of the road.

From the Seal Cove Pond parking area, ride up the hill on Western Mountain Road. This short, steep section is the hardest climb of the trip. In this area, the road passes through a small stand of hardwoods, with beech and maple trees lining

A cyclist rehydrates on the Western Mountains Loop trip. Always ride with 1 or 2 quarts of water per person.

small rushing streams. By the time you reach West Ledge Trail and enter the boreal forest, the makeup of trees begins to change. West Ledge Trail (hiking only) leads 1.6 miles to the summit of Bernard Mountain. This strenuous trail makes a great side trip, as it leads hikers to the island's best views of Blue Hill Bay.

Continue straight on Western Mountain Road until you reach an intersection at 0.7 mile. Turn right, following the sign that points to Seal Cove. At 1.2 miles, you will reach another intersection where you should turn left. (Turning right will lead you to a dead end in a few hundred yards.) Just before reaching Seal Cove Road at 1.6 miles, you enter a stand of tall red spruce, and the forest takes on a primeval feel. Keep your eyes open for moose! At Seal Cove Road, turn left.

The hard dirt surface of Seal Cove Road makes for easy riding. Despite its dirt surface, Seal Cove Road is a popular auto route for those driving between Southwest Harbor and Seal Cove. Ride single file for safety. The road passes through more spruce forest, although some deciduous trees, such as birch and downy serviceberry, have taken over the disturbed areas along the road. Common along streams, downy serviceberry, with its showy white flowers, was nicknamed "shadbush" by early colonists because it blooms at the same time that shad, a type of herring, swim upstream to spawn. At 2 miles, a small family cemetery from the nineteenth century is visible among the trees on the left. When visiting the cemetery, remember to follow the Leave No Trace ethics discussed in this book's introduction.

At 3.1 miles, you will reach another intersection. Turn left here to return to Western Mountain Road. At 3.5 miles, turn left again, following the sign for Seal Cove Pond. At 4.1 miles, the boreal forest is interrupted on the left by a northern white cedar bog, with a carpet of sphagnum moss hosting such hardy plants as partridgeberry and starflower. Sphagnum wetlands like this add a boost to Acadia's biodiversity, providing habitat for rare orchids and uncommon animals, such as the four-toed salamander.

At the next intersection, go straight to complete the final 0.7 mile back to Seal Cove Pond.

TRIP 25

LONG POND FIRE ROAD

NPS Rating ➤ Easy

Distance ➤ 5.5 miles

Elevation Gain ➤ 250 feet

Estimated Time ➤ 2 hours

Map ➤ AMC's Acadia National Park Map: E2, F2

An easy ride on a dirt road leads to a secluded cove on Long Pond.

DIRECTIONS

Head south on Route 102 in Somesville. Turn right at the flashing yellow light onto Pretty Marsh Road/Route 102. After 4.9 miles, park at the Pretty Marsh picnic area, which will be on your right. Long Pond fire road is on the east side of the road, about 0.1 mile south of the picnic area. There is no nearby Island Explorer stop for this trip. *GPS coordinates: 44° 19.845′ N, 68° 24.249′ W.*

TRIP DESCRIPTION

Long Pond is the largest body of freshwater on Mount Desert Island. On a calm day, its deep blue waters reflect the rounded shapes of Acadia's mountains like a mirror. The pond itself is a busy place in summer, with motorboats and personal motorized watercraft sharing the water with canoes and kayaks (Trips 40 and 44). This bike ride on one of Acadia's dirt fire roads brings you to a secluded cove on the bay formed by the pond's Southern Neck peninsula. Thick evergreen forests line the entire length of the road, adding to the feeling of seclusion on Mount Desert Island's "quiet side." This trip also has good wildlife-viewing opportunities, as it visits a boggy beaver pond and passes through some of the island's best moose habitat.

Begin your trip on the Long Pond fire road, just south of the Pretty Marsh picnic area. This dirt road is open to cars during summer and fall, but traffic is light. It is a fairly level ride for the 1.8 miles to Long Pond, with only a few short ups and downs. The forest is boreal, dominated by spruce and fir. There are a large number of small boggy areas where northern white cedar or alders grow. Vernal ponds, or temporary pools of water where amphibians breed, are also common, making this an interesting trip in spring. Pickerel and wood frogs make use of these small vernal pools to mate and lay eggs. Softball-sized clumps of gelatinous eggs can

The Long Pond Fire Road takes bike riders to this scenic vista of Long Pond.

be found floating free in the pools or attached to sticks or other debris. You will certainly hear the calls of these frogs as you pedal your way toward Long Pond. You may also see smaller egg clumps left by the salamanders that also use these temporary pools to breed.

From the shore of Long Pond, you'll have good views across the water to Cadillac Mountain. The bay to your right is formed by a peninsula of land called Southern Neck. The bay on the left is formed by Northern Neck. All of the shoreline on the Southern Neck side of the pond is part of Acadia National Park, making it seem much wilder than the rest of the pond, which is home to many summer cottages. Mallards, loons, and mergansers are common on the lake, and ospreys and bald eagles often soar high above it, looking for fish. Northern white cedar bogs are common along this part of the shoreline, with sphagnum moss carpeting the forest floor and pitcher plants surviving in the nutrient-poor soil by capturing and digesting insects.

After leaving the shoreline of Long Pond, the fire road soon reaches a fork, where you will bear right. Still in a forest of spruce and fir, you are experiencing the forested island much as it was before the great fire of 1947. This part of the island, with its thick forest peppered with bogs, is home to many of the moose in the park. Moose grow to about 6 feet tall and can weigh as much as 1,200 pounds. Only males have antlers, which can stretch as much as 6 feet across. Moose are not terribly dangerous, but do not to approach them, as they have been known to trample people when angry. If a moose puts its ears back or starts to move toward you, retreat immediately, and it will probably leave you alone. If you don't see moose around Long Pond, you are still likely to see their tracks in the road. Look for prints shaped like deer hooves but much larger, between 3 and 6.5 inches in length.

At 2.5 miles, a road on the right leads about 100 yards to Duck Pond, a small, boggy pond that appears to have been flooded by beavers at some point. The sunbleached trunks of scores of long-dead spruce stand in much of the pond, which is bordered by rhodora and blueberry shrubs. Pitcher plants and sundews grow from the bed of sphagnum moss that lines the shore. This is a good place to watch birds, with the pond and forest edge joining to form a habitat where you might see warblers, flycatchers, wrens, sparrows, wood ducks, hawks, and even bald eagles perching in the tall white pines circling the pond.

At 3.5 miles, the Great Notch Trail (hiking only) leads to the summits of Mansell and Bernard mountains on the left (Trip 14). In another 100 yards, turn left at the "T" intersection. The road continues through spruce-fir forest and cedar swamps, passing by Seal Cove Pond on the left and Hodgdon Pond on the right at 4.1 miles. At 4.4 miles, turn left onto the narrow paved road, which leads to Route 102 at 4.5 miles. Turn right on Route 102 for the final mile of this trip. Route 102 is not an extremely busy road, but it is narrow and the shoulder is soft, so you will need to be cautious on this final stretch.

TRIP 26

🚌 👫 🐕 ⛷ 📷 🏃

AMPHITHEATER LOOP

NPS Rating ➤ Moderate

Distance ➤ 5.5 miles

Elevation Gain ➤ 350 feet

Estimated Time ➤ 2 hours

Map ➤ AMC's Acadia National Park Map: E5, E6, F5, F6

Ride through an enchanting evergreen forest with streams lined with pink-granite stones.

DIRECTIONS

For this trip, park at the Brown Mountain gatehouse parking area on Routes 198/3, 0.5 mile north of Northeast Harbor. The parking area is stop E on the Island Explorer Brown Mountain route (route 6). *GPS coordinates:* 44° 18.681′ N, 68° 17.131′ W.

TRIP DESCRIPTION

The Amphitheater is a narrow valley walled in by the steep sides of Penobscot and Cedar Swamp mountains. Its cool streams and forests are the perfect place to escape summer's heat, and the carriage roads rise just high enough above the trees to give you good views of the ocean. This trip takes you from the Brown Mountain gatehouse on Route 198 around the southern end of Cedar Swamp Mountain and into the Amphitheater before heading south along the west side of Penobscot Mountain. Like the other carriage roads, this piece of Mr. Rockefeller's work features gentle grades, majestic bridges, and sweeping curves that seem to melt into the hillsides.

From the south end of the parking lot, just north of the gatehouse, pedal up the fire road, which leads about 50 yards to the carriage road. At post 18, turn right and make your way through the forest of tall red spruce. The road climbs quickly to post 19 (0.3 mile), where you will take another right. After about 1 mile, views begin to open up to the south. In the fall, hardwoods in the foreground create a beautiful contrast to the dark green spruce that covers the hills between you and the Cranberry Isles. The forest is so thick that it hides any signs of civilization, even though you are looking past Route 3 and the town of Northeast Harbor.

The road makes a gentle descent below the trees, where it reaches post 20 at 1.3 miles. Turn left here toward the Amphitheater. The road makes a graceful left turn toward Cedar Swamp Mountain in order to hug the mountain's contour. In the forest above the road are car-sized boulders covered in green, gray, and brown lichens. The ride eventually turns into a downward coast until you reach the Amphitheater Bridge at 1.8 miles. Built in 1931, the Amphitheater Bridge is 235 feet long, the longest in the carriage-road system. Turrets serve as viewing platforms for taking in the small waterfall, part of Little Harbor Brook. The bridge's single arch was designed to frame the waterfall from below. Characteristic of his love for nature, Rockefeller insisted that a 20-foot pine and a 20-foot hemlock both be left standing after the bridge's construction.

The bridge sits at the head of the valley known as the Amphitheater, which was named for its shape. The steep walls of Cedar Swamp and Penobscot mountains rise above and around the northern end of the valley, which gradually widens as it falls toward the ocean. Apparently, the early visitors who named the Amphitheater pictured giants sitting on the sides of the mountains, watching some grand event on Bear Island. As you continue south on the carriage road, take a look back at the mountains that form the Amphitheater. The road falls slowly through a mosaic forest of white pine, spruce, maple, beech, and birch. At 2.5 miles, turn right at post 21 then, in another 0.5 mile, turn right again at post 22. To the left of post 22, the carriage road enters private property where bikes are not allowed.

At 3.2 miles, the road parallels and soon crosses Little Harbor Brook, a small but beautiful stream lined with pink Cadillac granite. The small bridge that crosses

Cyclists cross one of several bridges found on Acadia's carriage roads.

the brook is a peaceful place to listen to birdsong and rushing water as you rest up for the steep climb that follows. The climb continues until you reach post 20 at 4.2 miles. During the climb, you'll get views of the east side of Cedar Swamp Mountain, which you traversed at the beginning of the trip. Looking at the mountain, it's impossible to discern where the carriage road travels. At post 20, turn left to retrace your route back to the parking area. Turn left again at posts 19 and 18 to complete the 5.5-mile loop.

TRIP 27

🚌 🧑‍🧒

ECHO LAKE TO SEAL COVE POND

NPS Rating ➤ Moderate

Distance ➤ 12 miles

Elevation Gain ➤ 400 feet

Estimated Time ➤ 2 hours

Map ➤ AMC's Acadia National Park Map: F2, F3, F4

The route uses new connector trails to traverse spruce woods between a lake and a pond. Bonus: Start or end your ride with a swim.

DIRECTIONS

From the intersection of Routes 102 and 198 in Somesville, drive 4.2 miles south on Route 102 and turn right on the road to Echo Lake. Parking is at the end of this road in 0.7 mile. This parking area is stop E on the Island Explorer Southwest Harbor route (route 7). *GPS coordinates:* 44° 18.898′ N, 68° 20.210′ W.

TRIP DESCRIPTION

This trip takes advantage of Western Mountain Connector, a multiuse trail that allows for easy bike access between the Echo Lake swimming area and Seal Cove Pond, as well as the hiking trails up Bernard and Mansell mountains (Trip 14). The ride primarily stays on dirt roads through thick spruce-fir forests, with one short singletrack jaunt and another 1.5-mile stretch on pavement—which you will appreciate on the steepest uphill of the trip. You can complete this trip as an out-and-back ride of about 10.5 miles, but we describe it here as a 12-mile loop to add some variety to the route. The 400 feet of elevation gain is spread out pretty evenly over the 12 miles, making for only a few short steep climbs.

From the parking area, ride back up toward Route 102 for 0.3 mile and turn right onto Lurvey Spring Road, a gravel fire road that soon enters a thick, green mossy forest of tall spruce trees. This road sets the tone for much of the trip, as this boreal forest is common on the western side of Mount Desert Island and will be the main habitat for most of the ride. The trees are tall and straight, without much growing in the understory other than ferns, blueberries, and bunchberries. The gravel surface is easy riding, and the terrain is gently rolling, two features common to all of the fire roads on this trip. Shortly before reaching the end of Lurvey Spring Road at 1.6 miles, an unmarked fire road comes in from the right; continue straight.

Lurvey Spring Road ends at Long Pond Road, but you will cross Long Pond Road and ride on Western Mountain Connector. This easy, singletrack, gravel trail passes some municipal buildings before heading downhill through more quiet spruce woods on its way to a right-hand turn onto a doubletrack road, 0.4 mile from Lurvey Spring Road. Western Mountain Connector is one of several village connector trails built in Acadia in the last decade as part of an effort to make it easier to gain access to the park without a lot of driving. Other connector trails include Great Meadow Loop and Schooner Head Path in Bar Harbor.

A bridge spans a carriage road near Eagle Lake.

After the right-hand turn onto the doubletrack road, Western Mountain Connector makes a short climb up to Western Mountain Road and a parking area known as Gilley Field (2.4 miles from Echo Lake). At Gilley Field, there are trailheads for trails that go to Long Pond and Bernard and Mansell mountains. These trails make great hikes, but bikes are not allowed. To ride to Seal Cove Pond, follow Western Mountain Road to the left, taking care to stay left at a fork 0.1 mile from Gilley Field. Like Lurvey Spring Road, Western Mountain Road is a gravel fire road that makes for easy riding over gently rolling hills through a beautiful forest of spruce and fir trees. It is a 2.8-mile ride from Gilley Field to Seal Cove Pond; stay straight at two intersections, 1.3 and 2.1 miles past Gilley Field. There is a nice view of Seal Cove Pond (Trip 41) from the end of the road. It is a quiet place, home to loons and visited by bald eagles.

To begin the return trip, turn around and ride back up Western Mountain Road for one of the longer uphill stretches of this trip. In 0.7 mile, turn right on a side road that leads to Seal Cove Road. About 1.6 miles from Seal Cove Pond, you'll reach Seal Cove Road, where you will turn left. Although still in the park, with that fire-road feel, Seal Cove Pond is a main auto route between Southwest Harbor and Seal Cove, so keep your eyes open for cars. At 0.6 mile after turning onto Seal Cove Road, you pass a small cemetery in the woods; the road then turns to pavement and goes through a more residential area before reaching Long Pond Road at 4.4 miles from Seal Cove Pond.

To finish the trip, turn left onto Long Pond Road and make the steep climb for 0.8 mile to Lurvey Spring Road. Turn right to follow Lurvey Spring Road back to Echo Lake. Hot and sweaty after your ride? Go for a swim at Echo Lake Beach, next to the parking area. Echo Lake has the warmest water for swimming on Mount Desert Island.

TRIP 28

AUNT BETTY POND LOOP

NPS Rating ➤ Moderate

Distance ➤ 6 miles

Elevation Gain ➤ 300 feet

Estimated Time ➤ 1.5 hours

Map ➤ AMC's Acadia National Park Map: D5, D6

This ride offers the possibility of seeing beavers and the certainty of having good views of Sargent Mountain and Eagle Lake.

DIRECTIONS

From the intersection of Routes 3 and 233 in Bar Harbor, take Route 233 west toward Cadillac Mountain. There are two parking areas for the carriage road in 2.1 miles, one on the right and one on the left. The parking area is stop B on the Island Explorer Brown Mountain route (route 6). *GPS coordinates:* 44° 22.648′ N, 68° 15.141′ W.

TRIP DESCRIPTION

This trip begins at the northern end of Eagle Lake then quickly veers away from the lake to visit Aunt Betty Pond and Gilmore Meadow, both of which offer good opportunities to see wildlife. A steep climb through cool evergreens is rewarded with a downhill coast to the western shore of Eagle Lake, with its stunning views of Cadillac Mountain, Pemetic Mountain, and the Bubbles. This trip easily can be combined with Eagle Lake Loop (Trip 29) or Giant Slide Loop (Trip 34).

If you park on the north side of Route 233, turn left onto the carriage road, which soon passes under Route 233. Go straight at post 6. If you park on the south side of Route 233, go right on the carriage road and turn left at post 6. From either direction, about 100 yards past post 6, turn right at post 9 to head toward Aunt Betty Pond. The road makes a moderate climb to views of Cadillac, Pemetic, and Sargent mountains before heading downhill for more than a mile on its way to Aunt Betty Pond. At 2.4 miles from the parking area, you'll reach the pond, which is surrounded by the dark green of spruce and the light green of white pine. There are at least two active beaver lodges in the pond, visible on the shore opposite the carriage road. Since beaver are nocturnal, your best chance of seeing them is at dawn or dusk.

At 2.8 miles, you reach post 11 and Gilmore Meadow, a grassy, freshwater meadow that is formed by a small stone dam at the bridge to the left of post 11. A narrow, meandering channel flows through the center of the meadow. Lincoln and swamp sparrows, sedge and marsh wrens, flycatchers, and warblers all feed on the insects that proliferate here in spring and summer. There's also an excellent view to the south of Sargent Mountain, the second-tallest mountain in Acadia. Turn left at post 11 for a short downhill before beginning a steep climb that crosses several streams and tops out at post 10, 3.9 miles from the parking area.

Turn left at post 10 and left again at post 8. The carriage road heads moderately downhill until it reaches the western shore of Eagle Lake, which it follows for the remainder of this trip. At 110 feet deep, Eagle Lake is one of the deepest lakes on Mount Desert Island, and its cold water provides the ideal habitat for cold-water fish, such as salmon and trout. Loons, mergansers, and cormorants ply the lake's surface, looking for fish. Bald eagles and ospreys fish from the tall spruce and pine circling the lake, and belted kingfishers can be heard chattering away between attempts at catching fish.

At 6 miles, you'll reach post 6 and the end of your trip.

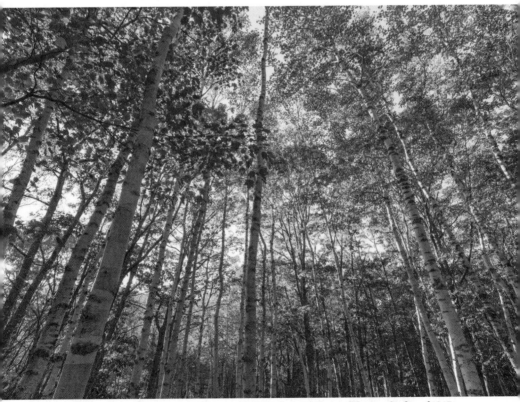

Paper birches are now common in some areas of Acadia that were burned during the fire of 1947.

EAGLE LAKE LOOP

NPS Rating >	Moderate
Distance >	6 miles
Elevation Gain >	350 feet
Estimated Time >	2 hours
Map >	AMC's Acadia National Park Map: D6

A route with only one long uphill stretch, this ride passes through rich woodlands, with mountain views from Eagle Lake.

DIRECTIONS

From the intersection of Routes 3 and 233 in Bar Harbor, take Route 233 west toward Cadillac Mountain. There are two parking areas for the carriage road in 2.1 miles, one on the right and one on the left. The parking area is stop B on the Island Explorer Brown Mountain route (route 6). *GPS coordinates:* 44° 22.648′ N, 68° 15.141′ W.

TRIP DESCRIPTION

Except for one long, gradual uphill stretch, this ride is relatively easy on the legs. It begins at the northern end of Eagle Lake, with its spectacular views of Cadillac and Pemetic mountains. This trip circles the lake in a counterclockwise direction in order to complete the climb up the west side of Conners Nubble at the beginning of the trip, making for an easy rest of the loop. While the views from higher up are limited, the mixture of forests provides beautiful scenery. As with Witch Hole Pond (Trip 23), Eagle Lake is very accessible from Bar Harbor and can be crowded during busy weekends, but the lake's undeveloped shoreline gives it a wilderness feel.

If you park on the north side of Route 233, turn left on the carriage road, which soon passes under Route 233. Go straight at post 6. If you park on the south side of Route 223, go right on the carriage road and turn left at post 6. About 100 yards past post 6, stay to the left at post 9. The carriage road makes a long and steady ascent for much of the 2.1 miles to post 8. The forest alternates between tall spruce,

The north shore of Eagle Lake provides a great view of Cadillac (left) and Pemetic mountains at dawn.

tall white pine, and mixed hardwood, occasionally providing views through the trees down to Eagle Lake.

Eagle Lake is the second-biggest lake on the island after Long Pond, and its deep, cold waters provide good habitat for salmon and trout. Osprey can often be seen circling above the lake while hunting for fish. In the forest, you are more likely to see and hear chickadees, juncos, and thrushes, and the noisy chattering of red squirrels. When you reach post 8, you have completed most of the climbing for this trip. Stay to the left and enjoy the ride back down to the shoreline of the lake, first through sweet-smelling spruce forest and then through a stand of large maple and beech.

As you round the southern end of the lake, you will notice the forest opens up. Tall hemlocks grow here, shading the ground so well that very little light reaches the forest floor, making it hard for shrubs and small trees to grow. The eastern hemlock is one of the more beautiful conifers in the Northeast, with its rich brown bark and feathery green-and-white needles. A hemlock's needles are flat and soft like those of a fir tree, but they are much shorter, only about 0.5 inch in length. Unlike fir trees, which live 70 to 100 years, eastern hemlocks can live up to 400 years and reach heights of 70 feet. They often grow in pure stands in cool, moist valleys and ravines, like the one at the southern end of Eagle Lake. These pure stands often form pockets in the midst of larger northern hardwood forests, creating an edge habitat that has a higher number of species than the rest of the forest.

Approximately 3.8 miles from the parking area, you'll come to post 7. Stay to the left and continue through a marshy area where the trees are smaller and closer together and views open up toward Cadillac Mountain. In spring, you can hear wood frogs making their quacklike mating call here. They are hard to spot, thanks to their brown coloring, but if you scan the small vernal pools near the road for moving shapes about 2 inches long, you should find some. After crossing a stream lined with white birch and sugar maple, the carriage road makes a short ascent followed by a fairly level return to the parking area. Beautiful stone retaining walls line the Cadillac Mountain side of the road. Just before the parking area, a mosaic forest of hardwoods and softwoods provides a good opportunity to look for pileated woodpeckers and yellow-bellied sapsuckers.

EARLY HUMAN HISTORY OF MOUNT DESERT ISLAND

Available archaeological evidence suggests that native people were living on Mount Desert Island at least 6,000 years ago. It is likely they were on the island even earlier, but Maine's wet coastal climate has caused any older evidence to decay into oblivion. Shell middens, or deep heaps of discarded clam and mussel shells that also harbor stone tools and other artifacts, can be found throughout this part of coastal Maine. The Wabanaki lived throughout Maine and spent at least part of the year on Mount Desert Island, which they called *Pemetic,* or sloping land. It was originally believed the Wabanaki spent summers on the island and wintered inland; however, archaeological evidence suggests the opposite was true. Avoiding the brutally cold winters of inland Maine, the Wabanaki most likely wintered on the coast, living off fish and shellfish. In the summers they moved inland to take advantage of Atlantic salmon runs. You can learn more about Maine's American Indian heritage at the Abbe Museum's two locations: inside Acadia National Park at Sieur de Monts Spring, and in downtown Bar Harbor at 26 Mount Desert Street.

It's possible that Leif Erikson and his crew of Viking sailors encountered Mount Desert Island around CE 1000 while seeking timber. Most of the known history of Mount Desert Island, however, begins with the Europeans, who arrived after 1500. Sailing on behalf of France in 1524, the Italian explorer Giovanni da Verazzano was the first European to make note of the island, although Samuel de Champlain generally is given credit for "discovering" Mount Desert Island. In 1604, he ran aground near Otter Point. Champlain, who was mapping the area for the French, named the island *L'Isle des Monts-Deserts,* or Island of the Desert Mountains. Maps of the region that predate his visit called the area *La*

Cadie, which derives either from the area's resemblance to the Arcadia region of Greece or from the Wabanaki word for "where it is plentiful." Most of what was to become New France, from Down East Maine to Nova Scotia, would be known for many years as L'Acadie, or Acadia.

The first permanent European settlement on Mount Desert Island was short-lived. In 1613, two French Jesuit priests, Father Biard and Father Masse, established a mission, possibly at Fernald Point, near the entrance to Somes Sound. They called their mission Saint Sauveur, now the name of the mountain just to the northwest of Fernald Point. The local Wabanaki, led by their chief, Asticou, welcomed the Jesuits' attempt to build a fort, plant corn, and baptize the natives. But before the Jesuits finished building their mission, an English ship under the leadership of Captain Samuel Argall destroyed the fledgling settlement. For the next 150 years, this part of Maine became disputed territory, as the French and English fought for control of North America. During this period, Mount Desert

Land titles on the eastern half of Mount Desert Island can be traced back to the French crown.

Island was used primarily as a landmark for passing ships—and some say as a hideout for pirates.

In 1688, the French king Louis XIV granted 100,000 acres on the Maine coast to Antoine de Mothe Cadillac, who briefly settled on Mount Desert Island before moving on to found Detroit. While Cadillac bestowed upon himself the important-sounding title of Sieur de la Mothe Cadillac, the French explorer had little influence on the history of Mount Desert Island. Shortly after the American Revolution, however, Madame de Gregoire, Cadillac's granddaughter, asked the United States to give her the land from her grandfather's grant. Feeling friendly toward the French after their help in the war, the Massachusetts legislature (which at the time included the land that now makes up the state of Maine) agreed to uphold part of her claim and granted her rights to the entire eastern half of Mount Desert Island. Mount Desert Island is the only place in the United States outside of Louisiana where land titles can be traced back to the French crown. Madame de Gregoire and her husband settled at Hulls Cove in 1788, but they proved ill-suited to the pioneer lifestyle. They gradually sold off their landholdings in order to support themselves, and their family grant was completely used up by the time of their deaths in 1810 and 1811.

The English began settling Mount Desert Island after their victory in the French and Indian War in 1759. In 1760, John Bernard, the governor of Massachusetts, obtained a royal land grant on Mount Desert Island and attempted to secure his claim by offering free land to settlers. Abraham Somes and John Richardson of Gloucester, Massachusetts, took advantage of Bernard's offer and settled in what is now Somesville. Bernard lost his grant as a result of the American Revolution, but the early U.S. government granted his son the western half of the island around the same time it deeded the eastern half to Madame de Gregoire. The grants of Bernard and de Gregoire had little effect on the settlers homesteading on the island, and by the middle of the nineteenth century, Mount Desert Island was thriving like much of the Maine coast, with a diverse economy revolving around farming, lumbering, and fishing.

TRIP 30

🚌 📷 🎿

BAR HARBOR TO OCEAN DRIVE LOOP

NPS Rating >	Moderate
Distance >	11.5 miles
Elevation Gain >	300 feet
Estimated Time >	2 hours
Map >	AMC's Acadia National Park Map: C7, C8, D8, E8

This moderate road ride delivers spectacular views of the Atlantic.

DIRECTIONS

This trip starts at the Village Green in downtown Bar Harbor, at the intersection of Mount Desert Street and Main Street. With the exception of the Loop Road and Schoodic routes, all Island Explorer bus routes stop at the Village Green. *GPS coordinates: 44° 23.252′ N, 68° 12.257′ W.*

TRIP DESCRIPTION

This ride is the only one in this book to follow pavement, but the spectacular views are worth sharing the road with cars. This trip takes you from Bar Harbor to the Schooner Head overlook's dramatic view of the Atlantic Ocean. It also visits Sand Beach, Ocean Drive, and the Tarn, a glacially carved pond beneath the steep cliffs of Dorr Mountain. The elevation gain is minimal for the length of the ride, making it easy to complete this loop in less than an hour, but we encourage you to take your time and drink in the ocean views and fresh salt air. Please note that the section of this trip on Park Loop Road is one-way.

Starting from the Village Green in Bar Harbor, follow Route 3 (Main Street) south, away from the harbor. The ride passes the outskirts of Bar Harbor on the way to Schooner Head Road at 1.2 miles, where you will turn left. Less trafficked than Route 3, Schooner Head Road passes Jackson Laboratory, a world-renowned supplier of lab mice, then enters woodlands filled with paper birch and white-tailed deer. At 3.5 miles from the Village Green, you'll cross the outlet of a large beaver pond with excellent views of the cliffs on Champlain Mountain.

Shortly after the beaver pond, you'll reach an intersection where a right turn brings you to Park Loop Road. You'll be going that direction soon, but first turn left for a 0.1-mile ride to the Schooner Head overlook and a great view of the open ocean. If you need a break from riding, walk down the 0.25-mile trail to Anemone Cave, where at low tide you can climb into the cave and look for the namesake sea creatures that live there. After taking in the views from Schooner Head, turn around and ride to Park Loop Road, where you must turn left. (This is the one-way section.) In about 0.5 mile, you will pass the parking area for Sand Beach on the left, where you can find bathrooms. The road then makes a short climb up to the pink-granite ledges that help make Acadia famous. This is the Ocean Drive section of Park Loop Road, and you will be compelled to get off your bike and explore the ledges. Here you'll have views of crashing surf, distant islands, and seabirds, such as guillemots and eiders. Thunder Hole, with its towers of sea spray, is the best-known attraction along Ocean Drive (at mile 5.2), but in our experience, any of the ledges or the intervening cobble beaches are worth a visit, especially if you want a little solitude.

At 0.6 mile past Thunder Hole, turn right off Park Loop Road and onto Otter Cliff Road (unmarked). In 0.2 mile, there is a picnic area with bathrooms on the left, but the majority of Otter Cliff Road is an uneventful, though pleasant, ride through woods and past a few houses, reaching Route 3 at mile 7.7 of the trip (1.9 miles from Park Loop Road). Turn right and follow Route 3 for the 3.8 miles back to the Village Green. Along the way, you may want to stop and explore the northern shoreline of the Tarn, a glacial pond tucked beneath the cliffs of the east face of Dorr Mountain. Just beyond the Tarn, you can turn left for a short ride to Sieur de Monts Spring and check out the Wild Gardens of Acadia, a native wildflower garden, as well as the Abbe Museum, dedicated to American Indian history.

The Village Green, this ride's starting point, lies opposite Bar Harbor's working waterfront.

TRIP 31

BAR HARBOR TO JORDAN POND VIA EAGLE LAKE

NPS Rating ➤ Easy

Distance ➤ 8.3 miles

Elevation Gain ➤ 200 feet

Estimated Time ➤ 2 hours

Map ➤ AMC's Acadia National Park Map: C7, C6, D6, E6

This route is an ideal first ride for those new to Acadia's carriage-road system.

DIRECTIONS

To Bar Harbor town pier. From the intersection of Mount Desert Street and Main Street, head north on Main Street, which dead-ends at the pier after 0.25 mile. With the exception of the Loop Road and Schoodic routes, all Island Explorer bus routes stop at the Village Green, which is about 0.25 mile from the town pier. *GPS coordinates:* 44° 23.484′ N, 68° 12.283′ W.

To Jordan Pond parking area. From the Hulls Cove Visitor Center, drive south on Park Loop Road for 7.3 miles. Be sure to continue straight at the intersections marked "Sand Beach" and "Cadillac Mountain." The Jordan Pond parking area will be on your right. The parking area is stop D on the Island Explorer Jordan Pond route (route 5) and stop F on the Loop Road route (route 4). *GPS coordinates:* 44° 19.332′ N, 68° 15.121′ W.

TRIP DESCRIPTION

The ride to Jordan Pond is an easy, rewarding trip that starts in Bar Harbor, follows the carriage roads at the Duck Brook Bridge, and proceeds past Eagle Lake on its way to Jordan Pond House. Even people without their "biking legs" should be able to ride this mostly flat route without having to get off and push. It is a great ride anytime, but we think it makes an ideal first experience for those new to the carriage-road system, particularly if you're staying in or near Bar Harbor. You can rent a bike from an outfitter in town and ride off, getting to the carriage roads in about fifteen minutes. If you feel strong after the two-hour ride to Jordan Pond, you can make this an out-and-back trip. Otherwise, you and your bike can

This easy ride takes you through Acadia's woods to Jordan Pond.

hop a ride back to Bar Harbor on an Island Explorer bus (route 5); check at the visitor center for a current schedule.

From the parking area at the town pier in Bar Harbor, ride west on West Street, which parallels the bay. In 0.6 mile, you will cross Route 3 and continue straight until you reach Duck Brook Road at 1.3 miles, where you will turn right. Note: As of 2016, this section of Duck Brook Road was open to bikes but closed to vehicles.

In another 0.6 mile, you will reach the carriage roads at Duck Brook Bridge, on the right. Ride over the beautiful granite bridge, complete with viewing turrets, and turn left at post 5. (For a longer ride, combine this trip with Trip 23, Witch Hole Pond.) About 1 mile from the bridge, turn left at post 4 and ride another mile to Eagle Lake, where you will quickly pass posts 6 and 9; continue straight at both intersections. Most of this ride's elevation gain comes during the next 2.1 miles, as you parallel the lake before climbing around Conners Nubble on the way to post 8.

Turn right at post 8 then left at post 10, in another 0.2 mile. From here it as an easy 2.5-mile ride to Jordan Pond House. On the way, you'll pass the Deer Brook Waterfall at the northern end of Jordan Pond and have excellent views of the pond and the Bubbles as the carriage road breaks into the open, under the cliffs of Penobscot Mountain. Just before reaching the end of the ride, be sure to continue straight at posts 14 and 15 then turn left at post 16. You will then come to Park Loop Road, with Jordan Pond House just a few hundred yards to the left.

TRIP 32
DAY MOUNTAIN

NPS Rating ➤	Moderate
Distance ➤	8 miles
Elevation Gain ➤	500 feet
Estimated Time ➤	2.5 hours
Map ➤	AMC's Acadia National Park Map: E6, F6, F7

This moderate ride on Acadia's only peak reachable by bike delivers great views of the Atlantic Ocean and the islands to the south and west of Mount Desert Island.

DIRECTIONS

From the Hulls Cove Visitor Center, drive south on Park Loop Road for 7.3 miles. Be sure to continue straight at the intersections marked "Sand Beach" and "Cadillac Mountain." The Jordan Pond parking area will be on your right. The carriage road for this trip begins next to the Jordan Pond gatehouse, across the road from Jordan Pond House. The parking area is stop D on the Island Explorer Jordan Pond route (route 5) and stop F on the Loop Road route (route 4). *GPS coordinates:* 44° 19.332′ N, 68° 15.121′ W.

TRIP DESCRIPTION

Day Mountain is the only peak in Acadia you can climb via the carriage roads. When John D. Rockefeller Jr. was having the carriage roads constructed, he decided against building them over mountaintops. He only agreed to this road because Day Mountain is a relatively small peak, 583 feet tall, and it was possible to build the road so it was not visible from any other peaks. Bikers visiting Acadia National Park are glad he made this decision. This trip is an enjoyable one, as you climb above the trees to sweeping vistas of the open Atlantic and the islands to the south and west of the park.

Begin this ride by heading east on the carriage road next to the Jordan Pond gatehouse, across Park Loop Road from Jordan Pond House. Rockefeller had the prominent New York architect Grosvenor Atterbury design the Jordan Pond gatehouse, which was constructed in the early 1930s. It was designed along the lines of a European hunting lodge in the French Romanesque architectural style. Another gatehouse was built near Lower Hadlock Pond, outside of Northeast Harbor. These

Day Mountain is the only mountain in Acadia that is accessible via the carriage roads.

gatehouses were built to provide a place for attendants to live while manning the gates that would allow in carriages but not automobiles. The gatehouses are no longer occupied, and the gates are closed to motorized traffic except for National Park Service maintenance vehicles.

The first 0.25 mile is a nice downhill coast before the road begins a long, gradual ascent. After passing above Wildwood Stables, the carriage road reaches post 17 at 1.2 miles. Turn right and cross the Triad-Day Bridge. Completed in 1940, this was the last of the carriage-road bridges to be built. Across the bridge, you will come to post 37. Turn right to circle around the west side of Day Mountain. You will need to watch your speed on the long downhill stretch here in order to maintain control and avoid accidents with horses or other bikes. At 1.8 miles you will reach post 38, where you will continue straight through a forest of spruce, fir, birch, and maple. From post 38, the road begins its gradual ascent toward the summit of Day Mountain. On your left you will see a low but beautiful retaining wall made of bowling-ball-sized boulders of pink granite.

At 2.5 miles, turn left at post 36 to ride the final 1.5 miles up to the summit. As you gain elevation, spectacular views open up of the Atlantic Ocean to the east and the Cranberry Isles to the south. The climb is steady but moderate, and long stretches of the carriage road are well above the trees, so the views are constant while you ride. At 3.7 miles, you'll reach the summit, which has excellent views to the south of the Cranberry Isles, Duck Island, Isle au Haut, and the western mountains. With its quiet woods and scenic vistas, Day Mountain is a great place for a picnic lunch.

Return down the carriage road to post 36, where you will turn left. You will have to watch your speed again on the descent, as there are many tight corners. Between post 36 and post 37 are more views of the Atlantic before you drop down for good into the shade of the cool forest. When you reach post 37, you are back at the Triad-Day Bridge, which spans Park Loop Road. Cross the bridge and turn left at post 17. About 100 yards past post 17, take the right fork in the road; the left fork is used as an access from Wildwood Stables. From here, retrace your route back to Jordan Pond House.

TRIP 33

🚌 🧍 🐕 ⛷ 🏞 📷 🏃

JORDAN POND–
BUBBLE POND LOOP

NPS Rating › Moderate

Distance › 9 miles

Elevation Gain › 500 feet

Estimated Time › 2.5 hours

Map › AMC's Acadia National Park Map: E6, D6

Take in the dramatic scenery of Jordan and Bubble ponds on a moderate ride that crosses two significant bridges.

DIRECTIONS

From the Hulls Cove Visitor Center, drive south on Park Loop Road for 7.3 miles. Be sure to continue straight at the intersections marked "Sand Beach" and "Cadillac Mountain." The Jordan Pond parking area will be on your right. The carriage road for this trip begins across the street from the Jordan Pond gatehouse. The parking area is stop D on the Island Explorer Jordan Pond route (route 5) and stop F on the Loop Road route (route 4). *GPS coordinates:* 44° 19.332′ N, 68° 15.121′ W.

TRIP DESCRIPTION

Jordan Pond is arguably the most scenic pond in Acadia National Park, with its deep blue waters reflecting the steep cliffs of Penobscot Mountain and the graceful curves of the Bubbles. Bubble Pond is smaller and more intimate, with dramatic scenery of its own, as the steep west face of Cadillac Mountain rises above the pond's eastern shoreline. This is one of the longer rides in the carriage-road system, but its grades are never steep. For this reason, it makes a great day trip for a family with older children who are comfortable spending the day on bikes. Of course, you can recharge following your ride with tea and popovers at Jordan Pond House.

Begin this trip by turning onto the carriage road across the street from the Jordan Pond gatehouse. Turn right at post 16 and go straight at post 15. At 0.3 mile, a small bridge crosses the outlet to Jordan Pond as the carriage road climbs up to post 14 at 0.5 mile, where you will continue straight. The road pursues its upward trek through a mixed forest until Jordan Pond and the Bubbles come into view at 1.25 miles. The road crosses a huge rock slide where giant boulders line the steep east face of Penobscot Mountain.

Deer Brook flows under Deer Brook Bridge, which you'll cross on this ride.

George Dorr, the first superintendent of Acadia National Park, feared that constructing a road through such a treacherous rock slide was a risky proposition. John D. Rockefeller Jr. and his contractor managed to assure Dorr no one would get hurt, and they were allowed to proceed. The views from this stretch of the carriage road are fantastic. The pond is about 150 feet below the road, and you can see the Bubbles, as well as the entire south ridge of Pemetic Mountain. You can also look straight up at Jordan Cliffs, home to one of Acadia's nesting pairs of peregrine falcons.

Upon reentering the forest, you will cross Deer Brook Bridge. This bridge, with its pair of tall, narrow arches, gives you a close-up view of Deer Brook cascading in a waterfall over large slabs of pink granite. Deer Brook Trail, on the south side of the bridge, makes its way up to Sargent Pond and Sargent and Penobscot mountains (Trip 13). After the falls, the ride levels out as you pass the north end of Jordan Pond and head toward Eagle Lake. At 2.5 miles, turn right at post 10. At 2.7 miles, turn right again at post 8. At this point, you are about 500 feet above and west of Eagle Lake, behind a small peak called Conners Nubble. At 3.2 miles, you'll cross a hiking trail; you might choose to take a quick detour on foot for a summit view of Eagle Lake.

After passing Conners Nubble, the road makes a long descent to the southern end of Eagle Lake, which is surrounded by thick spruce forest. This forest is a great place to look for finches, such as red crossbills, white-winged crossbills, pine siskins, and common redpolls. Except for redpolls, all of these finches breed in the park, but their numbers vary greatly. Boreal forest finches tend to migrate in waves, depending on the severity of the weather and the abundance of the seed crop, so their numbers in any one area can change from year to year.

At 4.5 miles, turn right at post 7, toward Bubble Pond. You will cross Park Loop Road at 4.8 miles and pass by the northern end of Bubble Pond. You will then ride over a bridge that seems to cross nothing but forest. The bridge was built to cross Park Loop Road, which was subsequently relocated because it passed too close to the pond. Bubble Pond Bridge was constructed of compressed rock, as opposed to the granite blocks used for the rest of the bridges in the park. After crossing the bridge, the road turns left and follows the shoreline of Bubble Pond. Pemetic Mountain rises steeply to the west. Across the pond to the east is the steep western face of Cadillac Mountain. Cedar and paper birch grow on the shoreline, as well as on the ledges on Cadillac. During the spring and fall migrations, you can see hawks, eagles, falcons, and vultures riding the thermals of warmed air above Cadillac. Turkey vultures are known to use the huge boulders at the southeastern end of the pond as a resting spot. They blend in well with the gray rocks, so you may need binoculars to spot them.

As the road continues past the pond, it passes through a variety of forest types: spruce-fir, northern hardwood, and cedar. In the northern hardwood forest, you will notice irregularly shaped and dying beech trees. These are infected with a blight that's a combination of a fungus and a scale (a sucking insect), introduced by European beech trees imported in the nineteenth century. While bad for the trees, the blight does benefit the insects that feed on the dying trees, as well as the woodpeckers and flickers that feed on the insects. Nonetheless, the loss of a large number of American beech trees would be devastating to the forest animals that depend on beechnuts for food. Scientists are still unsure as to the long-term effects of this blight on the beech forests of North America.

After rounding the southern end of a small peak called the Triad, go straight at post 17 (7.7 miles). The road then climbs for 0.5 mile as it traverses the west side of the Triad, behind Wildwood Stables, with views of the Cranberry Isles. From here it is an easy coast back down to the Jordan Pond gatehouse.

ACADIA'S MOSAIC FOREST

"Mosaic" is a word Acadia's naturalists use to describe much of the forest on the eastern half of Mount Desert Island. The term refers to a forest with a high diversity of tree species that does not fit into the normal forest-habitat categories (e.g., northern hardwoods or boreal). Acadia's mosaic forest came about after the great fire of 1947 (see page 25). Before the fire, a boreal forest of red spruce and balsam fir covered most of the island. The thick canopy of the spruce and fir made it nearly impossible for other trees to grow. With the spruce-fir canopy gone, sun-loving trees, such as birch, aspen, and maple, were able to take root. White pine also grew quickly, while spruce and fir saplings sprouted from the stumps of trees killed in the fire. The result is a forest that is part boreal, part northern hardwoods.

Acadia's mosaic forest defies the typical forest habitat categories such as northern hardwood or boreal and includes a mix of tree species from several forest types.

With a new forest of deciduous trees, Acadia became a different place and now experiences the brilliant fall foliage displays that make New England famous. Wildlife concentrations are also different. Beaver, which eat birch and aspen, are much more common in the park now compared to 70 years ago. Their presence has created an increase in wetland habitats, which in turn has attracted more river otters. These additional wetlands nurture fish, crayfish, and amphibians that attract birds, such as great blue herons and kingfishers, in addition to otters. The forest itself provides good habitat for myriad songbirds, including yellow warblers, scarlet tanagers, and northern orioles, as well as pileated woodpeckers and ruffed grouse. White-tailed deer numbers are up, as the deer feed on acorns and the twigs of young birches and aspens.

TRIP 34
GIANT SLIDE LOOP

NPS Rating > Difficult

Distance > 8.5 miles

Elevation Gain > 600 feet

Estimated Time > 2.5 hours

Map > AMC's Acadia National Park Map: E5, D5

This ride crosses rushing mountain streams to reach spectacular ocean and mountain views.

DIRECTIONS

Park at the Parkman Mountain parking area on Routes 198/3, 1.8 miles north of Northeast Harbor. The parking area is stop D on the Island Explorer Brown Mountain route (route 6). *GPS coordinates:* 44° 19.898′ N, 68° 17.653′ W.

TRIP DESCRIPTION

This trip begins with a long ride over relatively flat terrain to the northwest of Parkman and Sargent mountains. It then visits a beautiful meadow with views of the mountains before beginning a long, steep climb up the north side of Sargent. The 600-foot ascent is well worth the effort, though, as views open up all the way to the Camden Hills, 30 miles distant. With wetlands, streams, and several different forest types on view, this trip also provides excellent opportunities for nature study.

Starting at the Parkman Mountain parking area, follow the carriage road to the left, away from post 13. The 3.3 miles to post 11 is almost all downhill, following a gentle grade through an evergreen forest. The road crosses several small streams tumbling down from Sargent and Parkman mountains. As you get closer to post 11, wetlands begin to appear on the left and the forest changes, with deciduous trees, such as northern red oak, maple, and birch, taking over the flat valley floor. Northern red oak is the northernmost oak species in the eastern United States, and its range extends well into Quebec and Ontario, although it is most often associated with the oak-hickory forests to the south and west of Maine. Like most oaks, it can grow to be tall and stately, producing bumper crops of acorns every three or four years.

At post 11, you reach Gilmore Meadow, a freshwater wetland with a great view of Sargent Mountain. The meadow, with its grassy swamp surrounded by a meander-

On difficult rides, such as this one, take time to rehydrate along the side of Acadia's carriage roads.

ing channel, is a great place to look for small birds, such as sparrows, flycatchers, and warblers. Turn right at post 11 for a short downhill coast before beginning the steepest climb in the carriage-road system. Here the road enters a mixed evergreen and hardwood forest, passing through a grove of hemlocks as it makes several stream crossings over a series of uncharacteristic concrete and wooden bridges. At 4.4 miles, you will reach post 10, where you should turn right.

The steep climb continues as you wind your way up the north face of Sargent Mountain. At 4.9 miles, you reach Chasm Brook Bridge. Built in 1926, this bridge provides a welcome resting point, where you can listen to the rushing water of Chasm Brook as it cascades over a 40-foot waterfall. The road continues up the mountain, with switchbacks making the climb more amenable. As you get higher, the hills of northern and eastern Maine come into view. Climbing still, you'll see Blue Hill and Acadia's western mountains to the west. At 6.3 miles, the road crosses Sargent Northwest Trail then levels out.

As you round the north side of Parkman Mountain, you get wide-open views of Somes Sound and all of Maine to the west. The road stays in the open for much of its way down from Parkman Mountain. Pitch pines and white pines cling to the rock ledges amid clumps of blueberry bushes and lichen. At 8.1 miles, turn right at post 12. Turn right again at 8.4 miles, at post 13. The parking area is on the left in another 0.1 mile.

TRIP 35

🚌 🐕 🔍 📷 🥾

AROUND THE MOUNTAIN LOOP

NPS Rating ➤ Difficult

Distance ➤ 12 miles

Elevation Gain ➤ 1,000 feet

Estimated Time ➤ 4 hours

Map ➤ AMC's Acadia National Park Map: E5, E6, F5, F6

This ride has it all: three waterfalls, mountain and ocean views, and seven major bridge crossings.

DIRECTIONS

From the Hulls Cove Visitor Center, drive south on Park Loop Road for 7.3 miles. Be sure to continue straight at the intersections marked "Sand Beach" and "Cadillac Mountain." The Jordan Pond parking area will be on your right. The carriage road for this trip begins across the street from the Jordan Pond gatehouse. The parking area is stop D on the Island Explorer Jordan Pond route (route 5) and stop F on the Loop road route (route 4). *GPS coordinates:* 44° 19.332′ N, 68° 15.121′ W.

TRIP DESCRIPTION

It is not clear which mountain the person who named this loop had in mind, for "the loop" actually circles around six peaks: Penobscot Mountain, Cedar Swamp Mountain, Bald Peak, Parkman Mountain, Gilmore Peak, and Sargent Mountain. It begins and ends next to the deep blue waters of picturesque Jordan Pond. For 12 miles, it rises and falls through almost every forest type in the park, passes steep cliffs and waterfalls, and climbs to dramatic views of the area surrounding Acadia National Park. It is long by carriage-road standards and gains more elevation than any other loop in the park. Nevertheless, strong riders can complete it in less than half a day. It is easy, however, to spend the entire day studying nature's details and soaking in the long-distance views.

Begin this trip by riding west onto the carriage road across the street from the Jordan Pond gatehouse. Turn right at post 16 and go straight at post 15. At 0.3 mile, a small bridge crosses the outlet to Jordan Pond, as the carriage road climbs up to post 14 at 0.5 mile, where you will turn left. A short but steep climb brings you to the modest West Branch Bridge, with its single tall, narrow arch spanning

Around the Mountain Loop passes three waterfalls, including this one on Deer Brook.

a small stream tumbling down Penobscot Mountain. After climbing 1.2 miles, you will reach the 230-foot-long Cliffside Bridge, in the style of a fortress from the Middle Ages. Two large viewing turrets invite you to look out at Pemetic and Day mountains, as well as the Triad. Maples and other hardwoods dominate the foreground, while spruce and fir trees cling to the distant mountains.

As you round the southern end of Penobscot Mountain, you come to post 21, where you should continue straight toward the Amphitheater. The road gently rises through a mosaic forest, and views of the rounded ridges that make up the Amphitheater soon come into view. At 2.2 miles, you'll reach the head of the Amphitheater and the 235-foot-long bridge that crosses the small gorge there. Walking down a trail at the west end of the bridge will take you down to Little Harbor Brook, where you can look through the arch in the bridge to a small waterfall.

Continuing past the bridge, turn right at post 20 for a gradual climb up to views of the Cranberry Isles. As you ride toward post 19, notice the variety of lichens that grow on the rocks lining the road. Green target lichen grows in concentric rings. Brown-and-black rock tripe looks like lettuce gone bad. Reindeer lichen, with its greenish-white branches reminiscent of antlers, grows in bunches and is eaten by reindeer and caribou in the arctic environments where they live. There are also large clumps of rhodora, an evergreen shrub that grows in bogs and other areas with acidic soils. When you reach post 19, at 3.6 miles, turn right.

At 5 miles, you'll reach a pair of magnificent bridges that span Hadlock Brook and Maple Spring. Waterfall Bridge looks out at Hadlock Brook as the stream tumbles over 40 feet of granite. Hemlock Bridge spans Maple Spring, which is lined with tall hemlocks and white pines. An enchanted-forest feeling creeps in as you ride over these intricate bridges and through tall trees surrounded by the sounds of water and birdsong. The road then climbs to views of Upper Hadlock Pond and the Cranberry Isles at post 12 (5.5 miles). Turn right to begin one of the longest climbs in the carriage-road system.

From here, your route ascends for most of the next 1.8 miles, reaching an elevation of 800 feet. The road traverses the western shoulder of Parkman Mountain, climbing through a forest of pitch pine on its way to extensive views to the west and north. Somes Sound, the only fjord in the eastern United States, can be seen just to the west of the road, with Acadia, Beech, and Bernard mountains rising up to the west of the sound. As you get higher and round the northern end of Sargent Mountain, the wind gets a little stronger and the air a little colder. At this point, the views open up to include Mount Desert Narrows and northern Maine.

Once you pass Sargent Northwest Trail, at 7.3 miles, you are rewarded with a long, winding downhill coast that will take you back to Jordan Pond. It is easy to pick up a lot of speed on this stretch. Try to control it, because it's fairly likely someone will be stopped on the road, hidden behind a curve. You will have good views of Eagle Lake on the way down. Notice how the forest is sharply demarcated between spruce-fir and paper birch. Spruce-fir forests dominated the island before the great fire of 1947. After the fire, pioneer species, such as aspen, birch, and other hardwoods, grew back in place of the spruce and fir. In this area, thin soil has made it hard for trees to return, and the paper birch that do grow are very thin and spindly. By identifying the different forest types, it is easy to see where the fire did its damage.

At 8.7 miles, you'll cross a small bridge over Chasm Brook, which falls about 40 feet over the rocks to the south of the bridge. At 9.2 miles, go straight at post 10. A slight incline brings you to another waterfall and Deer Brook Bridge at 10 miles. The north end of Jordan Pond begins to come into view through the trees on the left. Continuing south, you will break out into the open as you pass through a massive rock slide on the east face of Penobscot Mountain. Here you will get a good look at Jordan Pond, the Bubbles, and Pemetic Mountain. Looming above you are Jordan Cliffs. At 11.3 miles, bear left at post 14, which completes the loop. To finish your trip, stay to the left at posts 15 and 16.

TRIP 36

AROUND THE MOUNTAIN LOOP II

NPS Rating ➤ Difficult

Distance ➤ 18.7 miles

Elevation Gain ➤ 900 feet

Estimated Time ➤ 5.5 hours

Map ➤ AMC's Acadia National Park Map: D5, D6, E5, E6, F5, F6

This long ride traverses gorgeous forests, skirts scenic ponds, and crosses the park's longest carriage-road bridge.

DIRECTIONS

From the intersection of Routes 3 and 233 in Bar Harbor, take Route 233 west toward Cadillac Mountain. There are two parking areas for the carriage road in 2.1 miles, one on the right and one on the left. The parking area is stop B on the Island Explorer Brown Mountain route (route 6). *GPS coordinates:* 44° 22.648′ N, 68° 15.141′ W.

TRIP DESCRIPTION

This ride follows the outer edge of the carriage-road system for most of its length, making it a long ride but one without the extensive or difficult uphill sections found on other routes in this book. Then again, 18.7 miles of riding on gravel roads that climb 100 feet every now and then requires a day's worth of exertion, so bring plenty of food and water to keep your energy levels high.

We describe this trip as starting at Eagle Lake, but you can just as easily start at Parkman Mountain, Jordan Pond, or Bubble Pond. In addition to all of the above, this ride also visits Aunt Betty Pond and crosses many of the magnificent stone bridges found on the carriage roads, including the 230-foot-long, fortress-like Cliffside Bridge. To trace out the route for this trip, start at the north end of Eagle Lake (grid D6 on the AMC map) and follow it to these carriage road intersections: 6, 9, 11, 13, 12, 19, 20, 21, 14, 15, 16, 17, 7, and back to 6.

If you park on the north side of Route 233, turn left on the carriage road, which soon passes under Route 233. Go straight at post 6. If you park on the south side of Route 233, go right on the carriage road and turn left at post 6. From either direction,

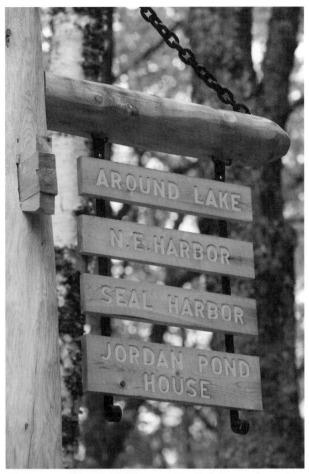
Acadia's signage makes for an easy-to-follow loop.

about 100 yards past post 6, turn right at post 9 to head toward Aunt Betty Pond. The road makes a moderate climb to views of Cadillac, Pemetic, and Sargent mountains before heading downhill for more than a mile on its way to Aunt Betty Pond. At 2.4 miles from the parking area, you'll reach the pond, where beavers make their home and conifers fill the surrounding forests. In another 0.4 mile, you will reach Gilmore Meadow and post 11. After taking in the views of Sargent Mountain, turn right and enjoy an easy ride through beautiful softwood and hardwood forests. At 6.1 miles, you will reach post 13, where you should turn left for a short, relatively steep climb to post 12 at 6.5 miles. Turn right here.

At 6.9 miles, you will reach Hemlock Bridge then Waterfall Bridge, two of our favorite bridges in the carriage-road system. Hemlock Bridge rises high above a small gorge populated with tall hemlocks, while Waterfall Bridge gives an unobstructed view of Hadlock Brook cascading beautifully over pink granite. After Waterfall Bridge, the carriage road bends to the south for a long, gradual descent, paralleling the south ridge of Cedar Swamp Mountain. At 8.3 miles, turn left at post 19 then left again at post 20 (9.3 miles). It is a relatively easy ride from here to Amphitheater Bridge at 9.8 miles. At 235 feet in length with an arch that spans 50 feet, this is the longest bridge on any of the carriage roads.

The carriage road then bends to the right and follows a contour on the west side of Penobscot Mountain, providing good views of unbroken forests and the ocean in the distance. At 10.5 miles, turn left at post 21. You will soon reach Cliffside

Bridge, where you can take a break in one of the viewing turrets that look out over the forests and mountains to the east. At 11.5 miles, turn right at post 14. Continue straight at post 15 then turn left at post 16, at 12 miles. You will cross Park Loop Road shortly after. If you need a break or want to recharge on the shores of Jordan Pond, turn left and follow the road a few hundred yards to Jordan Pond House, where there are restrooms, bike racks, a gift shop, and famous popovers. If you opt to skip Jordan Pond, continue straight across Park Loop Road and pass the elaborate gatehouse on the left.

Easy riding brings you to post 17 at 13.2 miles, where you will continue straight unless you have the energy for a ride up Day Mountain (Trip 32). The carriage road then skirts around the east side of the Triad and Pemetic Mountain, closely following the western shore of Bubble Pond, which has good views of the cliffs on the western face of Cadillac Mountain. At the north end of the pond, you will cross Park Loop Road and reach post 7 at 16.4 miles. Turn right, cross Bubble Brook, and enjoy the views of Eagle Lake as you follow its eastern shore on the way back to the parking area and the end of the ride.

ROAD BIKING TRIPS

While cycling enthusiasts of all types flock to Acadia's crushed-gravel carriage-road system, those seeking a road-bike experience will find several enjoyable trips on pavement around the island. Below are some of our favorites on the roads in and around Acadia National Park.

Park Loop Road (19 miles)

From Bar Harbor, take Kebo Road 1.2 miles to Park Loop Road. This ride must be completed in a clockwise direction, since much of Park Loop Road is one-way. This trip will take you to many of the park's highlights, including Champlain Mountain, Sand Beach, Otter Cliffs, and Jordan Pond.

Western Side, Routes 102/102A (26 miles)

Following Route 102 around the western side of Mount Desert Island gives you the opportunity to visit Long Pond, Bass Harbor Head Light, Seawall, Echo Lake, and the town of Southwest Harbor. From Somesville, follow Route 102 south, turning right at the blinking yellow light. Route 102 basically loops around this side of the island. Pass the little town of Tremont and turn right onto Route 102A, heading toward Bass Harbor and Seawall. Just before reaching Southwest Harbor, you reconnect with Route 102, which you can follow north back to Somesville.

Schoodic Peninsula (12 miles)

From Route 186 in Winter Harbor, follow Moore Road south along the very scenic coastline of Schoodic Peninsula. After passing the picturesque scenes of lobster boats in Bunker's Harbor and Birch Harbor, turn left on Route 186 to return to Winter Harbor.

Swans Island (16 miles)

An enjoyable, 40-minute ferry ride from Bass Harbor takes you to Swans Island. Here 16 miles of road provides plenty of opportunity for a day spent exploring the hills and valleys of the island's 7,000 acres. Hockamock Head Lighthouse is probably the most popular attraction on the island, with rural countryside and ocean views making up the bulk of the scenery.

These trips are a great way to get out of your car and see Acadia up close, but remember you are sharing the road with cars

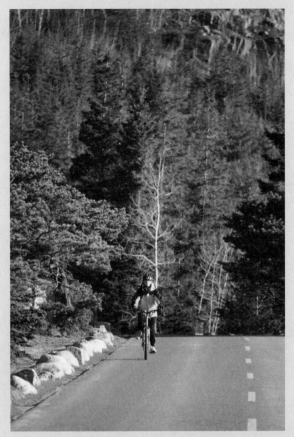

Take note that Park Loop Road, above, is one-way.

traveling at speeds of up to 55 miles an hour. Wear a helmet and bright colors, and follow the same rules of the road you would when driving.

QUIETWATER PADDLING

QUIETWATER PADDLING IN ACADIA NATIONAL PARK

Experiencing Acadia's quiet inland waters from a canoe or kayak offers a new perspective on the beauty of Mount Desert Island. From the grand vistas of Eagle Lake to the quiet comfort of Little Long Pond, all of these paddles are suitable for families and solo paddlers alike. These trips also provide excellent wildlife-watching opportunities. Loons and ducks and occasionally bald eagles, ospreys, and river otters all can be spotted in Acadia's inland waters. While we did omit a few of the island's smaller ponds, this chapter provides a fairly complete description of the quietwater paddling available in Acadia National Park. The following trips take you from serene glides through waterlilies to dramatic cliff-side paddling to meandering exploration in a bird-filled marsh.

PADDLING TIMES AND DISTANCES

The distances we've listed assume you will follow a pond's circumference for most of these trips. Distances will be shorter if you paddle from point A to point B and back, but we expect most people will explore the shoreline for at least part of a trip, looking for animals, flowers, and resting spots. Times vary widely according to paddlers' experience, physical conditioning, and curiosity. We have tried to come up with the time it would take a paddler of average strength and experience to complete these trips, with only one short rest break to eat a snack. If you have a group of very curious paddlers, expect your trips to take a bit longer.

STAND-UP PADDLEBOARDING

Stand-up paddleboarders will find several possibilities for outings in this chapter: Echo Lake (Trip 38), Seal Cove Pond (Trip 41), Northeast Creek (Trip 42), and Long Pond: North End (Trip 44).

SAFETY AND ETIQUETTE

Although paddling on Mount Desert Island is a fairly safe activity, cold and deep waters combined with regularly changing weather conditions require certain safety precautions. To ensure a safe and comfortable paddling experience, consider the following:

- Know how to use your canoe or kayak. Lakes and ponds such as those in Acadia are the perfect place for inexperienced paddlers to learn, but if you're new to the sport, at a minimum you'll want to have someone show you the basic paddling strokes, as well as how to enter and exit your particular boat. New paddlers should consider staying close to shore until they are comfortable with their paddling skills. Luckily, some of the most interesting aspects of the trips in this chapter are found close to shore.

- Turn around before the members of your party start to feel tired. Paddling a few miles after your arms are already spent can make for cranky travelers. All of the trips in this book start and end at the same location, so you can easily turn around at any time.

- Make sure everyone in your group is wearing a life jacket, also known as a personal flotation device or PFD. You are required by Maine law to have at least one PFD per person in your boat. We strongly suggest you wear your PFD while paddling. It is very easy to tip a canoe accidentally and, with Acadia's ponds reaching depths of 150 feet, it just makes sense to wear a PFD at all times. Children age 10 and under are required by law to wear a Class I, II, or III PFD in Maine, and parents should set a good example.

- Pay close attention to the wind. Wind as gentle as 10 miles per hour can create fairly large waves on all of the ponds on the island. Waves of 2 and 3 feet are not unusual on Eagle Lake, Long Pond, and Echo Lake. We even paddled in 1-foot waves on the fairly diminutive Jordan Pond. All of the ponds on the island run from north to south, making northerly or southerly winds even more problematic. Bring a windbreaker, as it can get cold in a canoe in the lightest of winds. Little Long Pond is probably your best bet on a windy day.

- Stay off the water if thunderstorms are nearby. Lightning is a serious danger to boaters. If you hear a thunderstorm approaching, get off the water immediately and seek shelter. For a current weather forecast, check your favorite weather website or smartphone app (we like wunderground.com and the wunderground iOS app), or call the weather line of the local radio station WDEA: 207-667-8910.

- Bring the following supplies with you to make your trip more comfortable. Why not, when you don't have to carry them on your back?

  ✓ Water: Bring 1 or 2 quarts per person, depending on the weather and the length of the trip.

  ✓ Food: Even for a short paddle, it's a good idea to have high-energy snacks, such as nuts, dried fruit, or snack bars. Bring a lunch for longer trips.

  ✓ Map and compass—and the ability to use them.

  ✓ Extra clothing: Rain gear, a wool sweater or fleece jacket, gloves, and a wool or fleece hat.

  ✓ Headlamp or flashlight, with spare batteries and light bulb.

  ✓ Sunscreen and hat: You will be at the mercy of the sun on a clear day.

✓ First-aid kit.

✓ Pocketknife.

✓ Binoculars for wildlife viewing.

In addition to the no-impact Leave No Trace techniques described in this book's introduction, please keep the following things in mind while paddling:

- Give wildlife a wide berth. Lakes and ponds are much different from forests, in that wildlife has less of an opportunity to hide from humans. The summer months see a lot of people in the water, and the ducks, herons, and loons waste a good deal of energy swimming or flying away from curious boaters. If you spot wildlife, remain still and quiet and let the animal decide whether to approach you. Use binoculars if you want a closer look. In spring, steer well clear of loons nesting along the shore.

- Respect private property. Much of the land surrounding the waters of Acadia is residential. We mention this fact in each of the relevant trip descriptions, but take a map that shows the park boundaries. Do not land your boat on private property and speak quietly when paddling near homes and cottages.

- Respect the purity of the water. Most of the ponds on Mount Desert Island are sources of drinking water for the surrounding communities. If you need to relieve yourself, do so on land, at least 200 yards from the shoreline. Echo Lake is the only pond in the park where swimming is allowed.

- Sound carries a long way on the water, so keep your conversations quiet in order to avoid disturbing wildlife, other paddlers, or nearby hikers.

You can thank the last ice age for the quietwater paddling on Mount Desert Island. Ice sculpted the landscape into deep cold-water ponds reflecting the rounded masses of pink granite that give Acadia its mountainous allure. Glaciers plowed through rock, creating cliffs that reach down to the water's edge on Long Pond, Jordan Pond, and Echo Lake. They created the deep waters of Eagle Lake, which remain cold enough throughout the year to support trout and salmon, which in turn support ospreys and bald eagles. The ice also left shallow depressions, such as Seal Cove Pond and Little Long Pond, that harbor marshes filled with wading birds and waterfowl, painted turtles, and green frogs. Surrounded by this enchanting scenery and abundant wildlife, you are sure to enjoy your time on the water!

TRIP 37

人 🐕 📷

LITTLE LONG POND

NPS Rating ➤ Easy

Distance ➤ 1.25 miles

Estimated Time ➤ 1 hour

Map ➤ AMC's Acadia National Park Map: F6

Take a short, easy paddle on one of Mount Desert Island's most picturesque ponds.

DIRECTIONS

From Bar Harbor, drive south on Route 3 for 8.8 miles. Little Long Pond will be on your right. You can park on the wide gravel shoulder next to the pond. *GPS coordinates: 44° 17.602' N, 68° 15.316' W.*

TRIP DESCRIPTION

Little Long Pond, with its gently sloping lawns and beautiful views of Penobscot Mountain, is an easy and quiet paddling destination that's suitable for the entire family. While the pond is only about 0.5 mile long, it provides a surprising amount of solitude during early-morning visits. Owned by the Rockefellers until David Rockefeller donated it to the park on his 100th birthday, in 2015, the pond and the surrounding lawns are open to the public and seem to have been landscaped for leisure. The lawns are an ideal spot to have a picnic, take a nap, and listen to the sounds of Mount Desert Island. You can also enjoy an easy walk around the pond on a wide, grassy path.

The route for this paddle is very simple. Put in at the southern end of the pond, along Route 3. Paddle straight ahead for 0.5 mile to the north end of the pond then return. Along the way, you will enjoy pink and white waterlilies and cattails hiding green frogs, mallards, and black ducks. The old boathouse on the eastern shore, built for John D. Rockefeller Jr., is an impressive structure for such a small body of water. The marshlike northern end of the pond is home to an active beaver lodge. Beavers are nocturnal, but early in the morning or late in the afternoon, you might see one or more swimming across the pond, carrying branches from a birch, maple, or willow tree. They store these branches underwater, near their lodges, and use them as food.

Beavers are not the only animals you might see here. Great blue herons wade near the shore, hunting for small fish, amphibians, and snakes. Belted kingfishers fly from tree to tree, making an occasional dive into the pond in search of fish. While onshore, watch and listen for the largest New England woodpecker, the pileated woodpecker. About the size of a crow, this black-and-white bird with a bright red crest on its head makes a loud *kuk, kuk, kuk, kuk, kuk* call. The pileated woodpecker excavates large rectangular holes in trees as it searches for ants and termites to extract from the wood with its sticky tongue. Unlike the similar-looking but extinct ivory-billed woodpecker, the pileated woodpecker has adapted comfortably to second-growth forests near small towns and is now common in the woods of Maine.

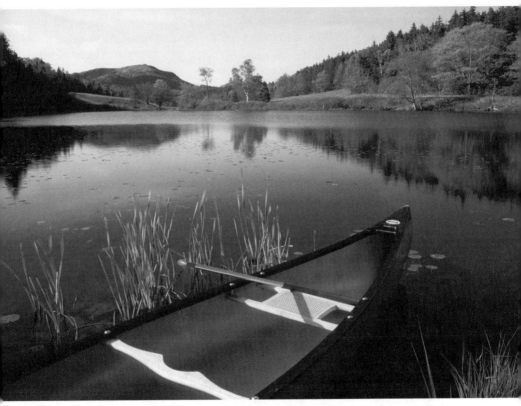

From Little Long Pond, you'll have a direct view to Parkman Mountain.

FROGS AND TURTLES

While visiting the freshwater ponds, swamps, and streams of Acadia, you may encounter frogs and turtles, from the diminutive spring peeper to the menacing snapping turtle. Seven species of frogs are known to live in Acadia. Five of these are relatively common: the spring peeper, bullfrog, green frog, pickerel frog, and wood frog. The gray tree frog and leopard frog are less common. As many as six species of turtles live in the park, but only two, the snapping turtle and the eastern painted turtle, are common. While paddling or hiking near water, keep your eyes and ears open for the following:

- Spring peepers are more likely to be heard than seen. Considered chorus frogs but also exhibiting characteristics of tree frogs, spring peepers fill the spring night air with their loud frog song. They prefer small, often temporary bodies of water near trees. These tiny frogs are less than 1 inch long and are usually brown or gray, with a dark "X" on their backs.

- Bullfrogs are the largest frogs in the United States, measuring 3.5 to 6 inches in length. They are either green, or brown and gray with a green background. They can be found in lakes, ponds, bogs, and streams and have a voracious appetite, eating almost anything they can swallow, including small snakes.

Frogs, including this wood frog, are common.

- Green frogs are smaller than bullfrogs, measuring 2.25 to 3.5 inches in length. True to their name, they tend to be greenish brown; in rare cases, however, they may be blue. Green frogs like shallower water than bullfrogs do, spending their time in brooks, small streams, and the edges of lakes and ponds.

- Pickerel frogs are 1.75 to 3 inches in length, with square spots arranged in two parallel rows down their backs. They often have bright yellow or orange coloring on their hind legs. Pickerels prefer the clear, cold waters of sphagnum bogs, rocky ravines, and meadow streams.

- Wood frogs are slightly smaller than pickerels but have an unmistakable "robber's mask": a dark patch around the eye. Wood frogs are generally brown, blending in well with leaf litter on the forest floor. They spend a lot of their time in moist woods, away from water.

- Snapping turtles reach lengths of 18 inches, weigh up to 50 pounds, and can live as long as 100 years. They are easily recognized by their large heads; beaklike mouths; long tails; and very rough, brownish-black shells. Snappers are voracious omnivores, eating small invertebrates, fish, reptiles, small birds, mammals, and vegetation. They will live in any permanent body of freshwater and spend a good deal of their time partially submerged in mud and shallow water. Luckily for swimmers, they tend to pull in their heads when underwater, letting people step on them and pass by unknowingly. On land, they will bite if harassed.

A note on changing species: In recent years, frogs have been found throughout the United States with severe physical deformities, most commonly an extra set of legs. Scientists have discovered that one cause of these deformities is a parasitic flatworm. While it has yet to be proven, scientists believe pollution may be an additional cause. Breathing through their moist skin, all amphibians may be especially susceptible to acid rain; airborne pollutants, such as mercury; and endocrine-system-disturbing chemicals, such as dioxin and PCBs. Acadia's frogs have yet to show these deformities, but if you happen to discover one with more than four legs, report it to a park naturalist.

TRIP 38
ECHO LAKE

NPS Rating > Easy

Distance > 1.5 miles

Estimated Time > 1 hour

Map > AMC's Acadia National Park Map: E3, E4

This short paddle passes below towering cliffs and offers a chance to see peregrine falcons.

DIRECTIONS

From Somesville, drive south on Route 102. At 2.7 miles from Pretty Marsh Road is a national park sign on the right for Ikes Point. Turn right into the driveway, which leads to a parking area and the put-in. *GPS coordinates:* 44° 19.009′ N, 68° 20.082′ W.

TRIP DESCRIPTION

Echo Lake is home to the Appalachian Mountain Club's Echo Lake Camp and Echo Lake Beach, the most popular place on the island to swim. At the southern end of the lake, Echo Lake Camp—with its comfortable tents, dining room, library, fireplace, and hot showers—is a great destination to bring the family for the week. Next to it is sandy Echo Lake Beach, with warm waters, lifeguards, and changing rooms. The lake itself runs up against Beech Cliff and Canada Cliff, both of which rise 150 feet straight up from the water's edge. The north end of the lake is fairly populated with cottages, and Route 102 runs next to the eastern shore for about 0.5 mile. For all of these reasons, this trip explores the southern end of the lake.

Put in your boat at Ikes Landing, on the west side of Route 102. There is plenty of parking in this lot, as Echo Lake is popular with both paddlers and motorboaters. From the put-in, paddle straight across the lake then turn left to follow the shore toward the cliffs of Beech Mountain. Keep the shoreline on your right for the remainder of this trip. In some years, peregrine falcons nest on the cliffs of Beech Mountain; point your binoculars skyward to search for these most efficient and speedy fliers. While they may hunt occasionally for ducks or other birds on Echo Lake, the falcons often head out to the shorelines around Mount Desert Island to hunt for seabirds. Common loons also frequent Echo Lake. While not endangered, these birds have been declining in number for most of this century. It is against the law in Maine to harass loons, so please do not approach them. Hearing their haunting call is just as exciting as seeing them up close.

Like most of the other ponds and lakes on the island, Echo Lake was created by glaciers during the last ice age. Carving out the lake to a depth of 65 feet, the ice also created the cliffs of Beech Mountain. Water ahead of the glacier filled cracks in the rock then froze. Freezing and thawing continued, weakening the granite until the glacier moved over the mountain and plucked boulders off the mountainside, creating the cliffs. The glacier also deposited the sand at the southern end of Echo Lake, creating Echo Lake Beach. The beach is popular with families, so pay attention for stray swimmers.

After paddling past the beach and the AMC camp, follow the shoreline north. As you paddle back toward the put-in, you will encounter about 0.5 mile of undeveloped national park shoreline, where you can pull over for a private lunch, a swim, or a quiet moment to yourself.

Fog rises over Echo Lake, home to AMC's Echo Lake Camp, at dawn.

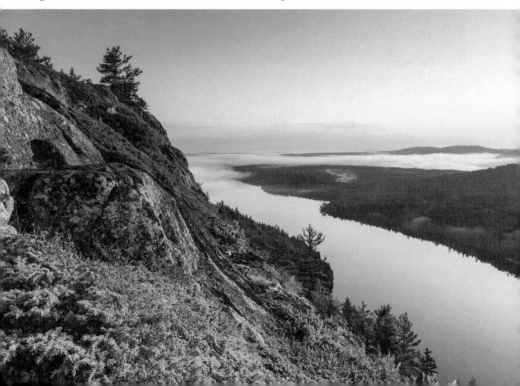

AMC'S ECHO LAKE CAMP

At the south end of Echo Lake, the Appalachian Mountain Club maintains Echo Lake Camp, a comfortable summer campground for families wishing to avoid the hustle and bustle of Bar Harbor. Accommodations are tents with board floors, beds, mattresses, pillows, and bedding. There is a shared bathhouse with hot showers, as well as a library, a recreation hall, a dining room, and a kitchen where your hosts cook up family-style meals. With access to Echo Lake outside your tent door, the camp provides rowboats, canoes, kayaks, and sailboats. There's a lobster picnic and clambake once a week, and twice a week you have the opportunity to participate in trail maintenance.

Guests swim in Echo Lake. The camp also provides canoes, kayaks, and rowboats. Photo: Sarah Aprea.

Echo Lake Camp is usually open July 4 weekend through Labor Day. A one-week stay, Saturday to Saturday, is required. The camp is not appropriate for children under 4, and pets are not allowed. Despite these restrictions, space fills up quickly, so make reservations before April. For current rates and reservation information, visit the Echo Lake Camp website at amcecholakecamp.org.

TRIP 39

👤 🐕 📷

JORDAN POND

NPS Rating ➤ Easy

Distance ➤ 2.5 miles

Estimated Time ➤ 2 hours

Map ➤ AMC's Acadia National Park Map: E7

Take an easy paddle on one of the most scenic ponds in Maine.

DIRECTIONS

From the Hulls Cove Visitor Center, drive south on Park Loop Road for 7.3 miles. Be sure to continue straight at the intersections marked "Sand Beach" and "Cadillac Mountain." The Jordan Pond parking area will be on your right. *GPS coordinates:* 44° 19.332' N, 68° 15.121' W.

TRIP DESCRIPTION

Jordan Pond has been a popular destination for visitors to Mount Desert Island ever since the first tourists started making their way to the island in the 1850s. One reason is undoubtedly Jordan Pond House, which has been serving afternoon tea at the south end of the pond since the 1870s. Of course, the incredible beauty is just as big a draw. Jordan Pond, at 150 feet deep, is the deepest of Acadia's ponds and lakes, scraped out by the same glacier that gave the Bubbles their rounded appearance at the pond's north end. The western side of the pond sits directly below Jordan Cliffs, a steep wall of granite on the east face of Penobscot Mountain. The long, sloping south ridge of Pemetic Mountain looms to the east. The pond is only about 1 mile long, making paddling trips here relatively short in duration; of course, that leaves plenty of time for tea and popovers at Jordan Pond House.

The put-in for Jordan Pond is not at the restaurant but next to the Jordan Pond hiker parking area (located just to the north of Jordan Pond House, on Park Loop Road). As you put in your boat on the eastern shore of the pond, you will be facing Penobscot Mountain and Jordan Cliffs. Blueberry bushes turn a fire-engine red in the fall on the side of Jordan Cliffs, which are home to one of Acadia's nesting pairs of peregrine falcons. As you paddle into the pond and turn to the right, you will be looking at one of Acadia's classic views: Jordan Pond and the Bubbles. The Bubbles are a pair of rounded, pink-granite peaks that are certainly bubblelike in shape. They are not particularly tall, reaching only 766 feet and 872 feet, but they

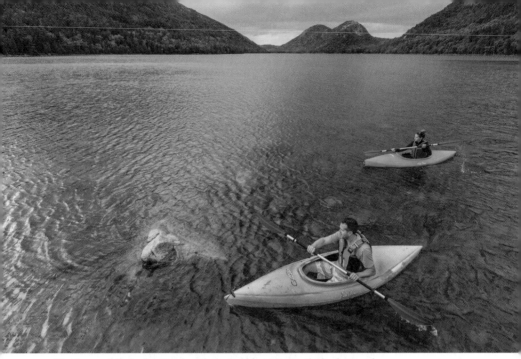

Kayakers paddle Jordan Pond, with the Bubbles rising in the background.

add a distinctive and beautiful silhouette to the pond's horizon. Like most of the features on Mount Desert Island, the Bubbles were shaped by glaciers during the last ice age, their granite composition stronger than the surrounding rock scraped away and deposited farther south.

Jordan Pond is home to both common loons and common mergansers in the summer. Female mergansers have rust-colored heads, gray backs, red bills, and red feet, while the males have white bodies, black backs, and greenish black heads. Mergansers nest around Jordan Pond, either in tree cavities or on the ground. Unlike loons, which share parenting responsibilities, male mergansers abandon the females while the latter incubate the eggs. Merganser chicks usually hatch by the Fourth of July, and those born in tree nests have to jump from the nesting cavity to the ground on their way to the pond. The female mergansers occasionally bring the fuzzy, cue-ball-colored chicks near Jordan Pond Trail, which follows the shore for most of the pond.

As you paddle toward the northern end of the pond, the cliffs of South Bubble loom closer. The forest beneath the cliffs is a northern hardwood, filled with maple, birch, and beech that turn the mountainside a spectacular red, yellow, and orange in the fall. At the northern end of the pond is a small stream that is not navigable by canoe or kayak. The footbridge over the stream is part of Jordan Pond Path. If you feel like taking a short hike up South Bubble for an elevated view of Jordan Pond, tie up your boat here. About 50 yards to the right of the footbridge is Bubbles Divide Trail, which leads 0.5 mile to the summit, a worthwhile side trip.

During the return trip, Jordan Pond House will be directly in front of you, while the hulking mass of Pemetic Mountain will be on your left.

TRIP 40

LONG POND: SOUTH END

NPS Rating > Easy

Distance > 3 miles

Estimated Time > 2 hours

Map > AMC's Acadia National Park Map: F3

This paddle beneath the steep cliffs of Beech and Mansell mountains explores the quiet end of Long Pond.

DIRECTIONS

From the center of Southwest Harbor, go west on Seal Cove Road. Take the first paved road on the right, Long Pond Road. Follow Long Pond Road through a residential area until the road ends at the south shore of Long Pond. There is a small parking area to the right of the pumping station. *GPS coordinates:* 44° 18.009′ N, 68° 21.032′ W.

Note: Stand-up paddleboarding is not allowed within 1,000 feet of the southern end of Long Pond.

TRIP DESCRIPTION

The southern end of Long Pond is nestled between the dramatic cliffs of Beech and Mansell mountains, granite walls hundreds of feet tall. This end of the pond is narrow (about 1,000 feet across) and quiet, as motorboats tend to stay at the larger, northern end of the pond. We found we could not help but stop paddling from time to time to stare up at the mesmerizing cliffs and cedar-lined shoreline. At 4 miles long, this is the largest body of freshwater in the park and is home to loons, mergansers, and other waterfowl. In some years, peregrine falcons nest on Beech Mountain and soar in the skies above the pond. Long Pond is also known as Great Pond; its shoreline has long been the home of summer cottages, much like the rest of Mount Desert Island, although here the homes are politely inconspicuous, often completely hidden from view.

The length of the pond and its north–south orientation can create some large waves at the southern end, when the wind is out of the north. During north-wind conditions, the northern end of the pond is a better bet for paddlers (Trip 44). The pond is used as a water source for the town of Southwest Harbor, so take extra care not to pollute. Swimming is not allowed in any part of the pond. Also, plan to ar-

Fog rises off Long Pond during an early-morning paddle.

rive early because parking is limited to about six or seven cars, and hikers climbing Mansell and Beech mountains also park here.

From the put-in at the southern end of Long Pond Road, begin your paddle by following the shoreline on your right. After passing a couple of private homes, you will be surrounded by Acadia National Park shoreline. The pond has a wild feeling here, as 30-foot-high granite cliffs drop straight into the water. These cliffs are the western shoulder of Beech Mountain, one of the more popular sites for hiking on the western side of Mount Desert Island (Trip 8). The cliffs eventually recede, and the forest comes down to the water's edge, with northern white cedars forming an impenetrable wall of green, their lower branches reaching over the water to collect as much sunlight as possible. With cliffs and cedars everywhere, it is difficult to land a boat, even a small kayak, on this side of the pond.

As the terrain starts to flatten out, you will see a small cottage on the right (eastern) bank. At this point, paddle over to the western shore of the pond for the trip back. The western side of the pond is also thick with cedars, but there are a few places to land a boat and take a break. If you hear voices, they probably belong to hikers on Long Pond Trail, which follows the shoreline from here back to the parking area. Near dusk and dawn, the shoreline of Long Pond is a good place to look for mink as they hunt for fish, frogs, snakes, and mice. About the size of ferrets, mink can swim underwater for distances up to 100 feet and occasionally will pop their heads out of the water near a canoe or kayak, providing a pleasant surprise for the boat's occupants.

As you paddle south along the western shore of the pond, the 700-foot-high cliffs of Mansell Mountain dominate your field of vision. At its narrowest point, the pond is only 700 feet across, with cliffs on both sides. You can almost see the glacier squeezing through the huge granite mounds on either side of the pond, scraping clean the sides of the mountain and pushing bits of rock and dirt ahead into a terminal moraine, which is now the hill behind the parking area. You can thank the last ice age for providing you with the peaceful paddling and dramatic scenery. The cliffs end just prior to your return to the put-in.

TRIP 41

SEAL COVE POND

NPS Rating ➤ Easy

Distance ➤ 4.5 miles

Estimated Time ➤ 2.5 hours

Map ➤ AMC's Acadia National Park Map: F2

This paddle on Mount Desert Island's westernmost pond offers the possibility of seeing waterfowl and bald eagles.

DIRECTIONS

From Route 102 in Southwest Harbor, drive east on Seal Cove Road. After 2.1 miles, turn right on a dirt National Park Service road. After 0.5 mile there is a sign for Seal Cove Pond. Follow this sign to the left. You are now on Western Mountain Road. In 0.8 mile, follow the right fork in the road toward Seal Cove Pond. The road ends at the put-in in another 0.7 mile. *GPS coordinates: 44° 17.513′ N, 68° 23.536′ W.*

TRIP DESCRIPTION

Like other ponds in Acadia, Seal Cove Pond is long and narrow, running in a north–south direction. Geologically, however, it is different from most of the other large ponds in the park, as it is shallow and marshy. It also lacks the dramatic scenery of Echo Lake or Long Pond, as there are no cliffs to speak of, and Route 102 runs along the western edge of the pond. That said, there are plenty of reasons to paddle this pond. Its shallow waters provide a diverse habitat for waterfowl, making this an excellent spot to watch for ducks and wading birds. The eastern shore of the pond is densely forested and has some large spruce trees that provide good perches for bald eagles. There are also fewer boats here than in the rest of the park.

The drive into the pond on the narrow dirt road known as Western Mountain Road is perhaps the most remote on the island. This is a good place to watch for moose. The parking area at the end of the road is fairly small, so try to arrive early. From the put-in at the southeastern end of the pond, it's about 1.75 miles to the north end. Before heading north, take some time to explore the marshy southern end. Cattails, fragrant waterlilies, and pickerelweed creep in from the shoreline, providing hiding places for ducks, herons, and egrets. The small stream in the cove directly across from the put-in drains Seal Cove Pond into Seal Cove, only 0.5 mile away. Seal Cove, a picturesque little harbor filled with sailboats and lobster boats, is worth a visit. You'll have to drive, though, as the stream from Seal Cove Pond is not navigable.

You might spot moose, like this cow, around Seal Cove Pond, but don't approach them—especially if they're with their young.

Once you have explored the southern end of the pond, paddle past the put-in toward the north end. Since the western shore is filled with houses, summer cottages, lawns, and driveways, the eastern shore is a much more interesting place. The eastern shore is also part of the national park, which makes it permissible to land your boat for a break. The western shore and the island in the middle of the pond are private property. As you head north, the shoreline is less marshy than at the southern end and takes on a rocky, forested character. The birdlife is still interesting, as loons and cormorants hunt fish in the deeper waters of the pond, and bald eagles sit patiently in the trees waiting for a fishing opportunity. The forest is thick with cedar, fir, spruce, birch, and maple. It is as wild as it looks, as no roads or trails traverse between the pond and the summit of Bernard Mountain, more than 1 mile to the east.

You can get good views of Bernard Mountain from the northwestern end of the pond. From here you can see a lush and uninterrupted forest that is home to moose and black bear, ruffed grouse, and black-backed woodpeckers. While the latter are common winter visitors, a few also live year-round and breed on Mount Desert Island. Though quite tame they are rarely seen, but the thick evergreen forest to the east of Seal Cove Pond is the type of habitat they prefer. Both sexes can be identified by their black backs, wings, and tails. (Both also have only three toes per foot.) Males have yellow caps. These birds feed by peeling the bark off dead and dying spruce trees and eating the underlying beetles and other insects. The boggy cedar-and-spruce woods at the northeast end of the pond are a good place to sit quietly and watch for these birds.

AIRBORNE ENEMIES: BALD EAGLES AND OSPREYS

Bald eagles and ospreys are both conspicuous but uncommon residents of Acadia and the islands surrounding Mount Desert Island. While these large birds of prey are dissimilar in appearance, they share many common habits and habitats. Their similarities often put them in proximity to each other, occasionally resulting in battles for prey and territory. Ospreys catch fish more than 50 percent of the time they try, and they rarely eat anything else. In contrast, bald eagles are less successful hunters and will feast on carrion every chance they get. Bald eagles also follow and harass ospreys in an attempt to steal the latter's catch. It was these habits that led Ben Franklin to observe: "I wish the bald eagle had not been chosen as the representative of our country. He is a bird of bad moral character; he does not get his living honestly. Besides he is a rank coward."

Although Ben Franklin may have disliked these huge birds, bald eagles are truly magnificent animals, soaring gracefully on thermals with an 8-foot wingspan, and possessing beautiful and regal coloring. Adults mate for life and share in parenting duties, raising broods of two chicks in huge nests they reuse year after year. The birds nest in the tallest trees they can find—in Maine, usually white pine or spruce—near any large body of water that is sufficiently free of human disturbance. Older nests can weigh as much as a ton and will usually end up killing the trees in which they are situated. The birds do not grow their distinctive white tail and head feathers until they are four or five years old. Until that time, they are either mottled in appearance or have completely brown coloring, resembling golden eagles. In Acadia, they nest on the smaller islands around Mount Desert Island but can be seen almost anywhere along the coast, soaring high on thermals or perching on tall trees where they can get a good view of their surroundings. In winter, some eagles will migrate south to congregate with other birds near open water and concentrated food; others, however, remain in the park year-round.

Like bald eagles, the smaller ospreys prefer to nest in tall trees near water in relatively wild areas. They are somewhat more adaptable than eagles, often nesting closer to civilization on telephone poles or other tall artificial structures that give them open views of the landscape. They are also more likely to nest next to small ponds rich in fish. Ospreys mate for life and, as with eagles, both parents raise the young. It is common to find eagles and ospreys nesting in sight of each other, which results in frequent aerial battles. While the birds seldom hurt each other, ospreys will harass and dive at eagles flying in the former's vicinity. Groups of ravens, peregrine falcons, and other birds of prey will also harass eagles in the attempt to drive eagles from an area. These displays are quite exciting to watch and usually end with the eagle deciding to catch a thermal and fly to more peaceful surroundings.

Bald eagle populations declined consistently from the time Europeans arrived in North America until the 1940s, as a result of persecution by hunters, anglers, and farmers. Ospreys, on the other hand, managed to escape some of this persecution because farmers believed the birds' presence kept away smaller falcons, such as merlins and kestrels, that preyed on domestic fowl. After World War II, both birds met considerable peril due to the widespread use of the pesticide DDT and other pollutants. These chemicals do not kill the birds but are stored in the birds' fatty tissue, eventually reaching a level that creates reproductive problems. Eggs laid by birds with high concentrations of DDT had thin shells that often ended up being crushed during incubation. Since DDT was banned in 1972, the birds' reproductive success has improved in most of the country. Bald eagles hit their population low in Maine in the

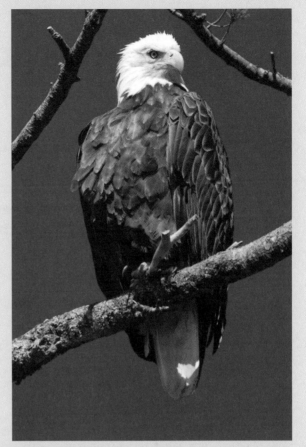

Look for bald eagles perched in the spruce along the eastern shore of Seal Cove Pond.

early 1970s (only 29 nesting pairs were found in the state in 1972), but have rebounded to more than 500 nesting pairs today. Osprey numbers have followed a similar trend, and the birds are now relatively common in the state. Today, the greatest threat to both birds is habitat loss.

It's possible to see bald eagles and ospreys in Acadia near the coast or above one of the bigger lakes. Your best chance is to get out on the water, whether in a sea kayak or on one of the nature cruises that leave from Bar Harbor. If you are kayaking, be aware that the National Park Service prohibits the landing of any boat on an island with an active bald eagle, osprey, or seabird nest. (Check at the visitor center beforehand for a list of islands with active nest sites.) Whether you are boating or hiking, never approach within 0.25 mile of a nest. These birds are very wary of people and will abandon a nest if disturbed often.

TRIP 42

👨‍👧 🐕 🏄

NORTHEAST CREEK

NPS Rating ➤ Moderate

Distance ➤ 5 miles

Estimated Time ➤ 2.5 hours

Map ➤ AMC's Acadia National Park Map: B4, C4

This quiet paddle on a narrow creek travels through extensive wetlands and prime wildlife habitat.

DIRECTIONS

From the Thompson Island Information Center (located on the west side of Route 3 on Thompson Island, between Trenton and Mount Desert Island,) follow Route 3 east for 2.5 miles to the bridge over Northeast Creek. A small dirt parking area lies immediately after the bridge on the right. Neither the creek nor the parking area is marked by signs. *GPS coordinates: 44° 25.490′ N, 68° 19.625′ W.*

TRIP DESCRIPTION

Northeast Creek is the only paddling trip in this chapter that explores a moving body of water. Fortunately, the current is negligible, as the creek drops a mere 5 feet from one end to the other. The creek's meandering nature makes paddling here a completely different experience than canoeing one of Mount Desert Island's big glacial lakes or plying the waters of the wavy Atlantic in a sea kayak. Much of this trip is spent in the narrow channel of an extensive boggy area, rife with wildlife and views of Acadia's mountains. Due to the open nature of the terrain for most of this paddle, windy days can create some uncomfortable paddling here, but since this is an out-and-back trip, you can turn around and return to the put-in at any time.

To start this trip, park at the dirt parking area on the inland side of Route 3, just east of the bridge that crosses the creek. A path descends the short hill leading to the put-in. The put-in area, as well as all of the land bordering the creek, is private property. Please tread lightly at the put-in and plan your trip so you don't need to land your boat once you're beyond the put-in. This creek has a small tidal influence, mostly confined to the portion of the creek on the Mount Desert Narrows side of the bridge.

Begin paddling on the inland side of the bridge and head toward the mountains. As you paddle south and east, you quickly leave the road and civilization behind. You are surrounded by private property, but you will only see one house and a few

Northeast Creek provides an opportunity for observing flora and fauna.

grassy lawns throughout your trip. The paddle makes its way through a mixed forest of maple, aspen, white pine, and oak. Keep your eyes open for white-tailed deer, black ducks, mallard ducks, and other waterfowl. You should watch also for the occasional large rock hidden just below the waterline for the first 0.75 mile.

After the creek turns sharply to the right, you leave the rocks and the woods behind. You have now entered Fresh Meadow, a boggy wetland of tall cattails, grasses, and sedges. Here the vistas open up to include Cadillac and Sargent mountains about 6 miles to the south. Summer finds great blue herons hunting amid the cattails at the edge of the creek. The chatter of belted kingfishers can be heard on most days as they busily fly from perch to perch, looking for fish. Lincoln's sparrows and swamp sparrows share the brushy surroundings with red-winged blackbirds and the occasional sedge wren.

About 1 mile from the put-in, Aunt Betsey's Brook enters on the right. In most conditions, Aunt Betsey's Brook is shallow, mucky, and difficult to explore. This trip stays on Northeast Creek, which turns left and heads north for a short distance before resuming an easterly course. For the next mile, Northeast Creek continues to meander through Fresh Meadow and its marshy expanse. Quiet paddling in this remote section of the creek can pay off with a muskrat, beaver, or river otter sighting. Beaver and muskrats are vegetarians, eating young trees, shrubs, and other plants, while river otters feed on fish, frogs, salamanders, and snakes. Beaver and muskrats often swim at the surface of the water, keeping their tails underwater as rudders. Otters, on the other hand, are more likely to be seen poking their heads out of the water in an attempt to get a better view of their surroundings.

After the creek flows past some higher land on the right bank, it turns right and heads due south for the final 0.5 mile of this trip. The creek narrows and becomes enclosed in an ever-increasing crop of cattails as it nears civilization and the houses along Crooked Road. While you can turn around at any point on this trip, you'll reach a definitive end when you can no longer navigate the cattails.

TRIP 43

EAGLE LAKE

NPS Rating > Moderate

Distance > 4 miles

Estimated Time > 3 hours

Map > AMC's Acadia National Park Map: D6

This moderate paddle on a scenic lake provides mountain views and proximity to wild shorelines.

DIRECTIONS

From the intersection of Routes 3 and 233 in Bar Harbor, take Route 233 west toward Cadillac Mountain. The parking area for Eagle Lake is at 2.1 miles on the left. *GPS coordinates:* 44° 22.648′ N, 68° 15.141′ W.

TRIP DESCRIPTION

Eagle Lake is the largest lake on the eastern side of Mount Desert Island and is a popular spot due to its proximity to Bar Harbor. All of Eagle Lake is part of Acadia National Park, giving it a wild shoreline with none of the cottages and camps you find on many of the island's other lakes. Its views of Cadillac and Pemetic mountains, as well as the Bubbles, are breathtaking. It is 4 miles around the edge of the lake, making it possible to spend a leisurely day taking in the scenery and watching for loons, mergansers, and ospreys. Carriage roads circle the lake and connect with hiking trails, creating the opportunity to spend the whole day in the area paddling, hiking, and biking. Swimming is prohibited, however, since the lake is the water supply for Bar Harbor.

A paddling trip on Eagle Lake begins at the north end of the lake, at the lake parking area on the south side of Route 233. Motorboats are allowed, but there is a 10-horsepower limit on motors. If you see motorized vehicles on the lake, they most likely will be slow-moving boats of anglers dropping lines into the 110-foot-deep water, trying to hook the salmon and trout that thrive in the cold depths. These fish make up the diet of the common mergansers and common loons that nest around the lake. The fish are also what draw ospreys to the wild southern end of the lake. Ospreys are impressive fishers, diving into the water talons-first and emerging with a catch more than half the time. It's no wonder bald eagles spend their time harassing ospreys in an attempt to get the latter to drop their prey.

Lying fully within the boundaries of Acadia, Eagle Lake's 4-mile shoreline remains wild and undeveloped.

Paddling Eagle Lake can take as much or as little time as you want. The shoreline is wooded and rocky, with just a few coves and inlets to explore. Either follow the shoreline for a 4-mile paddle or head straight across to the southern end of the lake, 1.75 miles away. As on all of the lakes on Mount Desert Island, a wind out of the north can create large waves at the pond's southern end. On a windy day, keep in mind that you will have to paddle against these waves on the return trip. At the southern end of the pond, directly opposite the put-in, a shallow gravel area makes it easy to land your boat and take a break onshore. Eagle Lake Trail is found here. Hiking the trail to the right makes for a flat, 0.5-mile walk along the southwestern shore of the lake. Following the trail to your left connects you to the Jordan Pond Carry, a 1.1-mile footpath through northern hardwood forest that ends at the northeastern shore of Jordan Pond. These trails also link up to the extensive system of crushed-gravel carriage roads. For biking around Eagle Lake, see Trip 29. For details on the short hike up Conners Nubble on the west side of the lake, see Trip 1.

Whether you follow the shoreline back or paddle down the middle of the lake, test if your hearing is as keen as that of painter Thomas Cole, who first visited Eagle Lake in 1844. According to *Mount Desert Island and Acadia National Park: An Informal History*, by Sargent Collier, Cole named the lake for the bald eagles that soared over his easel, and he once remarked that, at Eagle Lake, "one may fancy himself in the forests of the Alleghenies, but for the dull roar of the ocean breaking the stillness." From this point, the ocean is 3 miles away.

GRANITE DOMES AND GLACIAL LAKES

The story of what is now Acadia National Park began about 500 million years ago at the bottom of an ancient sea called the Iapetus Ocean. In this prehistoric ocean, silt and volcanic ash accumulated at the rate of 1 inch every 100 years until the material was thousands of feet deep. This matter solidified into shales and tuffs before the heat and pressure deep within the earth metamorphosed the rock into a dark gray or green schist composed of quartz, feldspar, and chlorite. This rock, now called Ellsworth schist, forms an incomplete ring around Mount Desert Island. It can be seen along the shore near the Thompson Island picnic area.

Around 400 million years ago, another round of silt accumulation formed a layer of sedimentary rock composed of sandstone and shale. Known as the Bar Harbor Formation, this rock is black to rusty brown and can be seen from the town pier in Bar Harbor, as well as around the Porcupine Islands and in Northeast Harbor. At about the same time, the Cranberry Island Series of sedimentary rock formed around the Cranberry Isles. This rock is lighter in color, with embedded rock fragments, and was formed by the sedimentation of volcanic ash.

These sedimentary and metamorphic bedrocks were an easily eroded covering that now makes up just a small part of the island. Between 380 million and 420 million years ago, the bulk of what is now Mount Desert Island literally bubbled up from deep within the earth. At this time, North America was colliding with what is known as the Avalonian plate. This collision, called the Acadian Orogeny, created the mountains of Acadia and caused great movements of magma (molten rock) below the earth's crust. Under Mount Desert Island, molten magma moved upward through the earth's crust, consuming and altering the existing layers of bedrock. At one point a huge balloon of magma, 8 or more miles in diameter, worked its way upward. This magma eventually cooled into what is now known as Cadillac granite, the rock that makes up much of the island and all of its mountains. The characteristic pink shading is due to a mineral called feldspar. Other minerals that are easily visible upon inspection of the granite are quartz, hornblende, and biotite.

As North America moved away from Europe and Africa, fissures occasionally formed in the crust. Molten black diabase rose from the earth's mantle to fill these fissures. These diabase dikes can be seen in many places around Acadia: on mountain summits, such as Pemetic Mountain, as well as on the shoreline. Schoodic Peninsula and Isle au Haut have some excellent examples.

While plate tectonics following millions of years of sedimentation are responsible for building the mountains and bedrock of Acadia National Park, it is the more recent phenomenon of glaciation that has shaped the park into its current form. Over the last 2 to 3 million years, New England has experienced 20 to 30 glacial cycles, each lasting about 100,000 years. Glacial periods take up about 80,000 years of that time, while interglacial periods last 15,000 to 20,000 years. During these glacial cycles, thick layers of ice up to 1 mile deep move over the landscape, breaking the weaker rocks and grinding them into sand and gravel. The dominant Cadillac granite in Acadia withstood this glacial grinding better than the weaker sedimentary and metamorphic rocks on Mount Desert Island. While the glaciers did not obliterate the granite, they were powerful enough to wear down Acadia's granite-topped mountains into the rounded shapes you see today.

The last ice age was named after the Wisconsin Glacier, which reached as far south as Long Island about 18,000 years ago. At this time, the ice had to be at least 1 mile thick, as it covered the entire 5,267 vertical feet of Katahdin in northern Maine. The ice was not stationary; it flowed toward the ocean, as all water does, and it wore its way through rock, creating deep "U"-shaped valleys like the one between Dorr Mountain and Huguenot Head. Between Acadia and Norumbega mountains, the glacier dug so deep it created the only fjord in the eastern United States, Somes Sound. Most of the lakes and ponds on Mount Desert Island are a result of glacial carving.

By 14,000 years ago, most of the ice had retreated from Mount Desert Island, leaving a treeless expanse of tundra surrounded by a constantly changing shoreline. As the glacial period ended, the ice melted, raising sea levels so that by 12,000 years ago, the shoreline of Mount Desert Island was much as it is now. Ice is heavy, however, and had depressed the island by as much as 0.3 mile. With the ice gone, the land began to rebound. By 11,000 years ago, the land had rebounded faster than the sea was rising, and Frenchman Bay and Blue Hill Bay were dry land. Ice continued to melt around the earth's polar regions, and sea level finally rose to its current level about 8,000 years ago. By then, all of the native tree species now present in Aca-

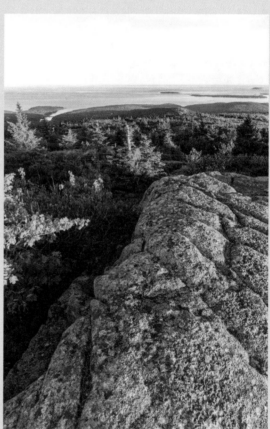

Glacial striations, such as these atop Cadillac Mountain, are etched into many of Acadia's granite domes.

dia had colonized the island. Since that time, most of the shaping of Acadia's landscape has been done by pounding surf, wind, rain, and people.

TRIP 44

🚶 🐕 🏄

LONG POND: NORTH END

NPS Rating ➤ Strenuous

Distance ➤ 7.5 miles

Estimated Time ➤ 4 hours

Map ➤ AMC's Acadia National Park Map: E2, E3

This long and popular paddle explores the wooded coves of Mount Desert Island's biggest lake.

DIRECTIONS

The parking area for the Long Pond put-in is on Pretty Marsh Road, 1.5 miles west of Route 102 in Somesville. *GPS coordinates:* 44° 21.288′ N, 68° 21.794′ W.

TRIP DESCRIPTION

If you do not have your own boat, this is the easiest place to paddle in Acadia, as National Park Canoe Rental is just across the street from the put-in, at the north end of Long Pond. (See Appendix D for a complete list of canoe outfitters.) With deep blue waters and scenic views of Beech, Bernard, and Mansell mountains, Long Pond is a beautiful place to paddle. You will not have the pond to yourself on a busy summer weekend, but there are plenty of quiet coves where you can find solitude and study the shoreline. This trip explores the northern end of the pond and its secluded coves, which are hidden by two peninsulas, Northern Neck and Southern Neck.

Begin the paddle at the boat launch on Pretty Marsh Road. The first 1.25 miles are a straight paddle up the narrow north end of the pond. The western mountains fill your views to the south, while the shoreline is edged with summer cottages. Boat traffic can get busy in this part of the pond, so stay near the shore and be prepared to ride the wakes of motorboats. The spit of land on your right is Northern Neck. As you come to the end of Northern Neck, the pond opens up to the right. At this point, Southern Neck is the narrow peninsula directly across from Northern Neck. Paddle your boat south toward Southern Neck. The shoreline of Southern Neck and all of the coves to the right of it are part of Acadia National Park.

This is the wildest section of Long Pond, with an undeveloped shoreline of white cedar, white pine, and balsam fir. Horsetail and fragrant waterlilies add color to the pond in the shallows. Black ducks, mallards, and common mergansers are numerous throughout this area, and the forest is filled with the songs of thrushes and wood warblers. Twenty-three species of warblers and thrushes nest in Acadia,

The paddle outfitter on Long Pond's north end rents stand-up paddleboards, increasingly common in Acadia.

including the colorful yellow warbler and the ovenbird, with its unmistakable forest-filling song of *teacher, teacher, teacher, teacher, teacher*. In late fall, America's smallest duck, the bufflehead, arrives in small groups that entertain paddlers by popping out of the water in all directions like black-and-white lobster buoys.

If you keep the shore on your left, eventually you will be heading north. As you enter the bay behind Northern Neck, the woods remain wild, although houses begin to appear behind the trees. With a couple of islands and some marshy shoreline, this bay is worth exploring, despite the summer cottages. From the westernmost part of the pond, you can even get a glimpse of Cadillac Mountain, 8 miles to the east. You can also look for small boggy areas filled with sphagnum moss and northern New England's most common carnivorous flora, sundews and pitcher plants. These plants trap insects and digest them with enzymes, delivering the much-needed nutrients not available in the acidic soil of bogs.

By keeping to the shoreline on your left, you will emerge from the western side of Northern Neck and find yourself back in the main part of Long Pond. From here, the put-in is 1.25 miles to the left (north).

LOON OR CORMORANT?

While common loons and double-crested cormorants have very different markings, it is difficult to distinguish the two in bright sunlight due to their similar shapes. With a little practice, however, it is easy to tell the two birds apart by looking at their bills. A loon's bill is much thicker than a cormorant's, and loons tend to hold their bills level with the water. Cormorants strike a somewhat "snooty" pose, with their bills pointed slightly upward.

Common loons, with their haunting call, are among the most popular birds in North America. They are seen in the waters surrounding Mount Desert Island, particularly from early fall through spring. Loons that are not old enough to breed often stay in the area year-round. In summer, mature loons nest on inland lakes and ponds, but during the rest of the year they feed in the ice-free waters of the Gulf of Maine. With their black heads, red eyes, black-and-white-striped necks, and black-and-white bodies, common loons are stunning birds. Occasionally red-throated loons, with their gray bodies and red throat patches, are also seen in the waters around Acadia.

Loons are present on both Acadia's inland ponds and the open ocean surrounding the park.

Double-crested cormorants are very common in Acadia from spring through late fall. Except for their yellow bills and throat pouches, double-crested cormorants are solid-black birds with an iridescent green or purple gloss. Like loons, cormorants are about the size of a goose and are excellent swimmers—much more adept in water than on land. Cormorants lack the oils that other ducks and seabirds have to keep their feathers dry. Instead, they perch on rocks, logs, and piers, holding their wings up to dry. Great cormorants can also be seen in Acadia. They are larger than double-crested cormorants and have a white chin or throat patch.

SEA KAYAKING

SEA KAYAKING THE WATERS OF MOUNT DESERT ISLAND

Acadia National Park is as much about water as it is about mountains, with the cold Gulf of Maine creating rich food supplies for large numbers of seabirds and mammals. Sea kayaking in the bays and narrows around Mount Desert Island is like no other experience in the park, with dramatic scenery and wildlife sightings practically guaranteed. Taking a naturalist cruise or a whale watch is a great way to see Acadia, but you get a much better look at the intricate details of the ocean ecosystem by sitting at water level in a kayak. You also gain a lot more freedom to explore the myriad inlets and coves that make up the shoreline of Mount Desert Island and the other islands in Frenchman Bay, Blue Hill Bay, and Somes Sound.

If you've never been in a sea kayak before, you can get an introduction to the sport by taking a guided tour offered by one of the outfitters listed in Appendix D. Taking a guided tour around the Porcupine Islands was our first experience in a sea kayak, and we have been hooked on ocean paddling ever since. For sufficient experience to paddle on your own, plan to take a multiday sea-kayaking class. You should also check out *AMC's Best Sea Kayaking in New England* by Michael Daugherty (AMC Books, 2016) for more trip ideas and sea-kayaking tips.

SAFETY AND ETIQUETTE

Registered Maine Guides, who are certified and licensed by the state of Maine to guide sea-kayaking activities, are excellent sources for kayaking information. The safety information in this chapter was compiled with the gracious help of Natalie Springel, a former lead kayaking guide at Coastal Kayaking Tours, and Elizabeth Ehrenfeld, another longtime Registered Maine Guide. You can enjoy sea kayaking in the waters around Mount Desert Island—but not without training and experience. At its warmest, the water temperature reaches the low 50s, and even at that temperature a submerged paddler can become hypothermic in minutes. The weather also can cause dangerous conditions, especially fog that can roll in off the ocean at any time, making strong navigation skills vital. Local outfitters will require you to prove your experience before renting you a kayak. In order to safely sea kayak in Maine, you should have the following, at a minimum:

- Previous paddling experience in a sea kayak.
- Knowledge of the basic paddle strokes: forward, reverse, sweep, skull, brace, and draw.

- Knowledge of how to use a nautical chart and compass.
- Previous practice of self-rescues and two-person rescues, and knowledge of how to use a paddle float.

How do you get this experience? Several local outfitters in Bar Harbor and Camden offer multiday classes on sea kayaking. Your local recreation department may offer introductory pool sessions, in which you can practice self-rescues in a controlled environment. AMC and other outdoor clubs offer regional kayaking workshops. Ask at the outdoors shops in your hometown if they know of classes you can take locally. Sometimes the stores themselves host classes if they sell sea kayaks. Of course, you can always ask an experienced paddler if he or she is willing to teach you.

Before putting your boat in the water, always check the tide and weather forecasts. Tides are listed in the local newspaper, *Mount Desert Islander* (mdislander. com). You can also buy official tide charts at local bookstores, find them at usharbors.com, and hear them on National Oceanic and Atmospheric Administration (NOAA) weather radio. NOAA is excellent for long-range forecasts, but for the best up-to-date Acadia weather information, check your favorite weather website or smartphone app (we like wunderground.com and the wunderground iOS app), or call the weather line of the local radio station WDEA: 207-667-8910.

In addition to checking the weather forecast, use your common sense and observe the conditions when you put your boat in the water. If you see whitecaps, it's probably too windy for a safe and pleasant paddle. Once the wind hits 10 knots, it can be exhausting to paddle for even an hour, constantly readjusting your course and fighting the wind and waves. Also, if it is foggy at your put-in, you should choose another trip. Besides causing navigational problems, fog can make you invisible to the many fishing and pleasure boats that travel through the area. A sunny day in the Gulf of Maine can quickly turn into a foggy nightmare. On the plus side, weather conditions surrounding Mount Desert Island, especially fog, can be very localized, and you can often drive to another part of the island and have a safe and sunny paddle. Even in sunny conditions, however, we advise keeping your group in a tightly knit formation, as this makes you much more visible to boats. Even small ocean swells can make it hard for other boats to see you. As Elizabeth Ehrenfeld says, "Boaters on the Maine Coast call sea kayaks speed bumps." Lastly, you should never paddle alone.

Everyone in your group should have the following essential gear with them:

- Personal flotation device (PFD). Wear a PFD—that is, a life jacket—while sea kayaking in Maine. If you end up in the water, a life jacket will allow you to save the precious energy you will need to stave off hypothermia. The few minutes a life jacket saves you while you try to get back into your boat could save your life. Consider a PFD to be required equipment.

- Whistle, attached to the outside of your PFD.

- Spare paddle.

- Paddle float.

- Sprayskirt.

- Bilge pump.

- Lunch, snacks, and emergency food.

- Water: Bring at least 1 gallon if you are out for the entire day.

- Sunglasses, sunscreen, and a hat.

- Appropriate clothing. Dress for the water temperature, not the air temperature. A wetsuit or a drysuit (a specialized waterproof paddling suit, usually made of Gore-Tex) is highly recommended, but at least wear synthetic materials and dress in layers. Neoprene or Gore-Tex gloves and booties are also good to have. Do not wear cotton. Even on an 80-degree day, a dunk in the 50-degree waters of the Gulf of Maine can cause hypothermia in minutes without the proper clothing.

- Dry bag to keep food and extra clothing dry.

- Headlamp.

- Binoculars for wildlife viewing.

The group should also carry at least one set of each of the following:

- Compass and charts.

- First-aid kit.

- Pocketknife.

- Foghorn.

- Flare gun.

- VHF radio, personal locator beacon (PLB), or cell phone, although cell phones do not work in all locations.

In addition to paying close attention to safety, kayakers in the waters around Mount Desert Island need to follow certain guidelines to avoid having a negative impact on the environment or local residents. First, it is important to respect private property and never land your boat near a house or on land marked, "No Trespassing." Land your boat only in the national park or on other public lands, except for the few locations where it is acceptable to land on private property, which are listed in the individual trip descriptions in this chapter. You may want to discuss your trip with an outfitter or a National Park Service ranger beforehand to learn of any possible changes in land status. Also, note that the National Park

Service prohibits the landing of a kayak on an island with an active eagle, osprey, or seabird nest.

Second, give wildlife a wide berth. Seals, in particular, are easily stressed by kayaks, possibly because kayaks are shaped like the seal's main predator, the killer whale. Never approach seals in a kayak, particularly if they have hauled themselves out onto rocks, where they feel especially vulnerable. Try to stay at least 0.5 mile away from basking seals. Also enjoy eagle and osprey nests from a distance, trying to stay at least 0.25 mile away from an active nest. If any animal changes its behavior as you approach, you are too close.

Third, practice no-impact Leave No Trace techniques, both on and off the water. Pack out all of your trash, including toilet paper and solid human waste. Urinating below the high-tide line is the most effective way to ensure quick dispersal of urine. Never urinate in a tide pool, as this can have negative consequences on the delicate life there. Try to stay below the high-tide line at all times to minimize your impact on fragile island habitats. Do not take rocks and shells home as souvenirs.

Finally, remember that fishers are out there trying to make a living. Always give them the right of way and try to stay out of their path. Do not go near lobster traps, and be as quick as possible while using local boat ramps. Theoretically, kayaks have the right of way when passing other boats, but larger boats do not always see kayaks or may be traveling too fast to change course quickly. Play it safe and move aside when possible.

This chapter highlights six possible trips that vary in length and difficulty. The islands in this part of Maine provide a great variety of scenery and wildlife habitat, and these trips explore many of them, from quiet, marshy coves to dramatic seaside cliffs and open ocean. The shorelines of Mount Desert Island and the surrounding smaller islands are a great place to study the intertidal zones of sea life present on rocky outcroppings. Students of geology will find the variety of rocks fascinating and will enjoy seeing evidence of volcanism, tectonics, and glaciation. Rocky ledges are interspersed with cobble and sand beaches, and in the shallows, low tide reveals mud flats that attract a variety of shorebirds and wading birds, such as sandpipers and great blue herons. Seals and porpoises frequent the spaces between islands, as do seabirds, including loons, guillemots, and cormorants. Soaring overhead and nesting in island trees are ospreys and bald eagles. And watching it all are paddlers in their quiet kayaks.

TRIP 45
MOUNT DESERT NARROWS

NPS Rating ➤ Difficulty depends on weather conditions

Distance ➤ 6 miles

Estimated Time ➤ 3 hours

Map ➤ AMC's Acadia National Park Map: B3, B4

This is a relatively sheltered paddle in shallow waters, with the chance to see seals, porpoises, and an eagle's nest.

DIRECTIONS

From the Thompson Island Information Center (located on the west side of Route 3 on Thompson Island, between Trenton and Mount Desert Island), drive east on Route 3 for 4 miles then turn left on Hadley Point Road. It is 0.6 mile to the end of the road, where there is plenty of parking. Note that during full-moon high tides, this parking area can flood. *GPS coordinates:* 44° 26.608′ N, 68° 19.151′ W.

TRIP DESCRIPTION

Weather and tide considerations: We recommend making this paddle during the hours around high tide. There are extensive mud flats near Thompson Island, as well as in Thomas Bay and surrounding Thomas Island and the Twinnies. At low tide, these mud flats may be filled with feeding shorebirds, but the mud flats also drastically reduce the amount of paddling you can accomplish, and make it quite difficult and unpleasant to land a boat there. Try to start your paddle at least two hours after low tide and plan to finish it at least two hours before low tide. The Hulls Cove Visitor Center can give you tide information. A strong southwest wind occasionally can cause some unpleasant paddling conditions, but in general, this is a good trip in windy conditions, as it is relatively sheltered. If you do not see whitecaps from Hadley Point, you should be all set. If you have strong navigational skills, this trip is a good choice in foggy weather, as there is not much boat traffic.

Mount Desert Narrows is the body of water that separates Mount Desert Island from the mainland. This paddle, which explores the narrows east of Thompson Island, is a good choice in strong winds. It also makes a great sunset paddle. Wildlife, such as harbor porpoises, great blue herons, and bald eagles, can be found in this area of uninhabited islands, mud flats, and salt marshes. Beginning at Hadley Point, this trip follows the shoreline of Mount Desert Island past Northeast Creek to Thompson Island before circling back around Thomas Island and the Twinnies. Please note that Thompson Island and Hadley Point are the only landing spots on this trip. The remainder of the shoreline on Mount Desert Island is private property, as are the islands in the narrows.

From the put-in at Hadley Point, follow the shoreline to your left (west). The first mile or so of shoreline is wooded and rocky, with eelgrass becoming more prominent as you make your way toward Thomas Bay. Approximately 1.3 miles from Hadley Point, the Twinnies will appear on your right. These two islands, named for their similar size and shape, are uninhabited and provide an important nesting site for bald eagles. Please remember that it is illegal to disturb nesting eagles. On the return portion of this trip, you can paddle near the Twinnies and take a look at the nest from a safe distance. For now, continue to follow the shoreline of Mount Desert Island on your left. Marshes and mud flats dominate your surroundings as you enter Thomas Bay, with the outlet of Northeast Creek providing a rare look, for Mount Desert Island, at an area where freshwater enters salt water. The marsh grasses and concentration of food—mollusks, crustaceans, and small fish—make this an area frequented by great blue herons, mallards and black ducks, and green-winged teals. To paddle up Northeast Creek, see Trip 42.

Continuing through Thomas Bay, you will run into a peninsula of land known as Israel Point. Paddle around Israel Point, keeping the shoreline on your left, and head toward Thompson Island, where you can see the bridge that connects Mount Desert Island with the rest of Maine. Thompson Island and about 0.5 mile of the

Lucky paddlers may see a porpoise up close while paddling Mount Desert Narrows, below.

surrounding shoreline on Mount Desert Island are part of Acadia National Park, and therefore it is acceptable to land your boat here to rest before heading into the deeper waters of Mount Desert Narrows. To start your return to Hadley Point, paddle past Israel Point toward the left side of Thomas Island, which is about 1 mile from Thompson Island.

As you paddle around the northern (left) end of Thomas Island, you will enter the deeper waters of Mount Desert Narrows, where you are most likely to see harbor porpoises surfacing to breathe. Harbor porpoises and seals use the narrows as feeding grounds when the tides are highest. Traveling in pods of two to five animals, porpoises may come quite close to your kayak, as they feel no threat from the small boats. If you hear a porpoise blow, which sounds like a loud sneeze, stay still and soak in the magnificent sight of these sleek animals passing nearby. In addition to seals and porpoises, seabirds, such as black guillemots, double-crested cormorants, and common loons, are also found in the narrows.

As you pass Thomas Island, follow its shoreline to the right. At this point, the Twinnies come back into view. Using binoculars, look for a gray mass of branches—a bald eagle's nest—at the top of a large spruce. The birds often can be seen perching in the area, but please do not approach them or their nest too closely, as they are very wary of people and will abandon a nest if disturbed often. Stay at least 0.25 mile away from the nest site. To complete this wildlife-rich trip, paddle to the left of the more northerly of the Twinnies then follow the shoreline of Mount Desert Island on your right for the final 1.2 miles back to Hadley Point.

HARBOR SEALS AND PORPOISES

While you'll have to take a whale-watching excursion to see dolphins and whales near Acadia, it's quite common to enjoy visits from harbor seals and harbor porpoises while kayaking the waters around Mount Desert Island. Of course, both seals and porpoises are mammals and need to breathe air, which means they have to show themselves at the surface every now and then. If you're lucky, they'll do this near your boat. Never approach seals, especially when they have hauled themselves onto rocks or a beach, hoping to rest in relative safety. They are easily startled and waste precious energy swimming back and forth between the rocks and the water when disturbed by careless paddlers. Give them 0.5 mile of breathing room.

Seals are much more comfortable in the water than on land and may come near a kayak to check it out. Whether you see seals in the water or not is very much up to them. The same can be said of harbor porpoises, which seem to go about their business with no regard to kayaks. If they need to swim near your boat to get where they are going, they will do so, but they probably won't hang around or display any curiosity whatsoever. Nonetheless, seeing the sleek black bodies and dorsal fins of a pod of porpoises within a few yards of your kayak is exciting. Harbor seals appear in all of the waters around Acadia, including Somes Sound. Harbor porpoises are similarly distributed, although you're most likely to see them during a paddle in Mount Desert Narrows, Bartlett Narrows, or Frenchman Bay around the Porcupine Islands.

A young harbor seal rests on a Maine coast mud flat.

While kayaking, you will usually hear harbor porpoises before you see them. Their exhalation blow is a sharp puffing sound that sounds almost like a sneeze and is probably responsible for the nickname "puffing pig." Usually in groups of two to five animals, harbor porpoises generally come up to breathe together, slowly arching their backs out of the water. While their undersides are white, most likely you'll see only their black or dark gray backs. Harbor porpoises are small for whales and porpoises, rarely exceeding 6 feet in length and weighing around 130 pounds. Harbor porpoises are found throughout the Northern Hemisphere in cold and subarctic coastal waters.

Like harbor porpoises, harbor seals are found throughout the Northern Hemisphere in cold coastal waters. They are year-round residents of the Gulf of Maine, where they feed on fish, crustaceans, and squid. Harbor seals have heads shaped much like a dog's, and they often poke their heads up out of the water to look around.

TRIP 46

📷

FRENCHMAN BAY AND THE PORCUPINE ISLANDS

NPS Rating ➤ Difficulty depends on weather conditions

Distance ➤ 6.5 miles

Estimated Time ➤ 3 hours

Map ➤ AMC's Acadia National Park Map: C7, C8

This exciting paddle circles the beautiful and wild Porcupine Islands.

DIRECTIONS

From the intersection of Route 3 and West Street in Bar Harbor, drive east on West Street for about 0.3 mile. Turn left at the first street, which is Bridge Street. Drop off your boat on the Bar Island Bar then park your car back on West Street. *GPS coordinates:* 44° 23.516′ N, 68° 12.592′ W.

TRIP DESCRIPTION

Weather and tide considerations: On this trip, tide is a concern only at the put-in on the Bar Island Bar. Do not expect to land your boat on the southern side of the bar during low tide due to extensive mud flats. This trip is not recommended during foggy conditions, due to heavy boat traffic in the area. Even during sunny weather, larger boats may have trouble seeing kayaks. This paddle has a fair amount of exposure to the open ocean and can be difficult in winds from any direction stronger than 10 to 15 knots. West winds, in particular, can make it slow going on the return leg of the trip. On windy or foggy days, consider paddling Trip 45 or Trip 49 instead.

Our first kayak trip in Acadia was a drizzly August ride through 5-foot swells around the Porcupine Islands in Frenchman Bay. Despite the wet weather and menacing seas, we were instantly hooked on the beauty of this place of 100-foot cliffs, seals, seabirds, and bald eagles. This trip passes near Bar Island and Sheep, Burnt, and Bald Porcupine islands, with a view of Long Porcupine Island thrown in for good measure. The mountains of Acadia provide the backdrop for some of the most scenic paddling on the Maine coast. This trip should be undertaken only by experienced paddlers, as there are several open-water passages up to 1 mile long; fog can creep in at any time; and large swells can roll in from the Atlantic. If you lack experience with open-ocean paddling, consider joining a guided trip for a safe group exploration of the Porcupines.

Begin this trip at the put-in on the Bar Island Bar, a gravel spit that connects Bar Harbor with Bar Island at low tide. You can drive a car on the bar at low tide or even hike across the bar to a short trail on the island. Take note that the bar does disappear underwater as the tide comes in, so park your vehicle back at the end of West Street. Start paddling on the left side of the bar and head for the eastern end of Bar Island. Paddle around the end of the island, turning right and following the northern shore. Daniel Rodick, whose fashionable Rodick House in Bar Harbor could accommodate more than 600 guests, bought Bar Island in the late 1800s. The island eventually was sold to the Rockefeller family, who in turn donated it to Acadia National Park. Except for one year-round resident, Bar Island is now populated only by spruce and birch, herons and hawks.

Once you are on the north side of the island, the hustle and bustle of Bar Harbor disappear, and you are immersed in the intricacies of the intertidal zones so apparent on Bar Island's rocky shore. Barnacles, periwinkles, and limpets share the rocks with seaweeds, such as bladder wrack and Irish moss, while crabs, starfish, and sea urchins forage on and around the rocks. The intertidal shorelines around Mount Desert Island can be as exciting a habitat to explore as the high subalpine meadows of Cadillac or Sargent mountains. You will notice that different plants and animals inhabit different layers of the intertidal zones, depending on their requirements for light, water, and air.

When you reach the end of Bar Island, you face the first of three open-water crossings on this trip. Sheep Porcupine Island is straight ahead, approximately 0.3 mile away. Aim for the left side of the island. Sheep Porcupine is home to nesting bald eagles, so you will want to keep your eyes open for flashes of white among the dark green of the spruce trees that cover the island. Only adult eagles have the distinctive white heads and tails, but you are likely to see immatures in the area as well. Bald eagles that are less than 4 or 5 years old are brown with a varying amount of mottled white feathers. You will recognize them as eagles, though, since they're just as big as adults, with wingspans up to 8 feet. The National Park Service has closed this island to foot traffic in order to give the eagles a better chance of successfully nesting. Stay at least 0.25 mile from the island.

During the crossing from Bar Island, you may also begin to see some of the other well-known wildlife that frequent Frenchman Bay, such as harbor seals and black guillemots. While not as popular as Atlantic puffins, which spend most of their time far at sea, black guillemots are easily seen in Frenchman Bay and are just as fun to watch. Only about 1 foot long, these true seabirds are built like torpedoes, with their bright red feet trailing a black body with white wing patches. Also known as sea pigeons or pigeon guillemots, they are expert swimmers, feeding on small fish and crustaceans. Harbor seals seem more wary than guillemots, but you can occasionally see them checking you out from behind. Other common animals in the bay are double-crested cormorants, common loons, harbor porpoises, gulls, and terns. Minke whales may also make an appearance in late summer.

Paddle around the north end of Sheep Porcupine, which was home to grazing sheep in the 1800s. The sheep are now gone and the forest has returned, as the island is now entirely a protected part of Acadia National Park. As you paddle around the northern end of the island, Burnt Porcupine comes into view. The crossing to Burnt Porcupine is about 0.5 mile in length, and it is fairly exposed to the seas coming in from the open Atlantic. A deep channel between the two islands is used extensively by boats, including the large yachts and cruise ships that visit the region in summer. Needless to say, steer clear of large vessels during this crossing, and if the fog is in, consider turning around and returning to Bar Harbor. Traveling in a compact group of kayaks can make you more visible to the larger boats and help reduce the possibility of an accident.

Burnt Porcupine is slightly larger than Sheep Porcupine, and its shoreline consists of a combination of cobble beaches, rocky stretches, and high cliffs. Burnt Porcupine has been preserved by The Nature Conservancy, making it possible to enjoy the beauty of the island's thick spruce forest and dramatic coast from the seat of your kayak for years to come. Paddle around the north end of the island and you will eventually see a small island just off the western edge of Burnt Porcupine. This island is called Rum Key and, though private, it's permissible to land on the cobble beach to take a break. Nonetheless, Rum Key is a fragile island environment, so try to remain on the rocks and below the high-tide line. From Rum Key you can see

A rainbow arches over paddlers and the Porcupine Islands in Frenchman Bay.

a receding set of islands to the southeast. The first two islands are Long Porcupine and Ironbound Island, the largest island in Frenchman Bay. The farthest island is not actually an island but Schoodic Peninsula, the only portion of Acadia National Park on the mainland.

You can spend a longer day exploring Long Porcupine and Ironbound, but our trip heads back to Bar Harbor via Bald Porcupine. To the south of Rum Key, you will see Bald Porcupine across a mile of open ocean. Like the crossing between Sheep and Burnt Porcupine, this crossing can have heavy boat traffic, as well as heavy seas, but it's also a good opportunity to paddle among seabirds and mammals. Head for the east end of Bald Porcupine, which will be on your left. Like the rest of the Porcupine Islands, Bald Porcupine has a gently sloping northern end, with steep cliffs on its south side. This shape is a landscape feature created by glaciers known as a roche moutannée (literally "sheep-rock," in French) or a whaleback. The cliffs on the southern end of Bald Porcupine are impressive, rising 100 feet up out of the waters of Frenchman Bay. Stay well clear of the cliffs, especially if there are winds or swells out of the south, as rebounding surf can topple a kayak.

As you paddle around the southern end of Bald Porcupine, you eventually come to a breakwater that leads toward the shore in Bar Harbor. During most tides the breakwater is not passable, so paddle its length toward the shore. At the end of the breakwater you can continue to the shore and turn right, keeping Bar Harbor on your left as you get a good look at some of the largest houses in town. This part of town was spared during the great fire of 1947, giving you a glimpse of the "cottage life" that existed before most of the large vacation homes were destroyed. As you follow the shoreline toward the harbor, you will need to maneuver around the sailboats, whale-watching boats, and lobster boats moored there. Once past the boats, you will be back at the Bar Island Bar, with Bridge Street on your left.

HUMPBACK WHALES

In *Moby-Dick*, Herman Melville wrote of the humpback whale: "He is the most gamesome and light-hearted of all the whales, making more gay foam and white-water than any other of them." Humpbacks are naturally curious about boats; one might sit in the water within a few feet of a boat for several minutes, slapping and waving its flippers, swimming under the boat, and sticking its huge barnacle-laden head out of the water in an apparent attempt to get a better look at the boat's occupants. Anyone who has seen one of these 25-ton behemoths breaching its entire body out of the water has been impressed with its size and agility. For these reasons, humpbacks have become the darlings of the whale-watching industry, and Bar Harbor is a great place to take a whale-watching cruise. Several tour companies have two or more whale-watching trips a day during the summer, and most of them guarantee a sighting.

Humpbacks live in all of the world's oceans and tend to favor coastal waters or shallower shelf waters out at sea. They are huge animals, with adults reaching 46 to 50 feet in length and weighing as much as 30 tons. Even at birth, they weigh 2 tons. Now, that's a big kid! Humpbacks generally migrate up to 5,000 miles between summer feeding grounds and winter breeding grounds. The animals that live in the Gulf of Maine during summer generally swim to the Caribbean Sea in winter to breed and give birth. Like most migratory whales, humpbacks bulk up in the food-rich waters of their summer feeding grounds since food is scarce in their warm-water breeding grounds. In winter, most yearling calves do not make the trip to the breeding grounds. Instead, they spend winter off the coast of Virginia, where they can continue to take advantage of more abundant food sources without expending the energy needed to make the long trip south. The young whales regroup with the mature whales during the spring migration north.

Humpbacks belong to the rorqual family of whales, which also includes minke, fin, blue, sei, and Bryde's whales, all relatively large baleen whales. Minke and fin, or finback, whales are also commonly seen during whale-watching excursions in the Gulf of Maine. Baleen whales feed by filling their mouths with tons of water then filtering out trapped fish or krill through their baleen. A substitute for teeth, this comblike plate hangs down from the whale's upper jaws and includes stiff hairs that aid in trapping the smallest of prey. These huge animals rarely eat anything larger than shrimp.

Humpbacks are unique among rorqual whales in that they have a fairly rotund appearance, as opposed to the long, sleek shape of the other members of this family. They also have very long flippers, up to 15 feet in length, with unique black and white markings that aid in animal identification. Using tail and flipper markings, scientists are meticulously identifying individual North Atlantic humpbacks in an attempt to better understand their behavior, breeding success, and longevity. Naturalists on the local whale-watching boats are familiar with most of the whales by name and contribute a great deal of information to the accumulating body of knowledge used to determine the overall health of the humpback population.

While you will not see a humpback from shore, if you take a whale-watching excursion you are likely to see one or more of the following behaviors:

- Breaching is perhaps the most exciting behavior to witness, as humpbacks propel their huge bulk out of the water. Humpbacks use their tails to shoot themselves out of the water sideways, with their flippers outstretched. They then arch their backs, do a half-turn, and land on their backs in what looks like a huge explosion. Why they breach is not known for sure. It could be to stun prey or to knock barnacles off their skin. It might also be just for fun.

- Lobtailing is when a whale repeatedly slaps the water with its tail. The rest of the whale's body remains underwater in a head-down position.

- Fluking is when a whale lifts its tail high above its body as a prelude to making a deep dive. If you see humpbacks, you will most likely witness this behavior. After fluking, a whale may stay under water for as long as 45 minutes.

- Flipper slapping gives many whale watchers the impression that a whale is waving at them. Sometimes a humpback will lie at the surface of the water on its side and simply slap the water repeatedly with its huge flipper. An individual occasionally will lie on its back and slap both flippers simultaneously.

- Spyhopping is what whales do when they just want to take a look around. While spyhopping, they slowly lift their heads straight out of the water until their eyes are above the surface. This is a common behavior for whales that voluntarily approach a whale-watching boat.

TRIP 47

📷

SUTTON AND BEAR ISLANDS

NPS Rating ➤ Difficulty depends on weather conditions

Distance ➤ 6 miles

Estimated Time ➤ 3 hours

Map ➤ AMC's Acadia National Park Map: F5, F6, G5, G6

This moderate paddle passes a remote lighthouse and a sea arch, providing a nice view of the mountains on Mount Desert Island.

DIRECTIONS

From downtown Bar Harbor, follow Route 3 south for 8.1 miles. Seal Harbor will be on your left. A public parking area is on the right. *GPS coordinates:* 44° 17.775′ N, 68° 14.417′ W.

TRIP DESCRIPTION

Weather and tide considerations: Tide is not an issue on this trip, but with heavy boat traffic in the area, it is advisable not to paddle here in foggy weather. Strong winds (above 10 to 15 knots) from the east or the west can cause problems, and winds out of the north can funnel through the mountains, making the return trip difficult. Winds from the southwest are the most favorable.

This 6-mile loop explores the shoreline of Mount Desert Island near Seal Harbor, as well as Sutton and Bear islands, which are part of the group of islands known as the Cranberry Isles. A lighthouse perches atop a cliff on the western side of Bear Island, while Sutton Island boasts a fascinating sea arch and sweeping views of the mountains on Mount Desert Island's eastern side. Like most of the waters surrounding Acadia, this area is rich in wildlife, giving any paddler a good chance to see guillemots, loons, seals, ospreys, and bald eagles.

The put-in for this trip is at the sand beach in Seal Harbor. While you may have a long walk across the beach at low tide, the sand is firm, and you do not have to worry about sinking up to your knees in muck. Seal Harbor is a picturesque spot, with sailboats filling the harbor, which in turn is enclosed by a gently curving shoreline populated by spruce and summer homes. The Cranberry Isles are directly across from the mouth of the harbor, inviting boaters of all types to escape the summer crowds of Mount Desert Island. Begin your trip by paddling toward the point of land on the southwest end of the harbor known as Crowninshield

Point. The very large house near this point should make it apparent that the shoreline here is privately owned and landing your boat is discouraged. Stay well clear of red bell 6 (a large red buoy) in this area. In the right conditions, a large rock underwater here can cause a rogue wave to topple a kayak. After rounding Crowninshield Point, keep Mount Desert Island on your right and follow the shoreline for about 0.75 mile, at which point you will be in a protected cove known as Bracy Cove. Other than Seal Harbor, Bracy Cove is the only allowable landing spot on this trip. Directly across the road from Bracy Cove is Little Long Pond, a picturesque body of water described in Trip 37.

Watch out for boat traffic on this paddle, including around the busy harbor of Little Cranberry Island.

Continue along the shoreline, which alternates between cobble beaches and rocky coast. Some of the larger summer homes on the island are in Seal and Northeast harbors, and this stretch of coastline boasts a few. To the southwest of Bracy Cove is Bear Island, the smallest of the Cranberry Isles. When opposite Bear Island, turn away from the coast and make the 1,200-foot crossing to the north end of the island. Like many of the islands in the area, Bear Island was used as sheep pasture for many years. Islands were popular for this purpose, because the sheep were easy to keep track of without building fences. As you paddle around the western end of the island, you will see a white lighthouse sitting among tall spruce 100 feet above cliffs, caves, and rocky rubble. Bear Island Light was built in 1839, rebuilt in 1889, and was attended until 1982, when its flashing beacon was deactivated and replaced with lighted buoys.

From the lighthouse and the west end of Bear Island, paddle due south for a little more than 0.5 mile to reach the west end of Sutton Island. While making this crossing, watch for black guillemots and double-crested cormorants. Keep an eye out for both harbor seals and their rare cousins, gray seals. While harbor seals are much more common on the Maine coast, gray seals do frequent this area. Much bigger than harbor seals, gray seals can grow to be 10 feet long and 650 pounds, while harbor seals reach 5 feet and 250 pounds. A gray seal's uniform black or gray color contrasts with the spotted fur of a harbor seal. Gray seals can dive to almost 500 feet while feeding on fish and cuttlefish.

On the northwestern corner of Sutton Island is an amazing osprey nest built on a rock outcropping that's separated from the island by a thin stretch of water. The nest may be as old as 100 years, and its component sticks are piled several feet high. Keep at least 0.25 mile from the nest, as the birds experience a lot of disturbance from boats in this area. If the adults are forced to leave the nest too often, the chicks may not survive. It's a wonderful experience, nonetheless, to sit in your kayak with binoculars and watch an adult osprey bring fish to its young and eager chicks. Instead of paddling around the western end of Sutton Island, turn left before reaching the osprey nest and follow the northern shore, keeping the island on your right. There is a cobble beach at the western end of the northern shore, but steep granite cliffs wall much of this side of the island. A sea arch is also visible from here. The arch, created by eroding waves, is about 40 feet tall.

As you reach the eastern end of Sutton Island, Little Cranberry island comes into view to the southeast. Great Cranberry island is farther away to the southwest. You'll have excellent views of Acadia's mountains by looking north. Turn your boat to the north in order to return to Seal Harbor. Crowninshield Point, at the entrance to Seal Harbor, is about 1 mile due north of the eastern end of Sutton Island. This is a long crossing in an area with heavy boat traffic. If you are traveling in a group, stay close together so that you're easier for boats to spot and avoid, and try to avoid making this crossing in foggy conditions. As you reenter Seal Harbor, keep an eye out for bald eagles, which sometimes soar above the harbor's shoreline.

TRIP 48
SOMES SOUND

NPS Rating ➤ Difficulty depends on weather conditions

Distance ➤ 7.5 miles

Estimated Time ➤ 4 hours

Map ➤ AMC's Acadia National Park Map: E4, E5, F4, F5, G4, G5

This unique paddle visits the only fjord in the eastern United States, with views of tall ocean-side cliffs and possibly wildlife.

DIRECTIONS

Just south of downtown Southwest Harbor, turn left off Route 102 onto Route 102A. After 1 mile, turn left onto Mansell Lane. At the end of the road, turn left onto Shore Road. The boat ramp is a short distance on the right. *GPS coordinates:* 44° 16.109′ N, 68° 18.509′ W.

TRIP DESCRIPTION

Weather and tide considerations: When the wind and tide are moving in opposite directions, ominous standing waves can develop in the shallow and narrow mouth of Somes Sound, known as the narrows. Otherwise, tides are not much of an issue in the sound. The wind is another story. Running north to south, with mountains rising up on both its eastern and western shores, Somes Sound experiences a strong wind-tunnel effect when winds are out of the north or south. These winds can make it very difficult to paddle, and you are better off trying an alternate trip, such as Mount Desert Narrows (Trip 45). Winds out of the east or west usually aren't a problem.

Somes Sound is a narrow finger of water that almost cuts Mount Desert Island in two. A glacier created Somes Sound, scouring a deep, "U"-shaped valley between Acadia and Norumbega mountains. The glacier carved through Mount Desert Island all the way to the ocean, and now the valley is filled with seawater. This paddling trip starts near the mouth of the sound, in the working harbor of Manset, where you can explore the shoreline of Greening Island before making your way up the sound to Valley Cove, Eagle Cliff, and a waterfall at Man o' War Brook. Like all of the kayaking trips around Mount Desert Island, Somes Sound provides good opportunities for seeing wildlife, such as seabirds, bald eagles, and seals.

From the boat ramp in Manset, Southwest Harbor is to your left, and Greening Island is across the water to the northeast. Straight ahead is a passage between Southwest Harbor and Greening Island that is the most direct route to Somes Sound. The water is shallow in this passage, which sometimes makes for a bumpy crossing. For this trip, head to the eastern tip of Greening Island and paddle around the northeastern side of the island before heading north into the sound. With Southwest Harbor to the west and Northeast Harbor to the east, the waters around Greening Island get a fair amount of boat traffic, so keep your group together and stay aware of your surroundings. Greening Island marks the entrance to Somes Sound, which is named after Abraham Somes, one of the first permanent settlers on Mount Desert Island, having built a log cabin at Somes Point after sailing to Somes Sound from Gloucester, Massachusetts, in 1761. Still privately owned, Greening Island has stunning views of Somes Sound and the mountains of Mount Desert Island.

As you paddle north from Greening Island, you will make your way through the mouth of Somes Sound, known as the narrows. Here the sound is only about 1,000 feet across and the water is very shallow—less than 10 feet deep in spots. If the wind is blowing against the tide here, there can be some fairly choppy water. Farther north in Somes Sound, the water attains depths of up to 150 feet. The gently sloping field on the western shore of the narrows is known as Jesuit Spring. A French colony settled on this site in 1613 was quickly attacked and destroyed by the

Dawn breaks over Somes Sound, Acadia's only fjord.

British, one of many skirmishes between the two naval powers in eastern Maine and Maritime Canada during the seventeenth and eighteenth centuries.

Just beyond Jesuit Spring, Flying Mountain rises 271 feet from the waters of Somes Sound. Follow the shoreline on your left around Flying Mountain and into Valley Cove, a sheltered inlet bordered by Flying Mountain on the south and the spectacular 400-foot face of Eagle Cliff on the west. This is one of the most sheltered coves on the island, and it is still used as a place to anchor boats in extremely rough weather. The shoreline here is part of Acadia National Park and makes an excellent spot to stop and take a break. Flying Mountain Trail is only a few yards from shore and takes you to the summit of Flying Mountain or the top of Eagle Cliff, both of which have excellent views of Somes Sound. We have never seen bald eagles on Eagle Cliff, but they are common visitors to the sound and could be seen at any point during this trip. To the north of Valley Cove is Acadia Mountain, and across the water to the northeast is Norumbega Mountain, which, at 850 feet, is the highest point above the sound.

From Valley Cove, continue north along the western shore of Somes Sound. Eagle Cliff and the northeastern shoulder of Saint Sauveur Mountain dominate the shoreline for much of the way to Man o' War Brook, which marks the low point between Saint Sauveur and Acadia Mountains. At Man o' War Brook, water rushes over steep rocks into the sound at a point where the water is deep enough for large boats. The deep water made it easy for schooners to sail into the sound, quickly collect freshwater, and head back out to sea. The easy access to freshwater in a hidden cove probably is responsible for the stories of pirate ships using this area. Today, Man o' War Brook is a scenic stop for boats, with its cool, cedar-lined shoreline flanked by the dramatic slopes of Acadia and Saint Sauveur Mountains providing beautiful visual relief.

From here you can return to Manset either by following the western shore or paddling across the sound to the rugged shoreline under Norumbega Mountain. South of Norumbega, the shoreline becomes gentler as you pass some of the biggest summer homes on Mount Desert Island, in the wooded outskirts of the town of Northeast Harbor. On your return paddle to Manset, keep your eyes peeled for guillemots, cormorants, and loons, as well as both harbor and gray seals. Looking south and east past Greening Island, you can see Sutton Island, the Cranberries, and out to the open Atlantic.

WHAT IS A FJORD?

Somes Sound is the only fjord on the East Coast of the United States. "Fjord" is a Norwegian word used to describe the deep bays and inlets that line the coast of Norway, on the Norwegian Sea. In addition to Norway, fjords are common in British Columbia, Alaska, and New Zealand. Most fjords were carved by glaciers during the last ice age, between 15,000 and 25,000 years ago. They are typically deep fingers of seawater surrounded by tall cliffs or mountains. In the case of Somes Sound, the mountains rise 850 feet above the surface, and the water reaches depths of 150 feet. If you drained Somes Sound, it would look much like the "U"-shaped valleys between Dorr Mountain and Huguenot Head, and Cadillac and Pemetic mountains. While a fjord is usually very deep for most of its length, it is often much more shallow at its mouth. At Somes Sound, when the Wisconsin Glacier retreated about 13,000 years ago, it left a pile of debris, called a terminal moraine, at the mouth of the sound. The water here is only about 10 feet deep. This narrow and shallow mouth makes it harder for water to leave and enter the sound during changes in tides, creating a unique mix of water and nutrients that supports a wide variety of wildlife, including lobsters, loons, seals, great blue herons, and bald eagles.

Acadia Mountain offers a view of the mouth of Somes Sound.

TRIP 49
SEAL COVE TO PRETTY MARSH

NPS Rating > Difficulty depends on weather conditions

Distance > 10 miles

Estimated Time > 7 hours

Map > AMC's Acadia National Park Map: G1, F1, E1

This paddle on the "quiet" side of Mount Desert Island is filled with wooded shoreline, beautiful islands, and bountiful wildlife.

DIRECTIONS

From the intersection of Seal Cove Road and Route 102 in Seal Cove, follow Route 102 north for 0.3 mile. Turn left onto Cape Road. Drive past the boat ramp in Seal Cove to a small turnout, about 0.5 mile down on the left. There is parking on the right. *GPS coordinates: 44° 17.144′ N, 68° 24.889′ W.*

TRIP DESCRIPTION

Weather and tide considerations: Low tide will make it necessary to paddle on the west side of Moose Island, but this will not add time to your trip. A strong wind out of the southwest can cause a fair amount of choppiness at the southern ends of Moose and Hardwood islands; otherwise, the wind and tides should not cause too many problems. There is a small amount of boat traffic in this area but much less than other areas around Mount Desert Island.

Mount Desert Island is bordered on the west by a body of water known as Blue Hill Bay. From Seal Cove north to Pretty Marsh, views to the west of Blue Hill Bay give way to the gentle shoreline of Bartlett Island as the bay funnels though the Bartlett Narrows. Here seals and porpoises regularly come to feed on the fish concentrated between the islands. There is much to explore here: the rocky intertidal zones of Mount Desert Island, the beautiful shoreline of Moose Island, and the pastoral views of the historically preserved farms of Bartlett Island. Trips of almost any length are possible in this area, but this one highlights the 5 miles between Seal Cove and Pretty Marsh Harbor. While there is a boat ramp in Pretty Marsh, parking is restricted to residents of the town of Mount Desert, so you must begin your trip in Seal Cove.

Sunset as seen from the town landing in Pretty Marsh.

This trip can take most of the day, so be sure to carry plenty of food, water, and extra clothing. Also note that all of the islands in Blue Hill Bay are privately owned, and landing on them for any reason is discouraged. One exception is Bartlett Island, which is owned by the Rockefeller family. If you land on Bartlett Island, try to remain below the high-tide line in order to minimize impact. The other exception is a small picnic area within the national park boundary on the eastern side of Pretty Marsh Harbor. The rest of Mount Desert Island in this area is private property. In addition to respecting private property, be sure to give a wide berth to any seals on the ledges of Bartlett Island and north of Pretty Marsh. Seals "haul out," or come out of the water onto land, in order to rest. They are very skittish of kayaks and lose a lot of valuable energy going in and out of the water. Stay at least 0.5 mile away from any seals hauled out on land.

With those logistical concerns out of the way, be prepared to enjoy a wonderful paddle. From the put-in at Seal Cove, paddle west to leave the cove then turn right around Reed Point. From here you can see Moose, Hardwood, and Bartlett islands to the north and west. Moose Island is particularly beautiful, with its gravel beaches giving way to heath and blueberry bushes before a forest of tall spruce takes over. Like many of the islands in Maine, Moose Island was used to graze livestock for much of the nineteenth century. Moose Island was particularly useful because a gravel bar connects it to Mount Desert Island at low tide. As a kayaker, you will need to pay attention to the tide in order to avoid having to carry your boat over the bar. The bar is usually above water during the two hours on either side of low tide. Of course, you can paddle around the western side of the island during any tide.

From Moose Island, paddle northwest, toward Hardwood Island. Hardwood Island is indeed named for its forest of hardwoods—in this case, birch, maple, and beech. Hardwood Island has a shoreline of gravel beaches with good views to the east of Mount Desert Island's western mountains. Paddle along the eastern shore of this island until you reach its northern tip. From here it is a 0.75-mile paddle to the southern end of Bartlett Island. Feel free to take a break on Bartlett Island but stay below the high-tide mark, pack out all of your trash, and refrain from building fires. Bartlett Island was first settled in the 1760s, and its fertile soil made it an excellent place to farm. By the early 1900s, however, most families had moved to the mainland or to Mount Desert Island, where access to services was much more convenient. The Rockefeller family bought the island in the early 1970s in order to prevent it from being developed into a resort community. Rockefeller family members now run the farm on the eastern side of the island that can be seen from the town landing in Pretty Marsh.

Follow the eastern shore of Bartlett Island by keeping the island on your left. You will see Folly Island to the east and the diminutive John Island to the northeast as you enter Bartlett Narrows. The waters and fish of Blue Hill Bay are funneled through this narrow passage between islands, creating an excellent feeding opportunity for harbor seals and harbor porpoises. This is one of the best areas around Acadia for spotting these marine mammals. Keep your eyes open for the periscoping, doglike heads of seals, and listen for the exhalations of porpoises, which sometimes will approach quite close to a kayak. Ospreys nest in the area and can be seen soaring above the water in search of fish. Double-crested cormorants and black guillemots are also frequent visitors to Bartlett Narrows.

Once you are past John Island, paddle east across Bartlett Narrows to the western shore of Mount Desert Island. Due east of John Island is the Pretty Marsh picnic area in Acadia National Park. While it is a steep climb to the picnic tables from the shore, you can stop here in all but the highest tides and take a break before heading back to Seal Cove. That said, the shoreline on Bartlett Island is more amenable to stopping and has good views of Acadia's mountains. No matter which location you choose for a break, return to Seal Cove by keeping the shoreline of Mount Desert Island on your left. This stretch of shoreline has small cobble beaches, interesting rocky outcrops with veins of quartz, and good opportunities to observe the different layers of the intertidal zones. After returning to Seal Cove, you may want to drive to the town landing at Pretty Marsh to take in the sunset over Bartlett Island.

INTERTIDAL ZONES

The tides around Mount Desert Island rise and fall between 8 and 10 feet. This gradual, twice-daily change in water levels creates unique habitats on the rocky ledges that surround the island. These habitats vary drastically in the amount of sunlight they receive and in the amount of exposure they have to the air. In 10 feet of rock at the water's edge, there are several different zones of life. Each zone supports a different group of organisms that has evolved to exploit varying amounts of sunlight, surf, air, and water. The intertidal zones all around Mount Desert Island and the surrounding islands can be studied, most easily from a kayak. If you prefer to visit them on foot, look along the shore below Ocean Drive, at the end of the Ship Harbor Nature Trail, or below Bass Harbor Head Light.

Intertidal zones generally break down into five distinct sections, each supporting a variety of life, from blue-green algae and periwinkles to kelp and sea urchins.

Spray zone: Just above the high-tide line, this zone is never submerged in seawater but receives a constant spray of salt water from crashing surf. Sometimes called the black zone, this zone is characterized by the presence of primitive blue-green algae (*calothrix*) and black lichen (*verrucaria*). The algae or lichen create a thin, black, very slippery covering over the rocks. A rough-shelled variety of periwinkle feeds on the algae in this zone and seeks shelter in crevices of rocks in both this zone and the barnacle zone.

Barnacle zone: Contrasting with the black spray zone is the barnacle zone, made up of masses of white acorn barnacles (*Balanus balanoides*). The barnacle

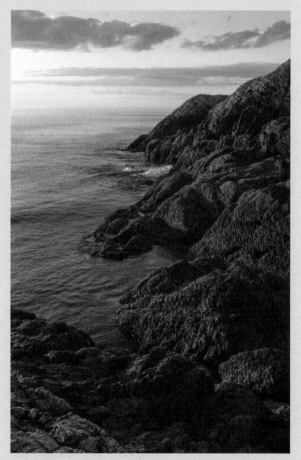

Intertidal zones break down into five distinct sections, each supporting a variety of coastal marine life.

zone drops below the water only at high tide, so the barnacles must be able to withstand long periods of exposure to the air, as well as to Maine's pounding surf. Barnacles are crustaceans, and they attach themselves to rocks with a cementlike substance they also use to build conical shells around themselves. At the top of this shell is a small valve a barnacle can close during low tide to protect itself from the drying effects of the air. At high tide, a barnacle opens this valve to feed, extending feathery comb-shaped arms to catch microscopic organisms.

Rockweed zone: This zone is out of the water about the same amount of time it is underwater. The rockweed zone is characterized by a covering of stringy, rubbery, brown algae known as rockweed. There are two dominant species of rockweed around Acadia: Bladder wrack is common in the upper level of the rockweed zone, while knotted wrack proliferates in the lower level of the zone. Both types use gas bladders filled with air to keep them suspended near the light during high tide so they can continue to photosynthesize. During low tide, they form a thick, protective covering inhabited by a wide variety of wildlife, such as common periwinkles, blue mussels, and dog whelks, which prey on both mussels and barnacles.

Irish moss zone: Exposed to the air only during low tide, this zone is characterized by red algae, such as Irish moss and dulse. Irish moss is a maroon-colored seaweed that has an iridescent sheen in bright sunlight. Dulse is a 6-inch-long red seaweed with broad, flat fronds. Irish moss is harvested around the world to make carrageenan, a thickener used in food and cosmetic products. The Irish moss zone also provides habitat for a number of shellfish and crustaceans.

Kelp zone: This zone is above water only during extreme low tides in the spring and fall. This diverse underwater community centers on kelp, a brown seaweed usually characterized by long, leathery blades. Kelp provides the ideal environment for aquatic animals, such as starfish and sea urchins. A starfish feeds on mussels, clams, and other shellfish by wrapping its arms around its prey, prying open the shell, inserting its stomach, and digesting the animal. Sea urchins are vegetarian, feeding mainly on kelp. Brittle stars, sea cucumbers, sea anemones, and crabs also inhabit the kelp zone.

TRIP 50
CRANBERRY ISLES

📷

NPS Rating ➤ Advanced
Distance ➤ 12 miles
Estimated Time ➤ 7 hours
Map ➤ AMC's Acadia National Park Map: F6, G6, G7, H6

This all-day paddle reaches historic islands and offers excellent views of the mountains on Mount Desert Island.

DIRECTIONS
From downtown Bar Harbor, follow Route 3 south for 8.1 miles. Seal Harbor will be on your left. A public parking area is on the right. *GPS coordinates:* 44° 17.775′ N, 68° 14.417′ W.

TRIP DESCRIPTION
Weather and tide considerations: Tide is not a major issue on this trip. At low tide, though, you will have to carry your boat farther to put in, and beware of submerged rocks in the Pool (a tidal salt marsh) at Great Cranberry. With heavy boat traffic in the area, we advise against paddling here in foggy weather, and fog is very common in these waters. Prevailing summer winds from the southwest often blow fog into this southern part of the Mount Desert Island area before any other waters near the island. Strong winds (above 10 to 15 knots) from the east or west can cause problems, and winds out of the north can funnel through the mountains, making the return trip difficult. Winds from the southwest are the most favorable, but only the most experienced paddlers should attempt this trip in winds stronger than 10 knots. In any case, the length and the exposed nature of some sections make this trip appropriate for experienced paddlers only.

The Cranberry Isles are five islands located off the southern coast of Mount Desert Island, near the entrance to Somes Sound. They have a rich history of settlement that goes back 150 years, when the islands were a tight-knit community of families who made their living from the sea. There is still a small population of fishing people living year-round on Great and Little Cranberry, but most of the houses on these islands are now used as summer homes and vacation rentals. Both islands have excellent museums that chronicle the history of these communities. This trip visits four of the five islands: Bear, Sutton, Great Cranberry, and Little Cranberry (also known as Islesford). The fifth island in the group, Baker Island, is also accessible by kayak but requires advanced paddling skills and ideal conditions, and is not described in this trip. Be aware that almost all of the shoreline along the Cranberry Isles is privately owned, so please respect the property and restrict your access to the area around the town docks on Great and Little Cranberry.

Like Trip 47, this paddling trip begins in Seal Harbor and proceeds to Bear and Sutton islands. From the beach at Seal Harbor, paddle out of the harbor then follow the shoreline to the right, to the cobblestones of Bracy Cove. About 0.5 mile past Bracy Cove, turn your boat to the left and aim for Bear Island, about 0.2 mile to the south. Paddle around the western shore of Bear Island, where you will pass the Bear Island Light House, then make the 0.5-mile crossing of Eastern Way to the western end of Sutton Island. Instead of following the northern shore of Sutton, as in Trip 47, stay to the west of Sutton Island to make the crossing to Great Cranberry.

By paddling due south from the western end of Sutton Island, you should reach the town dock on Great Cranberry in about 1 mile. Please remember there can be heavy boat traffic in this area. Once at Great Cranberry, if you want to stretch your legs and explore, you can beach your boat on the cobblestones just to the right of the town dock and walk into town. At the end of the dock, you will find a general store, and a 0.25-mile walk up the street takes you to the Preble-Marr Historical Museum, where there are public restrooms and excellent exhibits. There is also a 1-mile walking trail through beautiful, mature spruce woods behind the museum that leads to a secluded sandy beach on the western side of the island. Be warned,

Sunset as seen from the town landing on Great Cranberry Island.

however, that a walk on the streets of Great Cranberry will most likely cause you to dream of spending a week, a month, or a lifetime on the porch of a cedar-shingled home, overlooking fields with sweeping views of the Maine Coast.

To continue paddling, follow the shoreline east past the town dock for about 1 mile to Long Point. Following the shoreline to the right around Long Point brings you into the Pool, a tidal salt marsh that's a good place to watch for shorebirds and seabirds. (As mentioned at the beginning of this trip's description, be on the lookout for exposed rocks at the entrance to the Pool at low tide.) You will find this landscape unique in a paddle alternating between cobblestone beaches and inaccessible rocky shorelines.

Once you have returned to the entrance of the Pool, aim northeast across Cranberry Harbor for the docks at Islesford in Hadlock Cove, on Little Cranberry.

Caution: Do not paddle south and east through the so-called Gut and into the waters between the Cranberry Isles and Baker Island. This area features strong tidal currents and exposed ledges that are treacherous in certain conditions—especially without local knowledge and advanced paddling skills.

At Islesford, you also can land your boat at the beaches near the town dock and make your way into town on foot. Islesford has a few more amenities for visitors, including restaurants, galleries, and a bed-and-breakfast. Of real interest is the Islesford Historical Museum, which is run by the National Park Service and is home to excellent exhibits that describe life on the islands in the nineteenth century.

To make the return trip to Seal Harbor, paddle north from the dock at Islesford to Hadlock Point then head north-northeast to the eastern end of Sutton Island (about 0.6 mile). From there, make the 1-mile crossing to Seal Harbor, to the north. This is a lot of open water, so be wary of other boat traffic and keep your eyes open for gray and harbor seals, as well as black guillemots in the open water, and bald eagles and ospreys as you get closer to shore.

THE WARMING WATERS OF THE GULF OF MAINE

Mount Desert Island and Acadia are situated on the northern edge of the Gulf of Maine, the nutrient-rich, cold expanse of Atlantic Ocean that stretches northeast from the tip of Cape Cod in Massachusetts to Cape Sable, at the southern end of Nova Scotia. For hundreds of years, the Gulf of Maine has been one of the most productive fisheries in the world. This is due to a unique mix of nutrient-rich freshwater, ocean currents bringing down cold water from Labrador, and the world's largest tides, which churn it all together into a rich soup that feeds everything from lobster and cod to right whales and Atlantic puffins.

The ocean conditions, however, that provide this bounty are changing. During the last decade, sea-surface temperatures in the Gulf of Maine have risen faster than 99 percent of the world's oceans. This warming is causing changes in the populations and distribution of marine species throughout the region. According to a report published in the journal *Science* by the Gulf of Maine Research Institute, this warming is caused by "changes in the position of the Gulf Stream and to climate oscillations in the Atlantic and Pacific."

Cod fishing was the most lucrative fishery in Maine for more than 200 years. Estimates put the annual catch of cod in Maine in the mid-nine-

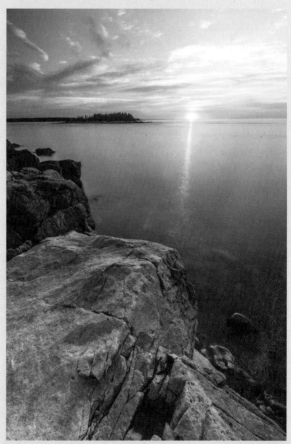

The waters on Maine's coast are warming faster than 99 percent of the world's oceans

teenth century at more than 75,000 metric tons per year. But by the late twentieth century, the fishery had collapsed, with overfishing a contributing factor. By 2015 the fishing quota for cod in Maine was a mere 386 tons. Now researchers believe even that quota is too high, as the warmer water in the region limits the reproductive capability of spawning females, with fewer young surviving to adulthood.

Other changes have been noted in recent years as well. Plunging populations of copepods, tiny crustaceans that thrive in cold water, have led to fewer already endangered right whales visiting the waters east and north of Mount Desert Island. The lack of copepods also has led to a decline in the herring population, which in turn has led to lower reproductive success in the Atlantic puffins that nest in the region. Invasive green crabs have decimated the soft-shell clam fishery in northern Casco Bay and are mowing down eelgrass beds there, while commercial fisherman are pulling in species previously common farther south, such as blue crabs and black sea bass.

On the other hand, lobster populations in the Gulf of Maine are booming as the cod population declines. (Cod are a main predator of lobster.) Lobster is the state of Maine's most lucrative fishery by far, bringing in more than $450 million a year to the state's fishers. Even lobster populations are likely to decline, though, if the waters of the gulf continue to warm.

There is likely little the state of Maine can do to stop warming effects due to climate change; the state accounts for 0.05 percent of the world's greenhouse gas emissions. But there are ways to strengthen the Gulf of Maine habitat to make it more resilient, such as limiting pollution in Maine's rivers, conserving coastal wetland buffers, and experimenting with commercially farmed kelp to reduce the acidity of sea water.

THE OTHER ACADIA

THE OTHER ACADIA: SCHOODIC PENINSULA AND ISLE AU HAUT

While Mount Desert Island may be the physical and social heart of Acadia National Park, the Schoodic Peninsula and Isle au Haut sections of the park are just as compelling. Schoodic Peninsula is the only part of Acadia on the mainland, its 2,100 acres of headland jutting out into the open Atlantic. Isle au Haut, perhaps the wildest part of Acadia, lies 10 miles off the Maine coast and features spruce-covered highlands and dramatic seashore cliffs. Both sections of the park receive considerably fewer visitors than Mount Desert Island due to their distance from the main section of Acadia.

SCHOODIC PENINSULA

Schoodic Peninsula is a secluded section of the Maine coast about an hour's drive east from Bar Harbor. It is the point of land that sits across Frenchman Bay from Mount Desert Island. Schoodic is a thickly forested headland, with a coastline that receives no protection from the relentless pounding of the Atlantic Ocean. Pink-granite ledges scoured free of vegetation line the peninsula. These ledges are good places to soak in ocean views and to get away from the crowds of Mount Desert Island. A visit to Schoodic Peninsula should start with a stop at the new Schoodic Woods Campground office, located on Park Loop Road, 0.9 mile south of ME 186 in Winter Harbor.

The 6-mile, one-way Schoodic Loop Road follows the coast, providing ocean views at every turn. Across Frenchman Bay, you can see the full expanse of Cadillac Mountain. About 3 miles from the park boundary, a rough gravel road on the left leads to the summit of Schoodic Head. This road makes a good hiking or mountain-biking trail for those without a four-wheel-drive vehicle. The views from the 440-foot summit are excellent.

Farther down Schoodic Loop Road is Schoodic Point. Its massive granite ledges are a must-visit. The rocks here show intense wear from the glaciers of the past, as well as from present-day pounding surf. Look for grooves in the granite caused by the grinding action of rocks stuck in glacier ice as it moved over the peninsula thousands of years ago. Today, Schoodic Point is at the mercy of the Atlantic Ocean, as there are no islands or reefs offshore to break up the waves that can reach heights of 30 feet during storms. While Thunder Hole on Mount Desert Island is a popular spot for watching geyserlike crashes, Schoodic Point may be the most reliable place in the park to see large waves making huge splashes. Like

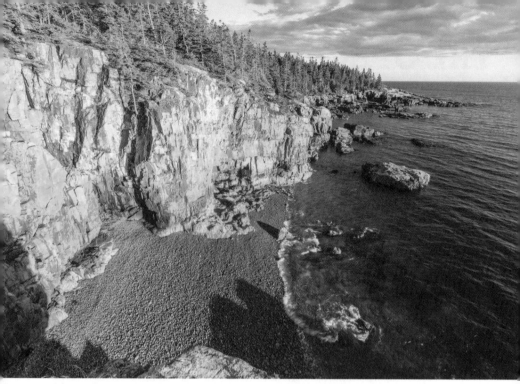
The evening sun strikes a pocket cobble beach on Schoodic's western shore.

Thunder Hole, standing at Schoodic Point can present some dangers. Be very careful to avoid falling into the water.

The remainder of the peninsula continues to provide breathtaking scenery. Several miles of hiking trails were recently added to this part of the park, primarily on Schoodic Head and Buck Cove Mountain, with access from both Schoodic Woods Campground and the Blueberry Hill parking area. (See Appendix A for trail descriptions.) More than 8 miles of carriage road-style bike trails opened here in late 2015. These trails are centered on the campground and provide access to Frazer Point, as well as Schoodic Point via Schoodic Loop Road. Trail maps are available at the Schoodic Woods Campground office. Sea kayaking in this area can be dangerous, with its exposure to the open Atlantic.

Getting There

To reach the peninsula from Mount Desert Island, drive back to Ellsworth via Route 3 north then turn right (east) on Route 1. Continue on Route 1 to West Gouldsboro and turn right on Route 186 south. Go straight until you reach Schoodic Loop Road, just beyond Winter Harbor. There's a ferry service from Bar Harbor to Winter Harbor in the summer months (Appendix C). From the Winter Harbor dock, you can take the Island Explorer bus (Schoodic route) into Schoodic. You can also bring a bike on the ferry or rent a bike in Winter Harbor. It's about a 3-mile ride from Winter Harbor to the Schoodic Woods campground.

ISLE AU HAUT

Isle au Haut has a unique wilderness character not found anywhere else in Acadia National Park. Dramatic 100-foot cliffs drop down to the Atlantic Ocean on the southern end of the island. Beautiful cobblestone beaches fill the spaces between the cliffs. Seals, eagles, loons, and guillemots are common along the shore, while deer, coyote, and numerous songbirds fill the interior boreal forest. Ten miles out to sea, Isle au Haut sees fewer than 10,000 visitors a year, a considerably smaller number than the 3 million who visit Mount Desert Island. The one road that circles the island does not intrude on the national park coastline. All of these factors contribute to making this an ideal place to find quiet solitude.

The island was named Isle Haut, or High Island, by the French explorer Samuel de Champlain during a voyage along the Maine coast in 1603. Like many of New England's outer islands, Isle au Haut was settled by fishing people who liked its proximity to fertile fishing grounds. At one point, the island had a community of around 300 permanent residents, but over the past century that number has dwindled to around 70. While the gas-powered engine made it less of an advantage for professional fishers to live on the island, fishing is still alive and well on Isle au Haut, accounting for the largest percentage of the island's economy. In the 1880s, residents of the big East Coast cities discovered Isle au Haut as a summer getaway. Unlike Mount Desert Island, with its proliferation of hotels, restaurants, and hectic social life, Isle au Haut was a quiet home away from home, with private summer cottages blending into the community. In 1945, descendants of one of these early summer visitors, Ernest Bowditch of Boston, donated almost

Isle au Haut, reachable by mail boat, provides an escape from the summer crowds at Mount Desert Island.

half of the island to Acadia National Park. Today, 2,728 acres of Isle au Haut (about 60 percent of the island) are part of Acadia.

Getting There

A visit to Isle au Haut involves taking the mail boat from the town of Stonington, at the southern tip of Deer Isle. It's a long day trip from Bar Harbor, as the drive takes about 1.5 hours and the boat ride is another 35 minutes. The mail boat makes two trips a day, three in the summer. For more information, contact Isle au Haut Boat Services at 207-367-5193 or isleauhaut.com. While day trips provide a good introduction to the island, the best way to experience it is to spend two or three nights in the Duck Harbor Campground, open annually from May 15 through October 15. Run by Acadia National Park, the campground has only five lean-tos and no tentsites. This limited space is highly coveted, so you will want to make reservations early. Call the National Park Service at 207-288-3338 or visit nps.gov/acad/planyourvisit/duckharbor.htm for the rules regarding reservations. Reservations currently are taken beginning April 1 for the following summer.

From the campground, you have access to 18 miles of hiking trails that explore both the dramatic seaside cliffs and the island's forested highlands. The island's high point, Mount Champlain, reaches a lofty height of only 556 feet and is completely forested, with no views. The best views on the island are from Duck Harbor Mountain, a short hike from the campground. From the ledges of this modest 314-foot peak, there are spectacular views of Penobscot Bay, with its deep blue waters surrounding scores of islands. The Western Head, Cliff, and Goat trails all provide excellent coastal hiking. Each of the three trails alternates between ascending rocky cliffs and traversing secluded cobble beaches. Harbor seals and gray seals can be seen feeding offshore, as well as black guillemots, loons, cormorants, common eiders, and harlequin ducks. (A complete list of hiking trails can be found in Appendix A.)

Experienced paddlers will agree that Isle au Haut is a great place to sea-kayak. The Isle au Haut Company can transport your kayak to the island, or you can paddle the 6 miles from Stonington. Contact the Maine Island Trail Association (see Appendix E) to learn about paddling opportunities around the other islands in Penobscot Bay.

Biking on Isle au Haut is limited to the 5 miles of paved roads and 7 miles of rough, unpaved roads on the island (mountain bikes are recommended.) Biking is not permitted on hiking trails. Bikes can be rented from Isle au Haut Boat Services.

Like the rest of Acadia, Isle au Haut is busiest during July and August. In these months, the mail boat drops visitors off at the campground in Duck Harbor. During the rest of the year, visitors debark at the town of Isle au Haut, a 5-mile hike from the campground. That means visiting the island in May and early June, as well as in the fall, takes a little extra effort, but the rewards are empty trails, fewer bugs, and peaceful solitude. Whenever you visit, you're sure to be charmed by the island's slow pace, relatively empty trails, and dramatic shoreline.

APPENDIX A

COMPLETE LIST OF HIKING TRAILS IN ACADIA NATIONAL PARK

The following brief trail descriptions list all of the well-marked, officially recognized, and maintained paths that give access to most of the summits and viewpoints on Mount Desert Island, Isle au Haut, and the Schoodic Peninsula. Many of these have been covered in the trip descriptions in Section 1 but are included here for those who would like to create their own routes. For the most part, you can reach the individual summits in comfortable half-day walks. To simplify references and to conform with Acadia National Park nomenclature, we have divided the hikes into an eastern district and a western district. The National Park Service (NPS) maintains all of the trails described here; trail markings include signs, cairns, and blue-painted blazes. In addition to the map in this guide, refer to the AMC Acadia National Park Map included with this book.

The National Park Service has rated each trail based on the following criteria:

Easy: Fairly level ground.

Moderate: Uneven ground with some steep grades and/or gradual climbing. Footing may be difficult in places.

Strenuous: Steep and/or long grades; steady climbing or descending. Sometimes difficult footing, difficult maneuvering.

Ladder: Iron-rung ladders and handrails placed on steep grades or difficult terrain. These trails are very difficult.

EASTERN DISTRICT (EAST OF SOMES SOUND)

CHAMPLAIN MOUNTAIN AREA

This area consists of Champlain (1,058 feet) and Gorham mountains, Huguenot Head, the Beehive, and Great Head, all of which provide excellent views. Champlain and the Beehive are the most popular due to exciting ladder trails that climb steep cliff faces overlooking the open ocean, but both peaks are also accessible by easier trails—better options for children or those with a fear of heights.

Precipice Trail

AMC's Acadia National Park Map: D8
NPS Rating: Ladder

Distances from Park Loop Road

to Orange and Black Path	0.4 mile	15 minutes
to Champlain summit	0.8 mile	1 hour

This trail starts from the Precipice Trail parking area, located 1.75 miles beyond the Sieur de Monts Spring entrance on Park Loop Road, at the foot of Champlain Mountain. The trailhead is located just before the entrance-fee station on Park Loop Road.

Following a rugged talus slope full of big boulders, the trail ascends northwest about 0.4 mile, where Orange and Black Path leads right to Champlain North Ridge Trail at 0.5 mile from the summit on the north ridge. From this intersection, Precipice Trail climbs southwest, rising steeply to a point directly west of the parking area, where the trail turns right (west-northwest.) Along this section of the trail, ladders and iron rungs help hikers negotiate precipitous vertical dropoffs. The final 500-foot climb to the summit follows gentle slopes and ledges. People afraid of heights should not climb Precipice Trail, and hikers less than 5 feet tall may have difficulty reaching some handholds.

Caution: It is most important that Precipice Trail hikers remain on the designated trail. Wandering off-trail can quickly lead hikers onto cliffs that require technical mountain-climbing skills and equipment.

Note: Precipice Trail may be closed for an undetermined amount of time each spring and summer due to nesting peregrine falcons on Champlain Mountain. Violators of the closure are subject to a $10,000 fine.

Orange and Black Path

AMC's Acadia National Park Map: D8
NPS Rating: Strenuous

Distances from Schooner Head Road

to Park Loop Road	0.2 mile	5 minutes
to Champlain North Ridge Trail (via spur trail)	0.5 mile	20 minutes
to Precipice Trail	0.9 mile	35 minutes

Orange and Black Path is a recently restored trail that connects Schooner Head Path to the trails on Champlain Mountain, effectively making it possible to hike Champlain Mountain from downtown Bar Harbor. The trail begins on the west side of Schooner Head Road, 1.2 miles south of Route 3.

The trail enters the woods and quickly crosses Park Loop Road in 0.2 mile. The trail then climbs moderately, then steeply, over rock ledge and through a forest of scrub oak and paper birch to views of Champlain Mountain and Frenchman Bay. At 0.4 mile, a spur trail leads right 0.1 mile to Champlain North Ridge Trail. The main trail turns left and stays just below the cliffs of Champlain Mountain en route to an intersection with Precipice Trail, 0.9 mile from Schooner Head Road.

Champlain North Ridge Trail

(formerly Bear Brook Trail)

AMC's Acadia National Park Map: D8

NPS Rating: Moderate

Distances from Park Loop Road

to Orange and Black Path	0.5 mile	30 minutes
to Champlain summit	1 mile	55 minutes

This trail begins on Park Loop Road, 0.2 mile east of the entrance to the Bear Brook picnic area. The trail ends at the summit of Champlain Mountain, where Champlain South Ridge Trail continues to Bowl Trail, located at the south end of the Bowl.

This trail climbs gradually from the parking area through a mixed forest of birch, pine, and spruce to a junction on the north slope of Champlain with Orange and Black Path on the left at 0.5 mile. Continuing right, Champlain North Ridge Trail steadily emerges from the forest canopy, giving outstanding views of Frenchman Bay and Schoodic Peninsula on the mainland to the east. At 1 mile the trail reaches the open, rocky summit of Champlain.

Champlain South Ridge Trail

(formerly Bear Brook Trail)

AMC's Acadia National Park Map: E8

NPS Rating: Moderate

Distances from Park Loop Road

to Precipice Trail	1.5 miles	1 hour
to Champlain summit and Champlain North Ridge Trail	1.6 miles	20 minutes
to Precipice Trail	1.6 miles	1 hour and 5 minutes

This trail provides a route from the Bowl (at the base of the Beehive) to the summit of Champlain Mountain. It begins at an intersection with Bowl Trail, 0.6 mile from Park Loop Road and the Sand Beach parking area. The trail skirts the southern edge of the Bowl, a small glacial tarn, before ascending to the ridgeline of Champlain Mountain's south ridge. The trail climbs moderately and soon enters an open-air forest of pitch pines. Climbing over pink Cadillac granite, the trail reaches open views and Precipice Trail, 1.5 miles above the Bowl, then the summit of Champlain Mountain and Champlain North Ridge Trail at 1.6 miles.

Beachcroft Path

AMC's Acadia National Park Map: D8
NPS Rating: Moderate

Distances from Route 3

to shoulder of Huguenot Head	0.4 mile	25 minutes
to Champlain summit	1.2 miles	1 hour and 5 minutes

Beachcroft Path makes a convenient route between Champlain Mountain and the area to the west. For the most part, the trail is entirely open. While the ascent to Huguenot Head from Route 3 is gradual and easily traveled, the character of the trail becomes more difficult on the actual ascent of Champlain.

The trail leaves Route 3 across the street from the north end of the Tarn and begins with a flight of granite steps on the east side of the highway. (There is parking above the north end of the Tarn, off the west side of the highway.) The trail then runs southeast, often on carefully placed stone stairs. Following switchbacks and stone steps, it rises up and across the west face of Huguenot Head. The trail passes to the south of (not over) the summit of Huguenot Head at about 0.4 mile. A brief, gradual descent into the gully between Huguenot Head and Champlain Mountain is followed by a sharp, difficult ascent over rocks up the northwest slope of Champlain Mountain to the summit at 1.2 miles.

Bowl Trail

AMC's Acadia National Park Map: E8
NPS Rating: Moderate

Distances from Sand Beach parking area

to Beehive Trail	0.2 mile	5 minutes
to Gorham Mountain Trail (eastern spur)	0.4 mile	10 minutes
to Gorham Mountain Trail (main spur)	0.5 mile	15 minutes
to the Bowl, and Beehive and Champlain South Ridge trails	0.7 mile	25 minutes

This trail leaves from opposite the Sand Beach parking area, located 3.25 miles beyond Sieur de Monts Spring on Park Loop Road. Bowl Trail is a gently sloping path that offers access to Beehive Trail and Gorham Mountain Trail. It connects Sand Beach to the Bowl, a lovely lake at the base of Halfway Mountain. At the Bowl, a connector trail to the Beehive bears right, and Champlain South Ridge Trail is on the left.

Beehive Trail
AMC's Acadia National Park Map: E8
NPS Rating: Ladder

Distances from Park Loop Road		
to the Beehive	0.5 mile	25 minutes
to return to Sand Beach parking area (via Bowl Trail)	1.4 miles	50 minutes

This trail begins 0.2 mile up Bowl Trail from the Sand Beach parking area. Take a sharp right at the sign marked, "Beehive." For 0.3 mile, the trail rises abruptly via switchbacks and iron ladders over steep ledges to the summit of the Beehive. This trail is challenging and not for those who are uneasy on precipitous heights. The views of Frenchman Bay, Sand Beach, and the Otter Cliff area are magnificent.

The trail continues northwest from the summit, soon reaching a junction with a spur trail that leads left toward Bowl Trail, making it possible to quickly loop back to Park Loop Road without visiting the Bowl. The main trail continues northwest, rising briefly to another open ledge and views of the Bowl, Champlain Mountain, and Cadillac Mountain before making a short, steep descent to the Bowl and Champlain South Ridge trails. Take the left fork (Bowl Trail) for 0.7 mile to return to Park Loop Road.

Gorham Mountain Trail
AMC's Acadia National Park Map: E8
NPS Rating: Moderate

Distances from Gorham Mountain Trail parking area		
to Gorham Mountain summit	1 mile	45 minutes
to Bowl Trail	1.6 miles	1 hour and 5 minutes

The trail starts at the Gorham Mountain Trail parking area (also known as the Monument Cove parking area) on Park Loop Road, 1 mile past Sand Beach. After 0.1 mile, the trail turns to the right at a junction with Otter Cove Trail (which leads 0.5 mile to Otter Cove on Park Loop Road). Gorham Mountain Trail rises gently over open ledges for 0.3 mile, to a junction with a side trail to Cadillac Cliffs (NPS rating: strenuous). The side trail is a loop that leads right and rejoins Gorham Mountain Trail 0.5 mile later, after passing under ancient sea cliffs and by a sea cave. Gorham Mountain Trail continues 0.3 mile over easy, open granite ledges to where the Cadillac Cliffs loop rejoins the main trail.

The main trail continues north another 0.4 mile to the Gorham Mountain summit, which is open and bare, with some of the finest panoramas on Mount Desert Island. Descending, the trail reaches a junction with a Bowl Trail spur in another 0.4 mile before reaching Bowl Trail proper 0.6 mile beyond the summit. For the Bowl, go left 0.2 mile. To reach the Beehive, turn right then left at the next junction, about 0.1 mile farther. Continuing straight ahead at this junction will bring you to Park Loop Road at Sand Beach.

Schooner Head Path

AMC's Acadia National Park Map: D8, E8
NPS Rating: Easy

Distances from the Dorr Point parking area		
to Old Farm Road	0.1 mile	5 minutes
to Orange and Black Path	1.3 miles	30 minutes
to Murphy Lane	1.8 miles	45 minutes
to Schooner Head overlook	2.5 miles	1 hour and 15 minutes

This recently completed path provides a pedestrian route from Bar Harbor to the Schooner Head overlook and nearby Sand Beach. It is very flat, and the trail is covered with crushed gravel for much of its length, making it an easy walk. It is also very close to Schooner Head Road for much of its length.

Access to Schooner Head Path is from the Dorr Point parking area on the east side of Route 3, 1 mile south of the Bar Harbor Village Green. Follow the trail into the woods, staying to the right at two trail junctions within 0.1 mile of the parking area. The trail soon crosses Old Farm Road then meanders through the woods for 0.6 mile before crossing Schooner Head Road near Jackson Laboratory.

From here, the path is basically a gravel sidewalk in the woods. It crosses the road a few times and is never far from the pavement, but the road is quiet and there are few interruptions. In another 0.7 mile, Orange and Black Path leads right to Champlain Mountain. In another 0.5 mile, you pass another trail on the right, Murphy Lane, which leads to Precipice Trail. After crossing the outlet of the pond, the trail crosses the road one last time and leads 0.1 mile through the woods to the Schooner Head parking area.

Great Head Trail

AMC's Acadia National Park Map: E8
NPS Rating: Moderate

Distances from the east end of Sand Beach		
to south end of peninsula (via millstone)	0.5 mile	15 minutes
to teahouse ruins	0.8 mile	20 minutes
to Schooner Head Road and Sand Beach path	1.3 miles	35 minutes
to return to Sand Beach parking area	1.6 miles	55 minutes

This scenic, short walk passes along cliffs directly above the sea. From the Sand Beach parking area on Park Loop Road, take the stairs down to the beach then walk the length of Sand Beach to the east end. A stream cuts through the beach just before the trail. Depending on the tide and the season, the stream can be completely dry or a couple of feet deep. Cross the stream and look for a series of granite steps ascending a high bank into the woods. The trail quickly reaches a huge millstone, where the trail turns sharply right (south), switchbacking up the cliff. The path continues to the extremity of the peninsula then turns northeast along the cliff to the high point, Great Head, where there are ruins of a stone teahouse. The trail descends northwest to a junction that offers hikers two choices: an alternate section of Great Head Trail that leads left (west) and ascends a rocky ledge in the middle of the peninsula before descending back to the east end of Sand Beach, or the main path that leads north and reaches an abandoned service road in about 0.3 mile. The road (now a dirt hiking trail), leads left (south) for about 0.3 mile, back to the east end of Sand Beach.

Ocean Path

(also called Shore Path)
AMC's Acadia National Park Map: E8, F8
NPS Rating: Easy

Distance from Sand Beach			
	to Otter Point	2.2 miles	1 hour and 5 minutes

Park at the large, lower Sand Beach parking area on Park Loop Road. From the parking area, follow the asphalt trail about 50 feet toward the beach. Where the staircase descends to the left, turn right to begin on Ocean Path. The trail leads uphill several hundred yards; crosses through a small, paved upper parking area; and continues south to Otter Point, paralleling Park Loop Road for 2.2 miles. Ocean Path offers spectacular shoreline scenery and follows a level grade. Of interest en route are Thunder Hole, Monument Cove, and Otter Cliffs.

Otter Cove Trail

AMC's Acadia National Park Map: F7, F8
NPS Rating: Easy

Distance from Otter Cove			
	to Gorham Mountain parking area	0.5 mile	15 minutes

Otter Cove Trail connects Otter Cove with the Ocean Drive section of Park Loop Road via Gorham Mountain Trail. The trail begins in Otter Cove, on the north side of Park Loop Road, and heads east into the woods for an easy walk to Gorham Mountain Trail in 0.5 mile. Continuing east (straight) on Gorham Mountain Trail will bring you to the Gorham Mountain parking area on Park Loop Road in another 0.1 mile.

DORR MOUNTAIN

Dorr Mountain (1,265 feet) lies immediately west of Sieur de Monts Spring, with four routes available up the mountain from the spring. Trails also ascend from the north and south over long ridges. The east and west slopes are steep. With properly placed cars, a party can have a good climb leaving from Sieur de Monts Spring, traversing Dorr, and continuing west to the summit of Cadillac Mountain (1,530 feet). The route descends to about 1,000 feet between the two summits. There is parking both at the nearby Tarn and on Cadillac's summit. Hikers are encouraged not to park at the very congested Sieur de Monts Spring parking area. There is a connecting path between the Tarn and the Sieur de Monts Spring parking areas for hikers wishing to visit or begin a hike at the spring.

Emery Path

(formerly Dorr Mountain East Face Trail, northern section)
AMC's Acadia National Park Map: D7
NPS Rating: Strenuous

Distances from Sieur de Monts Spring

to Homans Path	0.3 mile	20 minutes
to Kurt Diederich's Climb and Schiff Path	0.5 mile	30 minutes
to Dorr summit via Schiff Path and Dorr North Ridge Trail	1.6 miles	1 hour and 30 minutes

This trail starts behind the nature center at Sieur de Monts Spring. Follow the sidewalk to the right, crossing a stream on a small wooden footbridge. Emery Path will be on the right. The trail enters the woods and quickly begins its ascent, following a series of switchbacks up the northeast shoulder of Dorr Mountain. The first half has many stone steps. At 0.3 mile, Homans Path enters from the right. At 0.5 mile, Emery Path ends at its junction with Kurt Diederich's Climb, which leads left to the north end of the Tarn, and Schiff Path, which continues to the summit via Dorr North Ridge Trail.

Schiff Path

(formerly Dorr Mountain East Face Trail, southern section)
AMC's Acadia National Park Map: D7
NPS Rating: Strenuous

Distances from Emery Path and Kurt Diederich's Climb

to Ladder Trail	0.5 mile	20 minutes
to Dorr North Ridge Trail	1 mile	1 hour
to Dorr summit via Dorr North Ridge Trail	1.1 miles	1 hour and 5 minutes

This trail begins at the intersection of Emery Path and Kurt Diederich's Climb, 0.5 mile above Sieur de Monts Spring and the Tarn. The trail begins by traversing the east face of the mountain, ascending moderately, and reaching an intersection with Ladder Trail in 0.5 mile. Here the trail makes a sharp right and climbs steeply up to Dorr North Ridge Trail, 0.1 mile north of the summit, passing in and out of the trees on the way. There are excellent views to the east for most of the climb.

Homans Path

AMC's Acadia National Park Map: D7
NPS Rating: Strenuous

Distance from Hemlock Road		
to Emery Path	0.3 mile	5 minutes

This historic trail was restored and reopened in the summer of 2004. It allows a quick approach to Dorr Mountain for those walking from Bar Harbor via Jesup Path by bypassing Sieur de Monts Spring. The trail begins from Hemlock Road, a few yards west of Jesup Path, 0.1 mile from Sieur de Monts Spring. It rises steeply over switchbacks and stone steps to views of Great Meadow and Frenchman Bay, ending at the intersection with Emery Path at 0.3 mile.

Ladder Trail

(formerly Dorr Mountain Ladder Trail)
AMC's Acadia National Park Map: D7
NPS Rating: Ladder

Distances from Route 3		
to Schiff Path	0.4 mile	30 minutes
to Dorr summit via Schiff Path and Dorr North Ridge Trail	1 mile	1 hour and 10 minutes

This trail climbs from a parking area on Route 3, just south of Tarn, up the eastern side of Dorr Mountain. The trail is steep, with many stone steps and iron rungs. From the parking area, the trail immediately crosses Kane Path before making a steep ascent and ending at an intersection with Schiff Path at 0.4 mile. Continuing west on Schiff Path leads to the Dorr summit (via Dorr North Ridge Trail).

Kurt Diederich's Climb

AMC's Acadia National Park Map: D7
NPS Rating: Strenuous

Distances from the Tarn		
to Emery and Schiff paths	0.5 mile	30 minutes
to Dorr summit via Schiff Path and Dorr North Ridge Trail	1.6 miles	1 hour and 30 minutes

This trail takes a direct route from the south end of the Tarn to Schiff and Emery paths and the summit of Dorr Mountain. The trail starts at an intersection with Kane Path (reached via the Tarn parking lot on Route 3 or via a 0.25-mile walk from Sieur de Monts Spring). Look for an inscription in the stone stairs that reads, "Kurt Diederich's Climb." The trail climbs steeply via stone steps to good views and Emery and Schiff paths at 0.5 mile. Continuing west on Schiff Path leads to the Dorr summit (via Dorr North Ridge Trail).

Kebo Mountain Trail
(formerly Dorr Mountain North Ridge Trail, northern section)
AMC's Acadia National Park Map: D7
NPS Rating: Easy

Distances from Park Loop Road		
to Hemlock and Dorr North Ridge trails	0.9 mile	30 minutes
to Dorr summit via Dorr North Ridge Trail	1.8 miles	1 hour and 25 minutes

This trail begins on the south side of Park Loop Road, about 1 mile after the road becomes one-way. It climbs south over the summit of Kebo Mountain, traverses a second hump, and reaches its end at a junction with Hemlock and Dorr North Ridge trails at 0.9 mile from Park Loop Road.

Dorr North Ridge Trail
(formerly Dorr Mountain North Ridge Trail, southern section)
AMC's Acadia National Park Map: D7
NPS Rating: Moderate

Distances from Kebo Mountain Trail		
to Schiff Path and Cadillac-Dorr Connector	0.8 mile	50 minutes
to Dorr summit	0.9 mile	55 minutes

This trail (as well as Dorr South Ridge Trail) offers a less steep alternative to the summit of Dorr Mountain than the trails that climb its east face. Dorr North Ridge Trail begins as an extension of Kebo Mountain Trail 0.9 mile from Park Loop Road. It climbs the north ridge of the peak at a consistently moderate pace, reaching a junction with Schiff Path and Cadillac-Dorr Connector at 0.8 mile from Kebo Mountain Trail then reaches the summit in another 0.1 mile.

Dorr South Ridge Trail
(formerly Dorr Mountain South Ridge Trail)
AMC's Acadia National Park Map: D7, E7
NPS Rating: Moderate

Distances from Route 3		
to Canon Brook Trail	0.9 mile	20 minutes
to Dorr summit	2.2 miles	1 hour and 25 minutes

This trail diverges to the right from Canon Brook Trail 0.9 mile from Route 3 at the southern extremity of Dorr Mountain. It rises at a moderate grade over rocky ledges and through evergreen forest. Views of Champlain and Cadillac mountains and the ocean are frequent during the south-ridge ascent to the summit.

Cadillac-Dorr Connector

(formerly Cadillac-Dorr Trail)
AMC's Acadia National Park Map: D7
NPS Rating: Strenuous

Distance from Dorr North Ridge Trail		
to Gorge and A. Murray Young paths	0.2 mile	10 minutes

Combined with Gorge Path, this short trail links the summits of Dorr and Cadillac mountains. It starts just north of the summit of Dorr Mountain and runs east to west, connecting Dorr North Ridge Trail with Gorge Path at the intersection with A. Murray Young Path. It is only 0.2 mile in length.

From the intersection of Dorr North Ridge Trail and Dorr South Ridge Trail, 0.1 mile south of the summit, Cadillac-Dorr Connector descends the steep west face of Dorr Mountain, reaching the notch between Dorr and Cadillac mountains in 0.2 mile. From the notch, Gorge Path leads right (north) toward Park Loop Road, and A. Murray Young Path leads left. Continuing straight (west) on Gorge Path reaches the summit of Cadillac Mountain in 0.4 mile.

A. Murray Young Path

AMC's Acadia National Park Map: E7
NPS Rating: Moderate

Distances from Route 3		
to Canon Brook Trail	1.1 miles	25 minutes
to Cadillac-Dorr Connector	2.2 miles	1 hour
to Dorr summit via Cadillac-Dorr Connector and Dorr North Ridge Trail	2.5 miles	1 hour and 25 minutes
to return to Sand Beach parking area	1.6 miles	55 minutes

Ascending the narrow valley between Dorr and Cadillac mountains from the south, this trail leaves Canon Brook Trail 1.1 miles west of Route 3. It climbs gradually to Gorge Path near the junction with Cadillac-Dorr Connector. This point affords relatively quick (if strenuous) access to the summit of either mountain.

Jesup Path

AMC's Acadia National Park Map: D7

NPS Rating: Easy

Distances from Park Loop Road		
to Sieur de Monts Spring	0.8 mile	20 minutes
to the Tarn	1.1 miles	30 minutes

A pleasant, level woodland walk, this path begins on Park Loop Road, opposite the first road on the left after the beginning of the road's one-way section. Jesup Path follows the west margin of Great Meadow, which may be flooded as a result of beaver activity. The path passes through a mixed forest of hemlock and hardwood to Sieur de Monts Spring at 0.8 mile. Located here are the Abbe Museum, with displays of local Wabanaki culture; the Wild Gardens of Acadia, a formal garden of native plants; and the Acadia National Park Nature Center, with a bookstore and natural history exhibits. The trail terminates 0.3 mile farther, at the north end of the Tarn, where Beachcroft Trail and Kurt Diederich's Climb intersect.

Wild Garden Garden Path

AMC's Acadia National Park Map: D7

NPS Rating: Easy

Distance from the Tarn		
to Sieur de Monts Spring	0.3 mile	10 minutes

This short path connects the Sieur de Monts Spring area with the Tarn. To access the trail, park at the Tarn parking area and follow Beachcroft Path right for 0.1 mile. From here, Wild Garden Path heads right, following the outlet stream of the Tarn through a hardwood forest and crossing the stream about halfway to Sieur de Monts Spring, which is another 0.3 mile.

Stratheden Path

AMC's Acadia National Park Map: D7

NPS Rating: Easy

Distances from Park Loop Road		
to Hemlock Trail	0.7 mile	10 minutes
to Sieur de Monts Spring via Hemlock Trail and Hemlock Road	1.2 miles	20 minutes

This route runs from Hemlock Trail to Park Loop Road, providing an easy walk that bypasses the summit of Kebo Mountain. It begins on Park Loop Road, about 100 yards east of Kebo Mountain Trail, and follows a fairly level route through hemlocks on the way to Hemlock Trail, where it ends at 0.7 mile.

Hemlock Trail

AMC's Acadia National Park Map: D7

NPS Rating: Easy

Distances from Gorge Path

to Dorr North Ridge Trail	0.2 mile	5 minutes
to Stratheden Path and Hemlock Road	0.4 mile	10 minutes
to Sieur de Monts Spring via Hemlock Road	0.9 mile	20 minutes

This trail on the lower end of Dorr Mountain's north ridge connects Gorge Path to Dorr North Ridge Trail and Sieur de Monts Spring. It begins on Gorge Path, 1 mile below the Cadillac-Dorr notch and 0.4 mile above Park Loop Road. It travels east, rising slightly to meet Dorr North Ridge Trail in 0.2 mile. It then descends moderately to end at an intersection with Stratheden Path and a dirt road known as Hemlock Road (no cars allowed) at 0.4 mile. Sieur de Monts Spring is 0.5 mile south via Hemlock Road.

Great Meadow Loop Trail

AMC's Acadia National Park Map: D7

NPS Rating: Easy

Distances from Cromwell Harbor Road

to Hemlock Road	0.9 mile	20 minutes
to Jesup Path	1 mile	20 minutes
to return to Cromwell Harbor Road	1.9 miles	35 minutes

This path connects the streets of Bar Harbor to the trail system within the park. It begins on Cromwell Harbor Road, between Ledgelawn Avenue and Spring Street, just to the east of a large cemetery. Paralleling roads for most of its length, it enters the woods next to the cemetery and crosses a brook and a road at 0.2 mile. At 0.6 mile, the trail crosses the road again and runs along the Kebo Valley Golf Course. At 0.9 mile and 1 mile, respectively, Hemlock Road and Jesup Path lead left to Sieur de Monts Spring and the trails on Dorr Mountain. Over the next 0.6 mile, Great Meadow Loop Trail crosses two roads and a driveway then comes out on Cromwell Harbor Road at 1.8 miles, completing the loop in another 0.1 mile.

Kebo Brook Trail
AMC's Acadia National Park Map: D7
NPS Rating: Easy

Distances from Park Loop Road		
to Cadillac North Ridge Trail	0.1 mile	5 minutes
to Gorge Path	0.5 mile	10 minutes
to Kebo Mountain Trail	0.8 mile	15 minutes
to Stratheden Path	0.9 mile	20 minutes
to Great Meadow Loop Trail	1.1 miles	30 minutes

This newly built trail connects Great Meadow Loop Trail to Park Loop Road. Combined with Great Meadow Loop Trail, it provides walking access from Bar Harbor to the trails on the north sides of Dorr and Cadillac mountains.

The west end of the trail begins on Park Loop Road, 0.2 mile south of its intersection with Route 233, where there is a small parking area and an Island Explorer bus stop. For most of its length, Kebo Brook Trail descends gradually through woodlands just north of Park Loop Road, passing Cadillac North Ridge Trail, Gorge Path, Kebo Mountain Trail, and Stratheden Path. In 1.1 miles, the trail ends at Great Meadow Loop Trail on Kebo Street, between Cromwell Harbor Road and Harden Farm Road.

Kane Path
(formerly Tarn Trail)
AMC's Acadia National Park Map: D7
NPS Rating: Moderate

Distances from the north end of the Tarn		
to Ladder Trail	0.5 mile	20 minutes
to Canon Brook Trail	0.8 mile	25 minutes

This path leads from the north end of the Tarn south to Canon Brook Trail and links the Sieur de Monts Spring area to the southern trails of Dorr and Cadillac mountains while avoiding Route 3. At its start, the path runs south over a rocky talus slope, directly along the west side of the Tarn. After reaching the south end of the Tarn, Kane Path continues past Ladder Trail at 0.5 mile then ends at Canon Brook Trail at 0.8 mile.

Canon Brook Trail

AMC's Acadia National Park Map: E7

NPS Rating: Strenuous

Distances from Route 3			
	to Kane Path	0.2 mile	10 minutes
	to Dorr South Ridge Trail	0.9 mile	25 minutes
	to A. Murray Young Path	1.1 miles	30 minutes
	to Cadillac South Ridge Trail	2 miles	1 hour and 5 minutes
	to Bubble and Jordan Ponds Path	2.7 miles	1 hour and 40 minutes

From a pullout on Route 3 about 0.5 mile south of the south end of the Tarn, and about 2 miles north of Otter Creek Village, Canon Brook Trail runs west to join Bubble and Jordan Ponds Path in the valley south of Bubble Pond. It gives access (via Bubble and Jordan Ponds Path) to the Jordan Pond area, as well as to the trails running north to Dorr and Cadillac mountains.

From the highway, the trail descends west to Otter Creek and intersects Kane Path at 0.2 mile. Turn left (south) at the intersection and follow the trail in the valley of Otter Creek. After a brief, sharp rise from the valley, the trail reaches a junction with Dorr South Ridge Trail, which diverges right at 0.9 mile. Canon Brook Trail then descends to a junction with A. Murray Young Path, which goes right at 1.1 miles. The trail then runs steeply westward up the south bank of Canon Brook for about 0.5 mile. At this point, the trail swings away from the brook, passes a beaver pond, and ascends to a small pond known as the Featherbed, where it crosses Cadillac South Ridge Trail at 2 miles. Descending the west face of Cadillac Mountain, Canon Brook Trail ends in the valley between Cadillac and Pemetic mountains, at a junction with Bubble and Jordan Ponds Path at 2.7 miles.

CADILLAC MOUNTAIN

Cadillac Mountain (1,530 feet) is the highest point on the island. There is an auto road to the summit, where you'll find parking, a small gift shop, and bathrooms. Accessibility by car makes this summit the busiest in the park, but the tradeoff is commanding views.

North Ridge Trail, beginning on Park Loop Road, can be connected with Gorge Path, which ends on Park Loop Road, about 0.5 mile east of the North Ridge trailhead, creating a pleasant loop up and down Cadillac.

Cadillac South Ridge Trail

AMC's Acadia National Park Map: E7, F7

NPS Rating: Moderate

Distances from Route 3

	to Eagle Crag Spur	1 mile	40 minutes
	to Cadillac summit	3.5 miles	2 hours and 30 minutes (descending Cadillac summit to Route 3, subtract 45 minutes)

A relatively long hike for Mount Desert Island, this trail starts on the north side of Route 3, about 50 yards west of the entrance to the Blackwoods Campground. (A flat, 0.7-mile connector links the south campground loop to the trailhead, and a 0.3-mile connector links the north campground loop.) The trail climbs generally north. At 1 mile, a short loop trail on the right leads to Eagle Crag, which has good views to the east and southeast. The loop trail rejoins the main trail in 0.2 mile. After leaving the woods, Cadillac South Ridge Trail rises gently over open ledges. It crosses Canon Brook Trail about 2.3 miles from Route 3, in a slight col at the Featherbed. Continuing in the open, it passes close to a switchback in Summit Road and ends at the summit parking area.

Cadillac West Face Trail

AMC's Acadia National Park Map: E6, E7

NPS Rating: Strenuous

Distances from north end of Bubble Pond

	to Cadillac South Ridge Trail	0.9 mile	1 hour and 5 minutes
to Cadillac summit (via Cadillac South Ridge Trail)		1.4 miles	1 hour and 25 minutes

This steep trail, which starts at the north end of Bubble Pond, is the shortest route to Cadillac's summit. Begin where Park Loop Road passes north of Bubble Pond, using the short spur road off Park Loop Road to reach the pond and trailhead. The trail rises steeply through woods and over open ledges to a junction with Cadillac South Ridge Trail at 0.5 mile from the summit. For the summit, turn left (north).

Cadillac North Ridge Trail

AMC's Acadia National Park Map: D7

NPS Rating: Moderate

Distance from Park Loop Road			
	to Cadillac summit	2.2 miles	1 hour and 30 minutes

This trail follows the north ridge of Cadillac, quickly rising through stunted evergreens onto open ledges. To reach the trailhead, follow Park Loop Road south from the visitor center. Take the third left turn (about 3 miles), following the sign for Sand Beach and Park Loop Road Park at a paved pulloff on the north side of the road 0.4 mile beyond the intersection. You also can park at the eastern end of Kebo Brook Trail and hike 0.1 mile to the beginning of Cadillac North Ridge Trail. The trail starts on the south side of the road. It climbs steadily, always keeping east of the auto road, although it approaches road switchbacks on two occasions. For much of the distance, both sides of the ridge are visible. The views of Bar Harbor, Eagle Lake, Egg Rock, and Dorr Mountain are excellent.

Gorge Path

AMC's Acadia National Park Map: D7

NPS Rating: Moderate

Distances from Park Loop Road			
	to Dorr-Cadillac notch	1.4 miles	1 hour and 5 minutes
	to Cadillac summit	1.8 miles	1 hour and 35 minutes (descending Cadillac summit to Park Loop Road, subtract about 40 minutes)

Follow Park Loop Road south from the visitor center. Take the third left turn (about 3 miles), following the sign for Sand Beach and Park Loop Road. Gorge Path starts from a gravel pullout on the south side of Park Loop Road 0.8 mile beyond the intersection. The trail rises south, up the gorge between Cadillac and Dorr mountains, passing Hemlock Trail at 0.4 mile, and reaching a junction with Cadillac-Dorr Connector and A. Murray Young Path at 1.4 mile. At this point, the trail turns right and climbs steeply to the summit of Cadillac at 1.8 miles. Note: From the parking area, a spur trail leads 0.4 mile north to Kebo Brook Trail.

Bar Island Trail
AMC's Acadia National Park Map: C7
NPS Rating: Easy

Distance from Bridge Street		
to Bar Island summit	0.6 mile	20 minutes

This short trail leads from the Bar Island Bar to the summit of Bar Island. The trail must be hiked during low tide, as the Bar Island Bar is completely underwater at high tide. Return to Bar Harbor no later than two hours after low tide. The trail begins at the end of Bridge Street in Bar Harbor. Walk 0.25 mile across the bar to the island then follow a dirt road through the forest. After about 300 yards, Bar Island Trail leads to the left. At 0.2 mile from the road, it reaches the summit, offering good views of the harbor and the mountains of Acadia.

JORDAN POND AND SOUTHERN TRAILS AREA

Many trails on the eastern side of Mount Desert Island begin near Jordan Pond (274 feet). The view from Jordan Pond House across the pond to the Bubbles is justifiably famous.

Jordan Pond Path
(formerly Jordan Pond Loop Trail)
AMC's Acadia National Park Map: E6
NPS Rating: Moderate

Distances from Jordan Pond parking area		
to Bubble and Jordan Ponds Path (to Canon Brook Trail)	0.2 mile	5 minutes
to Jordan Pond Carry (to Eagle Lake)	1.1 miles	30 minutes
to Bubbles Trail (to South Bubble summit)	1.1 miles	30 minutes
to Bubbles Divide Trail (to Bubble Gap)	1.5 miles	45 minutes
to Deer Brook Trail (to Penobscot Mountain)	1.6 miles	50 minutes
to Jordan Pond parking area	3.2 miles	1 hour and 40 minutes

This circuit around Jordan Pond is level most of the way but crosses a rocky slope with occasional loose boulders at the pond's northeastern shore. It is 3.2 miles long; directions here are for traveling the eastern shore first. From the Hulls Cove Visitor Center, drive south on Park Loop Road for 7.3 miles. Be sure to continue straight at the intersections marked "Sand Beach" and "Cadillac Mountain." The Jordan Pond parking area will be on your right. Follow the boat-launch road to the south shore of the pond.

When you reach the pond, turn right to start the circuit. The trails listed below all diverge to the right, because the route described goes counterclockwise around the lake. Along the west side of the pond, the trail runs under Jordan Cliffs and loses the sun early in the day. The trail along the west shore also has many wet spots and exposed tree trunks. An alternative route is a carriage road that runs along the pond, uphill from the trail. Use Deer Brook Trail to reach the carriage road. The circuit is completed at the south end of Jordan Pond.

Jordan Pond Carry
AMC's Acadia National Park Map: D6, E6
NPS Rating: Moderate

Distances from Jordan Pond Loop Trail		
to Bubbles Divide Trail	0.4 mile	10 minutes
to Eagle Lake Trail	1 mile	20 minutes

This trail connects the northeastern shore of Jordan Pond with the southern shore of Eagle Lake. From Jordan Pond, the Jordan Pond Carry leaves Jordan Pond Path and climbs moderately to its junction with Bubbles Divide Trail at 0.4 mile. It then gently descends through forests to Eagle Lake and Eagle Lake Trail at 1.1 miles.

Jordan Stream Path
AMC's Acadia National Park Map: F6
NPS Rating: Moderate

Distances from Jordan Pond House		
to trailhead	0.1 mile	5 minutes
to cobblestone bridge	0.6 mile	20 minutes
to carriage road	1.3 miles	45 minutes

This walk along the outlet of Jordan Pond passes through pleasant cedar, maple, and spruce woods. The trailhead is reached by a short connecting path from Jordan Pond House. The path essentially parallels a carriage road, which hikers can take for the return trip.

At 0.6 mile, the trail passes under a cobblestone bridge and continues descending along the stream. The trail takes a sharp left from the stream at 1.2 miles and rises to end at a carriage road at the base of Lookout Ledge, close to Little Long Pond.

Jordan Pond Seaside Trail
AMC's Acadia National Park Map: F6
NPS Rating: Easy

Distance from Jordan Pond House		
to Seal Harbor	2 miles	1 hour

Jordan Pond Seaside Trail offers an easy, level walk between Jordan Pond House and Seal Harbor. Starting from the south side of Jordan Pond House, the trail passes through an evergreen forest. After crossing a carriage road at 0.2 mile, the trail continues on a level course to a private driveway just west of Seal Harbor. Follow the driveway south to Route 3 and Seal Harbor. The best option for spotting a car at the southern terminus of the trail is at the Seal Harbor entrance to Park Loop Road.

Asticou and Jordan Pond Path

(formerly Asticou Trail)
AMC's Acadia National Park Map: F5, F6
NPS Rating: Easy

Distances from Jordan Pond House		
to Asticou and Jordan Pond Path	0.1 mile	5 minutes
to Penobscot Mountain Trail	1.1 miles	30 minutes
to Asticou Ridge Trail	1.5 miles	50 minutes
to Sargent South Ridge Trail	1.8 miles	1 hour

Asticou and Jordan Pond Path is reached via a short connecting path from the west side of Jordan Pond House. This trail follows a level course for most of its distance but gains some elevation to reach Asticou Ridge Trail. It provides an important link to Eliot Mountain, as well as a potential leg of a loop over Sargent and Penobscot mountains.

Leaving from the trailhead, the trail goes through a mixed forest of birch, maple, white pine, and spruce. At 0.9 mile, the trail crosses a carriage road. At 1 mile, it crosses another carriage road, and at 1.1 miles Penobscot Mountain Trail leaves right, with Harbor Brook Trail entering from the left shortly after that. The trail then begins to climb up Asticou Ridge. At 1.5 miles, Asticou Ridge Trail leaves left toward Thuya Gardens, and the trail levels once again. Asticou and Jordan Pond Path follows straight ahead to a junction with Sargent South Ridge Trail at 1.8 miles. At 1.9 miles, the trail ends at a private drive.

Note: The private drive is not open to the public. It is recommended that hikers turn back or take other trails leading from Asticou and Jordan Pond Path to reach public areas.

Asticou Ridge Trail

AMC's Acadia National Park Map: F6
NPS Rating: Moderate

Distances from junction with Asticou and Jordan Pond Path		
to Eliot summit	0.8 mile	25 minutes
to monument	0.9 mile	30 minutes
to Route 3 spur trail	1.1 miles	35 minutes
to Thuya Gardens	1.4 miles	45 minutes

This trail is reached by following Asticou and Jordan Pond Path for 1.5 miles from Jordan Pond. Traversing a rocky ridge, this trail climbs over Eliot Mountain, offering views to the south and east of Day Mountain and the Triad, and beyond to the open ocean. Gradually descending from the summit, the trail reaches a monument to Charles William Eliot, one of the founders of the park, at 0.9 mile. Descending into the woods, the trail reaches a junction with a 0.4-mile side trail to Route 3. Keeping right, the trail descends into the beautiful Thuya Gardens.

Amphitheater Trail

AMC's Acadia National Park Map: E6, F6

NPS Rating: Moderate

Distances from carriage-road crossing between posts 20 and 22		
to Amphitheater Bridge	0.8 mile	25 minutes
to Sargent South Ridge Trail	1.6 miles	1 hour and 15 minutes
to Hadlock Brook Trail	1.9 miles	1 hour and 30 minutes

Amphitheater Trail connects Hadlock Brook Trail to Sargent South Ridge Trail and the carriage roads near Jordan Pond. It begins on a carriage road between posts 20 and 22, about 1.5 miles from Jordan Pond via Asticou and Jordan Pond Path and a carriage road. The trail parallels Harbor Brook, crossing the brook numerous times before and after passing under Amphitheater Bridge at 0.8 mile. Amphitheater Bridge is the largest carriage-road bridge in the park. After the bridge, the trail climbs more steeply to Birch Spring and an intersection with Sargent South Ridge Trail at 1.6 miles. Amphitheater Trail then descends 0.3 mile to its end at Hadlock Brook Trail.

Harbor Brook Trail

AMC's Acadia National Park Map: F6

NPS Rating: Moderate

Distance from Asticou and Jordan Pond Path		
to Route 3	2 miles	1 hour

Harbor Brook Trail connects Asticou and Jordan Pond Path with Route 3, between Bracy Cove and Northeast Harbor. Following the brook for its entire length, the trail passes through beautiful cedar groves and mixed forest. At 1.1 miles, a connector to Eliot Mountain and Asticou Ridge Trail leaves to the west. The trail ends on Route 3 at 2 miles.

THE BUBBLES

The finely shaped, almost symmetrical North Bubble (872 feet) and South Bubble (766 feet) rise above the north end of Jordan Pond. Formerly covered with heavy evergreen growth, they were swept by the great fire of 1947, leaving many open views. The best access is from the Bubble Rock parking area about 1.1 miles south of Bubble Pond on the west side of Park Loop Road.

Bubbles Trail

(formerly North Bubble Trail and South Bubble Trail)

AMC's Acadia National Park Map: D6, E6

NPS Rating: Strenuous

Distances from Jordan Pond Path

to South Bubble summit	0.4 mile	25 minutes
to North Bubble summit	0.9 mile	1 hour
to Conners Nubble	1.8 miles	1 hour and 30 minutes
to Eagle Lake Trail	2.2 miles	1 hour and 45 minutes

Like the Jordan Pond Carry, the 2.2-miles-long Bubbles Trail connects the north shore of Jordan Pond with Eagle Lake. Unlike the Jordan Pond Carry, Bubbles Trail takes the high route, climbing up and over both Bubbles and Conners Nubble in the process. The trail starts on the north shore of Jordan Pond at an intersection with Jordan Pond Path, 1.1 miles from the Jordan Pond parking area. It rises very steeply almost immediately, climbing over boulders and scrambling over ledges before leveling off just before reaching the summit of South Bubble in 0.4 mile. The views of Jordan Pond and beyond from the ledges before the summit are spectacular. At the summit, a spur trail leaves right for a short walk to Bubble Rock, a large glacial erratic seemingly perched on the edge of the mountain.

From the summit of South Bubble, the trail descends moderately for 0.2 mile then turns right, coinciding with Bubbles Divide Trail for a short distance. Bubbles Trail then turns left, making a steep climb to the summit of North Bubble at 0.9 mile. The trail continues north past the summit, descending at an easy pace over open ridgeline for several hundred yards. At 1.7 miles, the trail crosses a carriage road before making a short climb to the summit of Conners Nubble and its excellent views of Eagle Lake and Cadillac Mountain at 1.8 miles. The trail continues north over the summit and descends into the woods, reaching Eagle Lake Trail near the shore of Eagle Lake at 2.2 miles.

Bubbles Divide Trail
(formerly North Bubble Trail and South Bubble Trail)
AMC's Acadia National Park Map: E6
NPS Rating: Moderate

Distances from the Bubbles Rock parking area		
to Jordan Pond Carry	0.1 mile	5 minutes
to North Bubble summit via Bubbles Trail	0.5 mile	25 minutes
to South Bubble summit via Bubbles Trail	0.5 mile	25 minutes
to Jordan Pond Path	0.6 mile	30 minutes

Bubbles Divide Trail leaves the Bubble Rock parking area on Park Loop Road and heads east over the small notch between the Bubbles then down to the north shore of Jordan Pond. By providing quick access to Bubbles Trail, it is the quickest route to the summit of either mountain.

Eagle Lake Trail
AMC's Acadia National Park Map: D6
NPS Rating: Moderate

Distances from Eagle Lake parking area		
to beginning of Eagle Lake Trail	1.3 miles	30 minutes
to Jordan Pond Carry	2.5 miles	1 hour
to Carriage Road post 7	3.1 miles	1 hour and 15 minutes
to Bubble Pond parking area via carriage road	3.5 miles	1 hour and 30 minutes

This trail walks along the northern shore of Eagle Lake. It allows hikers to circumnavigate Eagle Lake via the carriage roads without making the climb up and around Conners Nubble. It begins from a carriage road 1.3 miles south of the Eagle Lake parking area. After about 100 yards, Bubbles Trail enters from the right. It follows the shoreline of the lake for 1.2 miles, ending at the carriage road near post 7, 0.4 mile north of the Bubble Pond parking area.

PEMETIC MOUNTAIN AREA
Pemetic Mountain (1,247 feet) is located roughly in the center of the eastern district of the island and offers some of Mount Desert Island's best views. Trails up the west side are short and relatively steep, while routes from the north and south are more gradual and wooded. For the trails from the south, park at the Jordan Pond parking area. From the north, park at Bubble Pond. From the west, park at Bubble Rock.

Pemetic North Ridge Trail

(formerly Pemetic Mountain Trail, Pemetic SE)

AMC's Acadia National Park Map: E6

NPS Rating: Strenuous

Distances from the Bubbles Rock parking area		
to Pemetic Northwest Trail	1 mile	55 minutes
to Pemetic summit	1.1 miles	1 hour

This trail ascends the mountain from the north. The views of Jordan Pond, the Bubbles, Sargent Mountain, and Eagle Lake are outstanding.

From the north, the trail leaves from the Bubble Pond parking area at the north end of Bubble Pond. It quickly climbs through spruce-fir forest to a junction with Pemetic Northwest Trail at 1 mile. The trail reaches the summit of Pemetic Mountain at 1.1 miles. There are excellent views of the Triad, Cadillac Mountain, and Jordan Pond from the summit. The trail continues down the south ridge, now called Pemetic South Ridge Trail (described below).

Pemetic South Ridge Trail

(formerly called Pemetic Mountain Trail, West Cliff Trail)

AMC's Acadia National Park Map: E6)

NPS Rating: Strenuous

Distances from Bubble and Jordan Ponds Path		
to Pemetic East Cliff Trail	0.6 mile	25 minutes
to Pemetic summit	1.2 miles	1 hour
to Bubble Pond via Pemetic North Ridge Trail	2.3 miles	1 hour and 45 minutes

This trail climbs to the summit of Pemetic via the mountain's south ridge. It begins at Bubble and Jordan Ponds Path, 0.5 mile east of the Jordan Pond parking area. It climbs steadily to a junction at 0.6 mile with Pemetic East Cliff Trail, which leads to the right. Pemetic South Ridge Trail continues straight, climbing over open ledges with spectacular views to the summit and reaches Pemetic North Ridge Trail at 1.2 miles.

Pemetic East Cliff Trail

(formerly a portion of Pemetic Mountain Trail)

AMC's Acadia National Park Map: E6

NPS Rating: Strenuous

This trail is short but steep, climbing from the intersection of Bubble and Jordan Ponds Path and Triad Trail to Pemetic South Ridge Trail in 0.3 mile and approximately 10 minutes.

Pemetic Northwest Trail

(formerly Bubbles-Pemetic Trail)
AMC's Acadia National Park Map: E6)
NPS Rating: Strenuous

Distances from Bubble Rock parking area

to Pemetic North Ridge Trail	0.5 mile	35 minutes
to Pemetic summit	0.6 mile	40 minutes

This trail begins at the Bubble Rock parking area, on the west side of Park Loop Road, about 1.1 miles south of Bubble Pond. The path enters the woods east of Park Loop Road and climbs in almost constant cover. Sometimes following a rocky streambed, the trail ends at a junction with Pemetic North Ridge Trail about 0.1 mile north of the summit.

Bubble and Jordan Ponds Path

AMC's Acadia National Park Map: E6, E7
NPS Rating: Moderate

Distances from Jordan Pond

Pemetic South Ridge Trail	0.5 mile	20 minutes
to carriage road	1.1 miles	40 minutes
to Canon Brook Trail	1.5 miles	1 hour and 5 minutes

Bubble and Jordan Ponds Path leaves the shore of Jordan Pond, traveling east, and crosses Park Loop Road at 0.1 mile. There is a small parking area at this crossing. Continuing through heavy woods via easy grades, the path swings into the valley between the Triad and Pemetic Mountain. It crosses Pemetic South Ridge Trail at 0.5 mile then turns left at an intersection with Triad Pass. It continues northeast to cross Pemetic East Cliff Trail at 0.8 mile and a carriage road at 1.1 miles. Continuing to climb for another 0.4 mile, the trail ends at Canon Brook Trail, which climbs to the south ridge of Cadillac Mountain, 1.2 miles south of the summit.

Triad Pass

AMC's Acadia National Park Map: E6
NPS Rating: Easy

Distances from Jordan Pond parking area

to start of trail via Bubble and Jordan Ponds Path	0.5 mile	20 minutes
to Hunters Brook Trail	0.7 mile	25 minutes

This short trail begins on Bubble and Jordan Ponds Path 0.5 mile east of Jordan Pond. From there, it heads southeast for 0.2 mile, ending at Hunters Brook Trail. This short link provides trail access from Jordan Pond to the Triad and Day Mountain.

Triad Trail

(the northern half of this trail was formerly called Pemetic Mountain Trail)

AMC's Acadia National Park Map: E6

NPS Rating: Moderate

Distances from Bubble and Jordan Ponds Path		
to Hunters Brook Trail	0.4 mile	15 minutes
to Day Mountain Trail	0.8 mile	25 minutes

Triad Trail provides a route from Pemetic Mountain to Day Mountain via a hill known as the Triad. The trail heads southeast from Bubble and Jordan Ponds Path (0.8 mile from Jordan Pond), where Pemetic East Cliff Trail heads northwest. Triad trail rises moderately for 0.4 mile and crosses Hunters Brook Trail before reaching the top of the Triad. It then descends for 0.4 mile before ending at a carriage road and Day Mountain Trail.

Day Mountain Trail

AMC's Acadia National Park Map: F7

NPS Rating: Moderate

Distances from Route 3		
to Day summit	0.8 mile	35 minutes
to carriage road	1.3 miles	50 minutes
to Pemetic summit via Triad, Pemetic East Cliff, and Pemetic South Ridge trails	3 miles	2 hours

Day Mountain Trail starts on the north side of Route 3, approximately 1.5 miles south of Blackwoods Campground. The parking area is located on the south side of the highway. Day Mountain Trail climbs moderately through the forest for its entire length. Periodically crossing carriage roads, the trail offers beautiful views of Hunters Beach and Seal Harbor from ledges 0.6 mile from the trailhead. The summit of Day Mountain is at 0.8 mile. (A carriage road also leads to Day's summit.) Descending into the forest quickly, the trail ends at another carriage road, at 1.3 miles, where Triad Trail continues north toward the Triad and Pemetic Mountain.

Hunters Brook Trail

(formerly Triad-Hunters Brook Trail)

AMC's Acadia National Park Map: E6, E7, F7

NPS Rating: Strenuous

Distances from Park Loop Road

to carriage road	1.4 miles	45 minutes
to Triad Trail	1.8 miles	1 hour and 15 minutes
to Triad Pass Trail	2.1 miles	1 hour and 25 minutes
to carriage road near post 17	2.6 miles	1 hour and 45 minutes

This trail begins on Park Loop Road near the southern overpass of Route 3. It follows along Hunters Brook, passing through a canopy of cedar, maple, and spruce. At 1.25 miles the trail bears west from the brook then climbs to a carriage road at 1.4 miles. Crossing the carriage road, the trail continues to climb to a junction with Triad Trail, near the Triad, at 1.8 miles. (Turning right onto Triad Trail takes you to the summit of Pemetic Mountain in an additional 1.3 miles.) Hunters Brook Trail then descends for 0.3 miles, passes Triad Pass Trail on the right, takes a left, and heads south, ending at a carriage road (0.2 miles west of post 17) at 2.6 miles.

SARGENT MOUNTAIN AND PENOBSCOT MOUNTAIN

Sargent Mountain (1,379 feet) and Penobscot Mountain (1,196 feet) are open summits about 1 mile apart. Sargent Pond, a pleasant mountain pond, lies between the two. From the south, the preferred starting point is the Jordan Pond parking area. The outlying territory to the southwest contains an interesting maze of trails and carriage roads around Bald Peak (974 feet) and Parkman Mountain (941 feet). Ample parking is available at two areas: on the west side of Route 3/198, about 0.3 mile north of Upper Hadlock Pond (a reservoir, no swimming); and at the Parkman Mountain parking area, on the east side of Route 3/198, about 0.5 mile north of Upper Hadlock Pond. Upper Hadlock Pond is approximately 2.5 miles south of where Route 3/198 splits from Route 233.

Penobscot Mountain Trail

AMC's Acadia National Park Map: E6

NPS Rating: Strenuous

Distances from Asticou and Jordan Pond Path

to Spring Trail	1.2 miles	1 hour
to Penobscot summit	2.2 miles	1 hour and 30 minutes
to Sargent summit	2.9 miles	2 hours

The lower section of this trail was recently rerouted to extend to Asticou and Jordan Pond Path, 1.1 miles west of Jordan Pond House. The original lower part of the trail, which starts near Jordan Pond House, is now called Spring Trail. Penobscot Mountain Trail heads north from Asticou and Jordan Pond Path, climbing at an easy pace and making three carriage road crossings in its first 0.3 mile. It then climbs more steeply, occasionally breaking out into the open with excellent views to the south. It reaches the south ridge of Penobscot Mountain and a junction with Spring Trail at 1.2 miles. The trail then climbs gradually over open granite ledges to the summit of Penobscot Mountain at 2.2 miles then continues north, descending to an intersection with Deer Brook Trail at 2.3 miles. The trail turns left and reaches Sargent Pond in about 100 yards. From the pond, the trail makes a short climb to Sargent South Ridge Trail at 2.5 miles.

Spring Trail

(formerly part of Penobscot Mountain Trail)

AMC's Acadia National Park Map: E6

NPS Rating: Strenuous

Distances from Jordan Pond House

to Jordan Cliffs Trail	0.3 mile	15 minutes
to Penobscot Mountain Trail	0.5 mile	30 minutes
to Penobscot summit via Penobscot Mountain Trail	1.5 miles	1 hour

This trail provides the quickest access to Penobscot Mountain from Jordan Pond House. It is short but very steep in places and should be avoided for descents, especially in wet conditions. The trail starts from the west side of Jordan Stream, about 100 yards west of Jordan Pond House at an intersection with a carriage road and Asticou and Jordan Pond Path. The trail runs west and passes Jordan Cliffs Trail at 0.3 mile, shortly before crossing a carriage road. It then climbs very steeply with the assistance of iron rungs and wooden handrails to Penobscot Mountain Trail at 0.5 mile.

Jordan Cliffs Trail

AMC's Acadia National Park Map: E6
NPS Rating: Ladder

Distances from Jordan Pond House			
to Jordan Cliffs Trail	0.3 mile	15 minutes
to Jordan Cliffs	1.1 miles	55 minutes
to Penobscot summit	1.8 miles	1 hour and 20 minutes
to Deer Brook Trail	1.8 miles	1 hour and 15 minutes
to Sargent summit via Sargent East Cliff Trail	2.5 miles	1 hour and 50 minutes

This challenging yet scenic trail leaves Spring Trail 0.3 mile west of Jordan Pond House, just northeast of the junction of Spring Trail and a carriage road. Bearing right soon after crossing the carriage road, Jordan Cliffs Trail heads north and rises up the east shoulder of Penobscot Mountain in gradual pitches, reaching the cliffs at 0.8 mile. The trail traverses Jordan Cliffs via ladders and handrails then reaches a junction with Penobscot East Trail at 1.2 miles. Turn left on Penobscot East Trail to reach the summit of Penobscot Mountain. While very steep, the trail is spectacular, with views of the Bubbles, Pemetic Mountain, and Jordan Pond.

Continuing straight past Penobscot East Trail, Jordan Cliffs Trail traverses the cliffs above Jordan Pond and ends at an intersection with Deer Brook Trail and Sargent East Cliff Trail at 1.5 miles.

Sargent East Cliff Trail

AMC's Acadia National Park Map: E6
NPS Rating: Strenuous

Distances from Deer Brook Trail		
to Sargent summit	0.7 mile	35 minutes

This short but steep trail connects Jordan Cliffs Trail to the summit of Sargent Mountain. It is recommended more for ascending than descending, especially in wet weather, when the steep climb down wet rocks and ledges can be troublesome. The trail starts at Deer Brook and an intersection with Jordan Cliffs Trail and Deer Brook Trail. It climbs quickly up the southeast face of Sargent Mountain and has excellent views for much of its 0.7 mile.

Deer Brook Trail

AMC's Acadia National Park Map: E6

NPS Rating: Strenuous

Distance from Jordan Pond House

to Penobscot Mountain Trail	0.8 mile	45 minutes

This is a steep, quick ascent of 0.8 mile to Sargent Pond from Jordan Pond Path at the north end of the pond. The route is entirely wooded and follows the course of Deer Brook, crossing a carriage road at 0.2 mile and reaching an intersection with the Jordan Cliffs and Sargent East Cliff trails at 0.3 mile. This trail joins Penobscot Mountain Trail in the valley between Sargent and Penobscot mountains, 0.8 mile from the shore of Jordan Pond.

Sargent South Ridge Trail

AMC's Acadia National Park Map: E6

NPS Rating: Moderate

Distances from carriage road

to Cedar Swamp Mountain spur	1.4 miles	1 hour
to Penobscot Mountain Trail	2 miles	1 hour and 40 minutes
to Hadlock Brook Trail	2.2 miles	1 hour and 55 minutes
to Maple Spring Trail	2.4 miles	2 hours
to Sargent summit	2.7 miles	2 hours and 15 minutes

This trail starts from a carriage road that leaves from the parking lot at the Brown Mountain gatehouse in Northeast Harbor, which is located about 1 mile south of Upper Hadlock Pond, on the east side of Route 3/198. From the parking area, follow the carriage road east, bearing right at post 18 and again at post 19 (toward Amphitheater Trail), reaching the trail 0.7 mile from the parking area. Here the trail heads south 0.1 mile to Asticou and Jordan Pond Path or north to the summit of Sargent Mountain.

On its way to the summit, Sargent South Ridge Trail rises over the wooded shoulder and passes just southeast of the summit of Cedar Swamp Mountain at 1.4 miles from the carriage road. A spur trail bears left to the summit. Sargent South Ridge Trail drops to cross Little Harbor Brook and Amphitheater Trail at 1.5 miles. The trail then leaves the woods and rises sharply 0.5 mile to a junction with Penobscot Mountain Trail, which comes in from the right. The trail continues north over open granite ledges, past junctions to the left with Hadlock Brook Trail at 2.2 miles and Maple Spring Trail at 2.4 miles. It reaches the summit of Sargent at 2.7 miles.

Giant Slide Trail

AMC's Acadia National Park Map: D5

NPS Rating: Ladder

Distances from Route 198

to carriage-road crossing	0.7 mile	15 minutes
to Parkman Mountain Trail and Sargent Northwest Trail	1.1 miles	45 minutes
to Maple Spring Trail	2.3 miles	1 hour and 30 minutes

This trail approaches the Sargent Mountain area from the northwest. Its beginning has been relocated to a trailhead on the east side of Route 198, 1 mile south of Route 233; limited parking is available on the west side of the road. The trail climbs through mature softwoods, up a gradual slope to a carriage road at 0.7 mile. The trail turns sharply right (south) and, following Sargent Brook, rises steeply over the tumbled boulders of Giant Slide. At 1.1 miles, Parkman Mountain Trail diverges right and Sargent Northwest Trail leaves left. Giant Slide Trail continues through the notch between Parkman Mountain and Gilmore Peak at an intersection with Grandgent Trail at 1.7 miles. It descends to end at a junction with Maple Spring Trail at 2.3 miles.

Sargent Northwest Trail

AMC's Acadia National Park Map: E5

NPS Rating: Moderate

Distance from Giant Slide Trail

to Sargent summit	1 mile	1 hour

Leaving Giant Slide Trail 1.1 miles from Route 198, this trail ascends east and crosses a carriage road at 0.3 mile. Continuing roughly east, it rises over slanting pitches for 0.3 mile before making a sharp right (south) turn. The final 0.4 mile to the summit crosses open ledges with spectacular views.

Hadlock Brook Trail

AMC's Acadia National Park Map: E5

NPS Rating: Strenuous

Distances from Route 198

to Maple Spring Trail	0.4 mile	10 minutes
to Amphitheater Trail	1.1 miles	40 minutes
to Sargent summit via Sargent South Ridge Trail	2.2 miles	1 hour and 30 minutes

Hadlock Brook Trail provides access to Sargent Mountain from the southwest and leads to several other trails without roadside access. From the east side of Route 198, just north of Upper Hadlock Pond and opposite the Norumbega Mountain parking area, Hadlock Brook Trail heads east, passing Bald Peak

Trail, Parkman Mountain Trail, a carriage road, Hadlock Ponds Trail, and Maple Spring Trail, all in the first 0.4 mile. From here, the trail follows the east branch of Hadlock Brook through mature forest for 0.4 mile before crossing a carriage road at Waterfall Bridge, with an excellent view of a 40-foot waterfall. The trail then gets steeper, continuing to parallel the brook over rough footing to a junction with Amphitheater Trail at 1.1 miles. The trail then climbs very steeply before reaching the open terrain of Sargent Mountain's South Ridge and Sargent South Ridge Trail at 1.7 miles.

Maple Spring Trail

AMC's Acadia National Park Map: E5
NPS Rating: Strenuous

Distances from Hadlock Brook Trail			
	to Giant Slide Trail	0.4 mile	15 minutes
	to Grandgent Trail	0.9 mile	40 minutes
	to Sargent summit	1.7 miles	1 hour and 20 minutes

This trail climbs to the south ridge of Sargent Mountain from the southwest, following the west branch of Hadlock Brook for much of its length. A recent relocation on the upper part of this trail means it now also provides access to Gilmore Peak via Grandgent Trail.

Reach the beginning of Maple Spring Trail by following Hadlock Brook Trail from the Norumbega Mountain parking area on Route 198 for 0.4 mile. Here Maple Spring Trail leads left. The trail closely follows Hadlock Brook, crossing it several times. In high water, there are some very nice cascades and small waterfalls before and after crossing under Hemlock Bridge, 0.3 mile from Hadlock Brook Trail. The trail climbs through a small gorge before reaching Giant Slide Trail at 0.4 mile then Grandgent Trail at 0.9 mile. (Gilmore Peak is 0.1 mile to the left via Grandgent Trail.) Maple Spring Trail makes a sharp right and climbs steeply, reaching the open south ridge and Sargent South Ridge Trail at 1.4 miles. Sargent's summit is 0.3 mile to the left via Sargent South Ridge Trail.

Grandgent Trail

AMC's Acadia National Park Map: E5
NPS Rating: Strenuous

Distances from Sargent summit			
	to Maple Spring Trail	0.5 mile	20 minutes
	to Gilmore Peak	0.6 mile	25 minutes
	to Giant Slide Trail	0.9 mile	35 minutes
	to Parkman summit	1.1 miles	45 minutes

This trail runs between the summits of Sargent Mountain, Gilmore Peak, and Parkman Mountain. From the summit of Sargent, the trail leaves west and steeply descends into a saddle at the base of Gilmore Peak, where there is an intersection with Maple Spring Trail at 0.5 mile. After a right turn and a short climb of 0.1 mile, the trail reaches Gilmore Peak. Then it gradually descends for 0.3 mile, crossing Giant Slide Trail before climbing another 0.2 mile to the summit of Parkman Mountain.

Parkman Mountain Trail

AMC's Acadia National Park Map: E5
NPS Rating: Moderate

Distances from Route 198		
to Parkman summit	1.5 miles	50 minutes
to Giant Slide Trail and Sargent North Ridge Trail	2.2 miles	1 hour and 10 minutes

Parkman Mountain Trail starts out with Hadlock Brook Trail but soon diverges north (left) for 1.5 miles through woods and over a series of knobs to Parkman's peak. The trail crosses a carriage road three times on the way to the summit. Bald Peak Trail joins from the right at 1.4 miles. At the summit, Grandgent Trail leaves right toward Gilmore Peak. Parkman Mountain Trail continues north over open ledges, then through the woods, crossing a carriage road 0.5 mile beyond the summit. The trail ends 0.3 mile farther, at the junction of Giant Slide Trail and Sargent North Ridge Trail.

Bald Peak Trail

AMC's Acadia National Park Map: E5
NPS Rating: Moderate

Distances from Route 198 via Hadlock Brook Trail		
to Bald Peak Trail	0.2 mile	10 minutes
to Bald Peak summit	0.9 mile	30 minutes
to Parkman Mountain Trail	1.1 miles	40 minutes

This trail is the most direct route up Bald Peak, one of several small, rocky, and open summits to the west of Sargent Mountain. Reach Bald Peak Trail by following Hadlock Brook Trail 0.2 mile from the Norumbega Mountain parking area on Route 198. At this point, Bald Peak Trail leaves left. Gradually climbing through the forest, the trail reaches the summit of Bald Peak at 0.9 mile. The trail reaches Parkman Mountain Trail 0.2 mile beyond the summit of Bald Peak.

NORUMBEGA MOUNTAIN

The summit of Norumbega Mountain (852 feet) is wooded, but the blueberries on the north slope make it attractive and appealing in season. The trail offers very good views of Somes Sound and the mountains west of the sound. Note: This area is honeycombed with abandoned and unofficial paths, and the names of existing trails have recently changed. Pay careful attention to trail markers and maps.

Goat Trail

(formerly a portion of Norumbega Mountain Trail)
AMC's Acadia National Park Map: E5
NPS Rating: Strenuous

Distance from Route 198		
to Norumbega summit	0.6 mile	45 minutes

This trail leaves the Norumbega Mountain parking area on the west side of Route 198, about 0.3 mile north of Upper Hadlock Pond. It ascends quickly and very steeply for the first 0.3 mile through woods to granite ledges, then swings south to the summit, 0.6 mile from the parking area. There are occasional views from the ledges prior to reaching the wooded summit and excellent views from Norumbega Mountain Trail about 150 yards beyond the summit.

Norumbega Mountain Trail

AMC's Acadia National Park Map: E5, F5
NPS Rating: Moderate

Distances from Norumbega summit		
to Golf Course Trail	0.8 mile	15 minutes (25 in reverse)
to Hadlock Ponds Trail	1.4 miles	30 minutes (45 in reverse)

This trail connects Hadlock Ponds Trail on the north shore of Lower Hadlock Pond to the summit of Norumbega Mountain. Beginning at Goat Trail and the summit of Norumbega, Norumbega Mountain Trail follows the south ridge over semiopen ledges with occasional views, descending moderately before entering the forest and reaching a junction with Golf Course Trail 0.8 mile below the summit. Veering left at this junction, the trail continues its moderate descent, reaching Lower Hadlock Pond and Hadlock Ponds Trail at 1.4 miles.

Hadlock Ponds Trail

(formerly Hadlock Trail)
AMC's Acadia National Park Map: F5
NPS Rating: Moderate

Distances from Hadlock Brook Trail

to Route 198	0.7 mile	15 minutes
to Lower Norumbega Trail	0.9 mile	20 minutes
to Lower Hadlock Trail	1 mile	25 minutes
to Norumbega Mountain Trail	1.5 miles	35 minutes

This relatively flat trail starts on Hadlock Brook Trail 0.3 mile from the Norumbega Mountain parking area on Route 198. From there, it follows the eastern shoreline of Upper Hadlock Pond; crosses Route 198; and continues to Lower Hadlock Pond, Lower Norumbega Trail, and Norumbega Mountain Trail. Views of the ponds from the trail are excellent.

Lower Norumbega Trail

(formerly part of Norumbega Mountain Trail)
AMC's Acadia National Park Map: E5, F5
NPS Rating: Moderate

Distance from Goat Trail

to Hadlock Ponds Trail	0.9 mile	30 minutes

This trail connects Goat Trail, just west of the Norumbega Mountain parking area, to Hadlock Ponds Trail near the northern shore of Lower Hadlock Pond. It is 0.9 mile long and traverses uneven terrain in a spruce forest while paralleling Route 198.

Lower Hadlock Trail

AMC's Acadia National Park Map: F5
NPS Rating: Easy

Distances from Hadlock Ponds Trail

to Hadlock Ponds Trail	0.7 mile	15 minutes
to southern terminus of Hadlock Ponds Trail	1.2 mile	25 minutes

This short trail follows the eastern shoreline of Lower Hadlock Pond. It starts at the inlet to the pond, where it leaves Hadlock Ponds Trail, crosses the stream, and follows the shoreline through an evergreen forest, reaching Hadlock Pond Road in 0.7 mile.

WESTERN DISTRICT (WEST OF SOMES SOUND)

ACADIA MOUNTAIN

The high point on the western side of Somes Sound, Acadia Mountain (681 feet) provides dramatic views of the sound and the Cranberry Isles from open ledges interspersed with pitch pines and scrub oaks. Hikers can loop the summit using Acadia Mountain Trail and Man o' War Brook fire road.

Acadia Mountain Trail

AMC's Acadia National Park Map: E4
NPS Rating: Strenuous

Distances from Route 102			
	to Acadia east summit	1 mile	45 minutes
	to Man o' War Brook	1.4 miles	1 hour
	to Route 102	2.3 miles	1 hour and 30 minutes

Parking is located at the Acadia Mountain parking area on the west side of Route 102, 3 miles south of Somesville and 3 miles north of Southwest Harbor. (Please do not block the fire road gates on the east side of Route 102.) Acadia Mountain Trail begins with a set of stone steps directly across the road from the parking area. At 0.1 mile, Saint Sauveur Trail leads to the right. Stay left to continue on Acadia Mountain Trail, which meanders through a forest of pine and spruce with an understory of blueberries and sheep laurel. At 0.2 mile, the trail crosses a dirt fire road then begins climbing steeply over granite ledges and stone stairs.

The trail ascends the west slope, soon leaving woods for open rocks and frequent views. It passes over the highest summit and reaches the east summit, with views of the sound, at about 1 mile. The trail then descends southeast and south very steeply to cross Man o' War Brook. A junction about 50 yards beyond the stream marks the end of Acadia Mountain Trail. To return to Route 102 via the fire road, go west (right) at the junction and proceed past trails to Saint Sauveur and Valley Cove, which diverge left about 100 yards east of the stream. The east end of the Man o' War Brook fire road is in another 200 yards. Follow the fire road west over gradual grades for 0.9 mile back to Route 102, 50 yards north of the parking area. You will cross Acadia Mountain Trail shortly before Route 102. Turn left onto the trail to reach the parking lot.

SAINT SAUVEUR MOUNTAIN

Saint Sauveur Mountain (690 feet) can be reached from the north via Man o' War Brook fire road (via NPS fire service road from Route 102), from Route 102 on the west, and from Fernald Cove Road on the south. There are good views of Somes Sound from Eagle Cliff, just east of the summit.

Saint Sauveur Trail

AMC's Acadia National Park Map: F4
NPS Rating: Moderate

Distances from Route 102			
	to Ledge Trail junction	0.9 mile	40 minutes
	to Saint Sauveur summit	1.2 miles	55 minutes
	to Fernald Point road	2.1 miles	1 hour and 20 minutes

This trail is an easy route to the summit of Saint Sauveur Mountain from the north. Follow the Acadia Mountain Trail description (above) to reach the parking lot and trailhead. Start 0.1 mile down Acadia Mountain Trail and go right at the fork.

The path runs south through evergreens and over open slopes, rising constantly for 0.8 mile to a junction where Ledge Trail enters on the right. From there, it is 0.2 mile to the summit. Saint Sauveur Trail continues past the summit, while a spur of Valley Peak Trail leaves left. Saint Sauveur Trail descends the south ridge of the mountain for 0.4 mile, where it ends at Valley Peak Trail, 0.5 mile from Fernald Point Road.

Ledge Trail

AMC's Acadia National Park Map: F4
NPS Rating: Moderate

Distances from Route 102			
	to Saint Sauveur Trail	0.6 mile	25 minutes
	to Saint Sauveur summit	0.8 mile	40 minutes

This trail begins at the Saint Sauveur parking area on the east side of Route 102, about 0.2 mile north of the entrance road to the NPS swimming facilities at the south end of Echo Lake. The parking area is also about 0.2 mile south of the access road to the Appalachian Mountain Club's Echo Lake Camp. (For more information, visit amcecholakecamp.org.)

Ledge Trail enters the woods and rises over ledges to its end. It meets the Saint Sauveur Trail 0.6 mile from the highway and 0.2 mile northwest of the summit.

Valley Peak Trail

AMC's Acadia National Park Map: F4

NPS Rating: Strenuous

Distances from the Valley Cove truck road			
	to Saint Sauveur Trail	0.4 mile	20 minutes
	to Saint Sauveur summit	0.8 mile	45 minutes
	to Acadia Mountain Trail	1.5 miles	1 hour and 10 minutes

Valley Peak Trail leaves the west side of the Valley Cove truck road a few yards north of the parking area at Fernald Cove. The trail rises steeply northwest through shady woods over Valley Peak (the south shoulder of Saint Sauveur Mountain), where Saint Sauveur Trail leads left. The trail then skirts the top of Eagle Cliff, with outstanding views of Valley Cove below and the mountains of Somes Sound to the east. At 0.7 mile, a spur path leads to the summit of Saint Sauveur Mountain, while Valley Peak Trail continues straight. It steeply descends the northeast shoulder of Saint Sauveur to end at a junction with Acadia Mountain Trail near Man o' War Brook and the east terminus of the Man o' War Brook fire road at 1.5 miles.

FLYING MOUNTAIN

A few minutes' climb to the open top of Flying Mountain (284 feet) gives a fine panorama of Somes Sound, Southwest Harbor, Northeast Harbor, and the islands to the south: the Cranberries, Greening, Sutton, Baker, and Bear.

Flying Mountain Trail

AMC's Acadia National Park Map: F4

NPS Rating: Moderate

Distances from Fernald Cove parking area			
	to Flying Mountain summit	0.3 mile	15 minutes
	to Valley Cove Trail and fire road	0.9 mile	25 minutes
	to Fernald Cove parking area	1.5 miles	45 minutes
	to Acadia Mountain Trail	2 miles	1 hour

This scenic trail over tiny Flying Mountain leaves the east side of the Fernald Cove parking area at the end of the Valley Cove truck road. From there, it rises quickly and steeply through spruce woods, reaching the summit of Flying Mountain in 0.3 mile, where there are nice views of Somes Sound. Another 0.3 mile past the summit, a short spur path leads right, to more open ledges and unobstructed views of the sound. The trail then descends to the shoreline of Valley Cove and follows the cove to the left, reaching Valley Cove Trail and the Valley Cove fire road at 0.9 mile. For an easy return to the Fernald Cove parking area, follow the fire road south about 0.6 mile.

Valley Cove Trail
(formerly part of Flying Mountain Trail)
AMC's Acadia National Park Map: F4
NPS Rating: Easy

Distances from Fernald Cove parking area			
to Valley Cove Trail	0.5 mile	10 minutes
to Acadia Mountain Trail	1.6 miles	45 minutes

This trail connects the Fernald Cove parking area to Acadia Mountain Trail. It starts on the shoreline of Valley Cove, at the end of the Valley Cove fire road, 0.5 mile from the parking area. From the fire road, Valley Cove Trail goes left, while Flying Mountain Trail goes right. Valley Cove Trail follows the shoreline under the ledges of Eagle Cliff high above. It ends at Acadia Mountain Trail in 1.1 miles.

BEECH MOUNTAIN

Beech Mountain (841 feet) lies between Echo Lake and Long Pond ("Great Pond," on some maps). Its summit is easy to reach from either the Beech Cliff parking area—located at the end of Beech Hill Road, in the notch between Beech Cliff and Beech Mountain—or the pumping station area at the foot of Long Pond. To reach the pumping station, follow Seal Cove Road west from Southwest Harbor. Take the first right, toward the landfill, and follow this road until it ends at the pumping station. You can also climb Beech Mountain via its southwest flank, beginning at the south end of Long Pond. An added attraction nearby is the Beech Cliff–Canada Cliff area, just east of the Beech Cliff parking area. These rugged cliffs offer spectacular views of Echo Lake.

Beech Cliff Trail
AMC's Acadia National Park Map: F3
NPS Rating: Ladder

Distance from Echo Lake beach parking area		
to Canada Cliff Trail and Beech Cliff Loop Trail	0.5 mile	40 minutes

This trail offers quick but extremely steep access to Beech Cliff from the beach parking area at the southern end of Echo Lake. The trail is usually closed from early spring through early August to protect peregrine falcons nesting on the cliffs, so check with park personnel to confirm that the trail is open. After about 0.1 mile of moderate hiking through the woods, the trail climbs very steeply for the rest of the way, ascending the cliff via a series of stone staircases and iron ladders. This trail reaches the level top of Beech Cliff 0.5 mile from the parking area, where the Canada Cliff Trail leads left. Beech Cliff Trail continues right for about 100 yards, where it ends at Beech Cliff Loop Trail. Views of Echo Lake and the mountains to the east are excellent.

Canada Cliff Trail

AMC's Acadia National Park Map: F3
NPS Rating: Moderate

Distances from Echo Lake beach parking area

to fork in trail	0.4 mile	10 minutes
to Valley Trail	0.6 mile	20 minutes
to Beech Cliff and Beech Cliff Loop trails	1 mile	35 minutes

This trail starts from the west side of the parking lot at Echo Lake beach and, via the right fork, leads to the top of Beech Cliff, where it ends at an intersection with Beech Cliff Trail. The left fork of the trail avoids the hike up the cliff and leads to Valley Trail, 0.3 mile south of the Beech Cliff parking area, at the end of Beech Hill Road. To reach the parking area, drive 4.2 miles south on Route 102 from its intersection with Route 198 in Somesville then turn right on the road to Echo Lake and AMC's Echo Lake Camp. Parking is at the end of this road, in 0.7 mile.

The trail starts next to the Echo Lake Island Explorer bus stop via a set of stairs. The trail parallels the road for 0.2 mile then turns right just before Lurvey Spring Road. It then begins to climb moderately, sometimes steeply, through a beautiful forest of evergreens and pink granite. At 0.4 mile, Canada Cliff Trail branches into two forks. The left fork leads 0.2 mile to Valley Trail. The right fork climbs over semiopen ledges 0.4 mile to Beech Cliff and an intersection with Beech Cliff Trail. From this intersection, it is an easy 0.2-mile walk via Beech Cliff and Beech Cliff Loop trails to Beech Cliff, with excellent views of Echo Lake and the mountains to the east.

Beech Cliff Loop Trail

AMC's Acadia National Park Map: F3
NPS Rating: Moderate

Distances from Beech Cliff parking area

to Beech Cliff and Canada Cliff Trails	0.2 mile	15 minutes
to return to parking area	0.8 mile	35 minutes

This trail climbs Beech Cliff from the Beech Cliff parking area at the end of Beech Hill Road. To reach this trailhead, follow Route 102 south through Somesville and take Pretty Marsh Road, the first right after the fire station. Follow Pretty Marsh Road west for about 0.5 mile, where the Beech Hill Road intersects from the left. Follow Beech Hill Road south until it ends at the trailhead, 3.2 miles from Pretty Marsh Road.

The trail leaves from the east side of the parking area, climbing moderately and sometimes steeply up the western, wooded slope of Beech Cliff. In 0.2 mile it reaches an intersection with Beech Cliff Trail and Canada Cliff Trail, both of which lead to the southern end of Echo Lake. Beech Cliff Loop Trail leads straight or left, depending on which direction you walk the loop. The loop is 0.4 mile long and follows the edge of the cliff for about half of its length. The views are spectacular to the east.

Beech Mountain Loop Trail
AMC's Acadia National Park Map: F3
NPS Rating: Moderate

Distances from Beech Cliff parking area		
to Beech summit (via north fork)	0.4 mile	30 minutes
to Beech Cliff parking area (via north then south forks)	1.1 miles	1 hour and 15 minutes

This trail leaves the northwest side of the Beech Cliff parking area and forks in 0.1 mile. The trail to the right (northwest) is 0.7 mile and provides a beautiful vista of Long Pond before climbing to the summit of Beech Mountain. The trail to the left (south) is 0.4 mile and climbs more steeply to Beech's summit, with its fire tower. The two trails can be combined to form a scenic loop hike.

From the summit, Beech West Ridge and Beech South Ridge trails depart to the southwest and south, respectively, providing access to the parking area at the south end of Long Pond.

Valley Trail
AMC's Acadia National Park Map: F3
NPS Rating: Moderate

Distances from Long Pond parking area		
to Beech South Ridge Trail	0.7 mile	15 minutes
to Canada Ridge Trail	1.3 miles	40 minutes
to Beech Cliff parking area	1.5 miles	50 minutes

This graded path is a convenient link between the Long Pond area and the Beech Cliff parking area, which is located in the notch between Beech Cliff and Beech Mountain. It also permits either a circuit or a one-way trip over Beech Mountain, since it provides direct access to Beech South Ridge Trail.

The trail starts at the parking area next to the pumping station at the south end of Long Pond. From there, it crosses a service road in 0.3 mile. Via easy grades over wooded slopes, the trail runs north briefly then swings east (right) before entering a series of switchbacks on the south slopes of Beech Mountain. At 0.7 mile, Beech South Ridge Trail to Beech Mountain leaves left. Continuing east, Valley Trail soon swings north to maintain altitude as it runs up the valley separating Beech Mountain and Canada Cliff. At 1.3 miles Canada Cliff Trail comes in from the right. Continue directly ahead to reach the Beech Cliff parking area at 1.5 miles.

Beech South Ridge Trail

AMC's Acadia National Park Map: F3

NPS Rating: Moderate

Distances from Long Pond parking area

to Beech South Ridge Trail	0.7 mile	15 minutes
to Beech summit	1.5 miles	45 minutes

This well-marked trail diverges left from Valley Trail about 0.7 mile east of the Long Pond parking area and steadily ascends the south ridge to the summit along open ledges, offering views to the south.

Beech West Ridge Trail

AMC's Acadia National Park Map: F3

NPS Rating: Moderate

Distances from Long Pond pumping station

to Beech Mountain Loop Trail	0.9 mile	40 minutes
to Beech summit (via Beech Mountain Loop Trail)	1 mile	45 minutes

Leaving from the east side of the Long Pond pumping station, this trail skirts the edge of Long Pond for 0.3 mile. At this point, the trail begins to climb from the shore, rising steeply at times. Ledges offer good views of the pond and Mansell Mountain. The trail reaches Beech Mountain Loop Trail at 0.9 mile.

WESTERN MOUNTAINS

BERNARD MOUNTAIN AND MANSELL MOUNTAIN

This area has two main summits: Bernard Mountain (1,071 feet) to the west and Mansell Mountain (938 feet) to the east. Both summits are wooded, and extensive views are rare. You can reach all of the southern approaches from the parking area at the foot of Long Pond, near the pumping station. To reach the pumping station, follow Seal Cove Road west from Southwest Harbor. Take the first right, toward the landfill, and follow this road until it ends at the pumping station.

Great Notch Trail

(formerly Great Notch and Western Mountain trails)
AMC's Acadia National Park Map: F2, F3
NPS Rating: Moderate

Distances from Long Pond (Great Pond) fire road

to Long Pond fire road	1.1 miles	1 hour and 5 minutes
to Great Notch	1.5 miles	1 hour and 25 minutes
to Gilley Trail	2 miles	1 hour and 40 minutes
to Gilley Field parking area via Gilley Trail	2.6 miles	2 hours and 5 minutes

This is the only trail providing access to the western mountains from the north. There are no open vistas. To reach the trailhead, go about 1 mile east from the western loop of Route 102 on the Long Pond (Great Pond) fire road. Parking is available here. The fire road crosses Route 102 just north of Seal Cove Pond. Great Notch Trail starts on the southeast side of the road, about 0.1 mile beyond the Pine Hill turnaround and parking area.

The trail trends southeast and rises by easy grades to a junction with Long Pond Trail, entering from the left, 1.1 miles from the fire road. It reaches Great Notch at 1.5 miles, where Bernard Mountain Trail leads right toward Bernard Mountain, and Razorback Trail leads left toward Mansell Mountain. Great Notch Trail continues through the notch and down to Gilley Trail at 2 miles, 0.6 mile from the Gilley Field parking area.

Gilley Trail

(formerly part of Great Notch Trail)
AMC's Acadia National Park Map: F3
NPS Rating: Easy

Distances from Gilley Field parking area

to Razorback Trail	0.1 mile	5 minutes
to Great Notch and Sluiceway trails	0.6 mile	15 minutes

This trail starts at the Gilley Field parking area, at the eastern end of the Western Mountain fire road. It provides access to Mansell and Bernard mountains via Razorback, Great Notch, and Sluiceway trails. The trail starts next to Mansell Mountain Trail, but instead of climbing the peak it follows easy grades to the west, passing Razorback Trail in 0.1 mile, crossing a fire road at 0.3 mile, then turning north and climbing moderately to its end, at Great Notch and Sluiceway trails at 0.6 mile.

Long Pond Trail
(formerly Great Pond Trail)
AMC's Acadia National Park Map: F2, F3
NPS Rating: Easy

Distances from pumping station

to Perpendicular Trail	0.2 mile	5 minutes
to Great Notch Trail	2.9 miles	1 hour and 40 minutes

This excellent footpath starts at the parking area at the south end of Long Pond. Following the west shore of the pond, Long Pond Trail reaches an intersection with Perpendicular Trail (which leads left to the summit of Mansell Mountain) in 0.2 mile. Long Pond Trail continues along the shore of the pond for another 1.3 miles, before turning southwest, passing through a beautiful birch forest and following Great Brook to a junction with Great Notch Trail, 2.9 miles from the parking area. This route to Great Notch Trail leads to the complex of trails on Bernard and Mansell mountains, and completes a circuit back to the parking area.

Perpendicular Trail
AMC's Acadia National Park Map: F3
NPS Rating: Strenuous

Distances from Long Pond parking area

to Perpendicular Trail	0.2 mile	5 minutes
to Mansell summit	1.2 miles	1 hour and 10 minutes

This trail up Mansell Mountain leaves left from Long Pond Trail on the western shore of Long Pond, 0.2 mile north of the parking area. It follows a steep course up the east slope of Mansell, crossing a rock slide, passing over stone steps, and climbing a few iron rungs and one iron ladder. The upper portion has an excellent view southeast. At an open ledge near the top, watch for a sign marked, "Path," where an abrupt left turn leads down sharply into woods and marsh before ascending to the actual summit, which is wooded. To make this a loop, take Mansell Mountain Trail south from the summit to Cold Brook Trail (at Gilley Field), which you can follow back to the parking area.

Sluiceway Trail

AMC's Acadia National Park Map: F3

NPS Rating: Strenuous

Distances from Mill Field parking area		
to Great Notch and Gilley trails	0.4 mile	25 minutes
to Bernard Mountain Trail	0.9 mile	50 minutes
to Bernard summit	1.1 miles	1 hour

This trail starts at Mill Field on the Western Mountain fire road. To reach Mill Field, follow Seal Cove Road west from Route 102 in Southwest Harbor. The pavement ends at the Acadia park border. Take the first right off the dirt road, bear right at the first fork, and left at the second fork. The road ends at Mill Field. The trail runs north 0.4 mile to a junction with Great Notch and Gilley trails. At this junction, Sluiceway Trail swings northwest and climbs rather steeply to a junction with Bernard Mountain Trail 0.5 mile farther. To reach Bernard Peak, follow Bernard Mountain Trail left (south) for 0.2 mile.

Bernard Mountain Trail

(formerly South Face Trail)

AMC's Acadia National Park Map: F2

NPS Rating: Strenuous

Distances from Mill Field parking area		
to West Ledge Trail	1 mile	1 hour
to Bernard summit	1.5 miles	1 hour and 20 minutes
to Great Notch	2.2 miles	1 hour and 50 minutes

This trail also starts at Mill Field on the Western Mountain fire road. (For directions to Mill Field, see the Sluiceway Trail description, above.) As do many of the trails on the western mountains, it runs through a magnificent spruce-fir forest and affords fine views of western Mount Desert Island and Blue Hill Bay. It leads west for 1 mile, where West Ledge Trail enters from the left and Bernard Mountain Trail turns right. From here it rises north to Bernard summit at 1.5 miles and reaches a junction with Sluiceway Trail at 1.7 miles. The trail continues straight, passing over Knight Nubble before descending to Great Notch at 2.2 miles.

Razorback Trail

AMC's Acadia National Park Map: F3

NPS Rating: Strenuous

Distances from Gilley Field

to Razorback Trail	0.2 mile	5 minutes
to Mansell Mountain	1.3 miles	50 minutes
to Great Notch	1.1 miles	40 minutes

Razorback Trail leaves from Gilley Trail, which in turn begins at the Gilley Field parking area, at the east end of the Western Mountain fire road. To reach Gilley Field, follow Seal Cove Road west from Route 102 in Southwest Harbor. The pavement ends at the Acadia park border. Take the first right off the dirt road, bear right at the first fork, and right at the second fork. The road ends at Gilley Field. Follow Gilley Trail for 0.2 mile, to where Razorback Trail bears right.

This moderate hike climbs the western side of Mansell, offering views of Great Notch and Bernard Mountain. The trail climbs over ledges and through softwood forest to reach a fork between Mansell and Great Notch at 0.7 mile. The left fork leads 0.2 mile to Great Notch. The right fork leads 0.2 mile to Mansell Mountain Trail, which is 0.2 mile below Mansell Mountain.

Cold Brook Trail

AMC's Acadia National Park Map: F3

NPS Rating: Easy

Distance from Long Pond parking area

to Gilley Field	0.4 mile	15 minutes

This trail is an important link between the parking area at the south end of Long Pond and the western mountains. Running between Long Pond Trail and Gilley Field, it's an easy hike, following the lowlands around Mansell Mountain. It provides access to Mansell Mountain and Gilley trails. More importantly, it is a natural beginning or finish to a circuit hike over both Mansell and Bernard—a lovely woodlands walk.

Mansell Mountain Trail

AMC's Acadia National Park Map: F3

NPS Rating: Moderate

Distances from Gilley Field

to Razorback Trail	0.8 mile	30 minutes
to Mansell summit	1 mile	35 minutes

This trail leaves from Gilley Field, offering a beautiful hike up Mansell Mountain. Gradually climbing from the trailhead, the trail passes through softwood forest.

It continues to climb, reaching ledges with views to the east and south: Southwest Harbor, Beech Mountain, Long Pond, and Northeast Harbor. At 0.8 mile, Razorback Trail enters from the left. From here it's a short walk to the summit of Mansell.

West Ledge Trail

AMC's Acadia National Park Map: F2
NPS Rating: Strenuous

Distances from Western Mountain Road

to Bernard Mountain Trail	1.1 miles	45 minutes
to Bernard summit via Bernard Mountain Trail	1.6 miles	1 hour and 5 minutes

West Ledge Trail connects the west end of Western Mountain Road to the system of trails on Bernard and Mansell mountains. The views to the west of Blue Hill Bay, the Atlantic Ocean, and the islands south and west of Mount Desert Island are spectacular. The trail begins from Western Mountain Road, approximately 0.3 mile east of Seal Cove Pond. This road is closed to cars during winter and early spring. West Ledge Trail begins climbing moderately up the west face of Bernard Mountain, reaching open ledges very quickly. It briefly reenters the woods twice before beginning a very steep climb over open granite ledges. From here, the views stretch from Bass Harbor to the Camden Hills, 30 miles to the west. After entering the woods, at 1.1 miles, the trail ends at its intersection with Bernard Mountain Trail.

Western Mountain Connector

AMC's Acadia National Park Map: F3
NPS Rating: Easy

Distance from Long Pond Road

to Gilley Field	0.8 mile	20 minutes

This wide gravel path connects Long Pond Road, across from Lurvey Spring Road (0.8 mile from Seal Cove Road in Southwest Harbor), to the trails at Gilley Field. During the course of its 0.4 mile, the trail passes a municipal building and a view of the town dump before entering a grove of beautiful spruce. The trail ends at a dirt road that leads right 0.4 mile to Gilley Field.

SEAWALL AREA TRAILS

There are two coastal trails near the Seawall Campground on the western side of Mount Desert Island: Ship Harbor Trail and Wonderland Trail. Both are relatively flat and short but provide access to excellent ocean views, ledges, and tide pools. Part of Ship Harbor Trail was recently renovated and is now accessible to those in wheelchairs.

Wonderland Trail

AMC's Acadia National Park Map: H4

NPS Rating: Easy

Distance from Route 102A parking			
	to Wonderland ledges	0.6 mile	15 minutes

Parking for Wonderland Trail is on the south side of Route 102A, 4.1 miles south of Route 102 in Southwest Harbor. The trail starts out as a wide footpath, with a gravel bed from its days as a fire road. At times the footing gets a little rocky and bumpy, but overall it is a flat and easy walk. At 0.6 mile from the parking area, the first of several side trails leads through the shrubs to the rocky ledges of Wonderland. From the ledges, you can see the Duck Islands to the southeast and Great Cranberry Island to the northeast. This is a good place to bring kids for rocky tide-pool exploration. The trail loops around and in another 0.25 mile rejoins itself, turning right to return to the parking area.

Ship Harbor Trail

AMC's Acadia National Park Map: H4

NPS Rating: Easy

Distances from Route 102A parking			
	to beginning of first loop	0.1 mile	5 minutes
	to beginning of second loop	0.4 mile	15 minutes
	to ocean ledges	0.7 mile	25 minutes
	to return to parking area	1.3 miles	45 minutes

Parking for Ship Harbor Trail is on the south side of Route 102A, 4.4 miles south of Route 102 in Southwest Harbor. Ship Harbor Trail is basically two loops in the form of a figure-eight. The loop closest to the parking area is accessible. From the parking area, the trail enters the woods and reaches the top of the first loop in 0.1 mile. This loop is approximately 0.5 mile in length. The second loop is 0.6 mile in length. Both loops follow the shoreline of Ship Harbor on the west side of the loop and are in the woods on the east side of the loop. The second loop reaches a series of beautiful granite ledges that look out over the Gulf of Maine.

SCHOODIC PENINSULA

Schoodic is best known for its dramatic coastline, primarily accessed via Park Loop Road. There is, however, a low ridge of hills on the eastern side of the peninsula that the National Park Service has recently developed for recreation. The ridge extends from Birch Harbor Mountain near the Schoodic Woods Campground, south for several miles over Buck Cove Mountain and Schoodic Head, then drops back down to sea level at the southern tip of the peninsula at Blueberry Hill. There are few views along this ridge, save for those atop Schoodic Head (440 feet) and the

Anvil, a rocky ledge just south of Schoodic Head. Several trails leave from Park Loop Road and ascend Schoodic Head, and it is now possible to hike to this peak from Schoodic Woods Campground via Buck Cove Mountain Trail.

Buck Cove Mountain Trail
NPS Rating: Moderate

Distances from Schoodic Woods Campground

to final carriage road crossing	1.8 miles	1 hour
to Buck Cove Mountain	2.2 miles	1 hour and 15 minutes
to Schoodic Head Trail overlook	3.2 miles	1 hour and 45 minutes

This trail starts from the parking area adjacent to the group camping area at Schoodic Woods Campground and travels south to Schoodic Head. It heads east, soon crosses a carriage road, then crosses it again as the trail turns to the south. The trial gradually rises and falls through spruce woods on its way to another carriage road crossing, 1 mile from the campground. At 1.2 miles, the trail reaches another carriage road, following it to the right for about 100 yards before reentering the woods on the right. The trail rises and falls through scrub evergreen habitat and rock ledges with blueberries, rhodora, jack pine, and spruce before crossing a carriage road for the last time at 1.8 miles.

The trail makes a gradual ascent to the summit of Buck Cove Mountain (no views) at 2.2 miles. After a short descent, Buck Cove Mountain Trail climbs more steeply to Schoodic Head Trail and an overlook just below the summit of Schoodic Head, at 3.2 miles. From this overlook, there are excellent views to the north and east.

Schoodic Head Trail
NPS Rating: Moderate

Distances from Alder Trail

to Anvil Trail	0.5 mile	15 minutes
to summit and East Trail	0.6 mile	20 minutes
to Buck Cove Mountain Trail	0.7 mile	25 minutes

Schoodic Head Trail begins from a dirt road called Blueberry Hill Road, but most people hike to the trailhead via Alder Trail from the Blueberry Hill parking area on Park Loop Road, which is 4 miles south of the Schoodic Woods Campground.

The trail begins on the north side of Blueberry Hill Road, about 50 yards west of the end of Anvil Trail. It climbs, sometimes steeply, over rocks, roots, and stone steps. It reaches open ledges with obstructed views shortly before reaching an intersection with Anvil Trail (left) in 0.5 mile. The trail flattens out and turns left, passing a spur path that leads left to Schooner Head Road, then reaches the wooded summit and East Trail (right) at 0.6 mile. The trail continues north as it drops down to a scenic overlook with good views north and east at 0.7 mile. Here Buck Cove Mountain Trail leads north to the Schoodic Woods Campground.

Alder Trail

NPS Rating: Easy

Distance from Blueberry Hill parking area			
	to Schoodic Head Trail	0.6 mile	10 minutes

Alder Trail begins across the street from the Blueberry Hill parking area on Park Loop Road, 4 miles south of the Schoodic Woods Campground. The trail is wide, level, and grassy, with only occasional tree roots to challenge hikers. It parallels an alder swamp and spruce forest, ending at Blueberry Hill Road and Schoodic Head Trail at 0.6 mile.

Anvil Trail

NPS Rating: Moderate

Distances from Blueberry Hill parking area			
	to the Anvil	0.3 mile	5 minutes
	to Schoodic Head Trail	0.8 mile	25 minutes

Anvil Trail begins across the street, and to the right, from the Blueberry Hill parking area on Park Loop Road, 4 miles south of the Schoodic Woods Campground. It's a short but steep climb through a spruce forest to a spur path that leads a few yards left to the Anvil, a rock ledge with nice views to the west at 0.3 mile. Continuing straight, the main trail makes a short descent before climbing over rock ledges peppered with jack pine. After a final, steep climb, Anvil Trail ends at Schooner Head Trail, 0.8 mile from the parking area and just south of the Schooner Head summit.

East Trail

NPS Rating: Moderate

Distances from Park Loop Road			
	to Schoodic Head	0.4 mile	20 minutes
	to overlook	0.5 mile	25 minutes

East Trail climbs to Schooner Head from a parking area on the eastern side of Schoodic, about 1 mile past the Blueberry Hill parking area. The steepest of the Schoodic trails, East Trail climbs quickly from Park Loop Road, requiring the occasional scramble, before it reaches the wooded summit of Schoodic Head, 0.4 mile from the parking area. Turn left on Schoodic Head Trail for a 0.1-mile walk to an overlook with views to the north and east.

Lower Harbor Trail
NPS Rating: Easy

Distances from Schoodic Woods Campground

to north end of trail	1.1 miles	40 minutes
to return to campground	2 miles	1 hour

This trail explores the shoreline to the east of the Schoodic Woods Campground. Parking is at the campground, which is on Park Loop Road, 0.9 mile south of Route 186 in Winter Harbor.

The trail enters the woods on the west side of Park Loop Road, opposite the entrance to the campground, and descends moderately for 0.2 mile. Here it reaches the shoreline of a protected cove south of Winter Harbor. The trail turns right and parallels the shoreline about 20 yards from the water. There are several spots along the route with access to the shoreline itself. At 1.1 miles, the trail reaches its northern terminus at Park Loop Road, about 0.6 mile north of the campground entrance. To return to the parking area, cross the road and follow the trail for 0.1 mile to a carriage road, where you can turn right for a 0.8-mile walk back to the parking area.

ISLE AU HAUT

On Isle au Haut, a range of mountains extends for 6 miles, the length of the island. Mount Champlain (543 feet), near the island's north end, is the highest summit. Farther south along the ridge are Rocky Mountain (500 feet), Sawyer Mountain (480 feet), and Jerusalem Mountain (440 feet). Near the island's southwest tip is Duck Harbor Mountain (314 feet).

The island is reached by mail boat from Stonington (45 minutes); make sure to check the schedule locally (Section 5).

About half of the island is within Acadia National Park. The National Park Service maintains a camping area at Duck Harbor, on the southwest side of the island and about 4 miles from Isle au Haut Village. There are five lean-tos (no tentsites), which are available by reservation only. The NPS has established daily limits on the number of people allowed to visit Isle au Haut. For the latest information and reservations, which are available no earlier than April 1 for the following summer, call the park headquarters on Mount Desert Island at 207-288-3338 or write to Acadia National Park, P.O. Box 177, Bar Harbor, ME 04609. You can also find a reservation request form at nps.gov/acad/planyourvisit/duckharbor.htm.

The 12-mile road that runs around the island is partly paved. Some sections, however, are very rough and not recommended for bike riding. The road passes the foot of Long Pond, where there is a place to swim.

Numerous trails offer opportunities to explore wild and rocky shoreline, heavily wooded uplands, marshes, and mountain summits. For current hiking information, write to Acadia National Park at the address above, stop at the park visitor center in Hulls Cove, or pick up a map from the mail-boat operators. From mid-May to mid-October, park rangers will meet the mail boat and provide you with detailed hiking information. Isle au Haut and Schoodic Peninsula are covered at the bottom of the Eastern Mount Desert Island side of the map found in the pocket of this book.

Goat Trail

NPS Rating: Moderate

Distances from main road

to Median Ridge Trail	0.9 mile	30 minutes
to Duck Harbor Mountain Trail	1.8 mile	1 hour
to Western Head Road	2.2 miles	1 hour and 15 minutes

This trail runs from the southern portion of the main road to Western Head Road. It parallels the shoreline and offers spectacular views of Head Harbor, Merchant Cove, Barred Harbor, Squeaker Cove, and Deep Cove.

The trail begins in a marshy lowland and gradually rises to the coastal ridge. After passing through an evergreen forest, the trail emerges onto a rocky beach at 0.6 mile. Shortly thereafter, the trail climbs again and passes the southern terminus of Median Ridge Trail at 0.9 mile. Once again, the trail passes intermittently through both beaches and highlands, offering a variety of perspectives on the island's southern coast.

Cliff Trail

NPS Rating: Moderate

Distances from Western Head Road

to Western Head Trail	0.7 mile	40 minutes
to Western Ear	0.8 mile	45 minutes

This trail leaves from Western Head Road. It offers the shortest possible route to Western Ear, a small island accessible only during low tide. Cliff Trail begins by climbing steeply (50 feet) to the coastal ridge. It then follows the ridge, passing through an evergreen forest. At 0.6 mile, the trail traverses a rocky beach, offering views of Deep Cove and the coast.

Western Head Trail
NPS Rating: Moderate

Distances from Western Head Road

to view of rock outcroppings	0.7 mile	45 minutes
to cliffs	1.2 miles	1 hour
to Cliff Trail	1.6 miles	1 hour and 15 minutes

This trail follows the western shore of Western Head. It offers spectacular views of the ocean and rock outcroppings in Western Bay from ocean-side cliffs. Combined with Cliff Trail, Western Head Trail offers a very nice loop around Western Head. The trailheads are a short walk apart on Western Head Road.

The trail begins in lowlands. At 0.2 mile, it starts to climb gradually to a shoreline ridge. Shortly thereafter, it crosses an active stream. As it continues to ascend through an evergreen forest on a ledge, views of the coast are visible to the west. At 0.4 mile, the trail descends onto a rocky beach. The trail continues along the coast, ascending and descending between ridge and beach.

Duck Harbor Trail
NPS Rating: Moderate

Distances from the park ranger station

to Bowditch Trail	1.5 miles	45 minutes
to town road	1.5 miles	45 minutes
to National Park Service cabin	2.2 miles	1 hour and 10 minutes
to side trail to Deep Cove	2.7 miles	1 hour and 20 minutes
to second town road junction	3 miles	1 hour and 30 minutes
to views of harbor and ocean	3.7 miles	1 hour and 50 minutes
to Duck Harbor	3.9 miles	2 hours

This trail begins at the park ranger station on the north end of the island. As a major connector, this trail offers access to Duck Harbor, Moore's Harbor, Eli Creek, Bowditch Trail, the Nat Merchant Trail, and the Duck Harbor Campground.

Following the marshy lowlands, this trail passes through mature stands of softwoods. At 0.9 mile, a small pond appears to the left. At 1.5 miles, Bowditch Trail bears to the left. Shortly thereafter, another junction with the town road cuts off to the right. The trail crosses a sandy beach at 1.9 miles, offering views of the western coast. At 2.2 miles, a National Park Service cabin is visible. A small side trail with views of Deep Cove bears off to the right at 2.7 miles. After crossing the road, the trail offers outstanding views of the ocean and harbor.

Duck Harbor Mountain Trail
NPS Rating: Strenuous

Distances from Western Head Road

to Duck Harbor summit	0.4 mile	35 minutes
to Goat Trail	1.2 miles	1 hour and 30 minutes

This trail begins on Western Head Road and is one of the most physically challenging trails on Isle au Haut. It climbs over Duck Harbor Mountain, offering terrific views of the harbor, as well as the southern end of the island. The trail begins on rapidly ascending ledges. At 0.2 mile, the trail briefly crests. Then, at 0.3 mile, after a short descent, the trail again ascends steeply. It passes through a mixture of softwood forest and open ledge to the summit of Duck Harbor Mountain. After the summit, this trail continues along the ridge. It goes over the Puddings, offering more views, and descends rapidly through softwood forest and ledges down to a junction with Goat Trail.

Median Ridge Trail
NPS Rating: Moderate

Distances from main road

to south spur and Goat Trail	0.3 mile	25 minutes
to north spur and Nat Merchant Trail	1 mile	45 minutes
to north spur and Long Pond Trail	1.6 miles	1 hour and 30 minutes

This trailhead is located on the main road in the southern part of the island. This trail has two spurs, north and south, from this point: The south spur soon connects at 0.3 mile with Goat Trail by following low marshlands; the north spur quickly ascends to the ridge. At 0.3 mile, a blue blaze marks the park boundary. Median Ridge Trail proper follows the ridge into a Japanese garden, offering views to the east. At 0.7 mile, there are excellent views from a ledge area surrounded by small conifers. The trail then descends into a bog. At 1 mile, it crosses Nat Merchant Trail. The trail continues through marsh, evergreens, and a cedar bog to a junction with Long Pond Trail.

Nat Merchant Trail
NPS Rating: Moderate

Distances from main road

to Median Ridge Trail	0.8 mile	25 minutes
to main road	1.2 miles	45 minutes

Nat Merchant Trail is located on the main road on the western shore of the island. This trail begins by entering low marshlands covered in cedar and pine. It crosses several intermittent streams until it meets with Median Ridge Trail at 0.8 mile. After this junction, the trail begins to climb gradually. It passes over a boulder field and crests at the top of the field, offering fine views. After this ridge, the trail passes through a softwood forest then ends at the main road on the island's eastern side.

Long Pond Trail
NPS Rating: Strenuous

Distances from main road

to Median Ridge Trail	0.4 mile	15 minutes
to old foundation	1.1 miles	35 minutes
to Long Pond via south leg	1.7 miles	55 minutes
to summit and Bowditch Trail via south leg	2.4 miles	1 hour and 30 minutes
to complete the loop	3.2 miles	2 hours

This trailhead is located on the main road on the western portion of the island. While this trail is relatively flat to begin, once on the loop the change of elevation is quite severe. Despite the difficult climb, this trail offers wonderful views of the largest pond on Isle au Haut, not to mention access to the summit of Bowditch Mountain, Bowditch Trail, and Median Ridge Trail. The trail forms a nice loop for a day hike.

Beginning at the road, the trail follows a low, wet area for 0.4 mile, where it meets Median Ridge Trail (entering right) and splits into the two legs of the loop. The southern loop follows along an old streambed for quite some time. At 1.1 miles, the trail passes over the old foundation of a building, follows along a stone wall, and gradually climbs onto a ridge. At 1.7 miles, you will see Long Pond. The trail follows Long Pond north for a short time, bears west, and climbs gradually through evergreens to the summit of Bowditch Mountain. At the summit, Bowditch Trail enters from the right. Long Pond Trail continues straight ahead and returns to the junction with the southern leg of the loop and Median Ridge Trail.

Bowditch Trail

NPS Rating: Moderate

Distances from Duck Harbor Trail

to ledges	1.6 miles	1 hour
to summit and Long Pond Trail	2 miles	1 hour and 30 minutes

This trail runs between Duck Harbor Trail and Median Ridge Trail, offering spectacular views from Bowditch Mountain. Beginning from Duck Harbor Trail, Bowditch Trail follows low marshlands for its first 0.8 mile, where it crosses an active stream and turns onto an old firebreak. After following the firebreak, the trail begins to climb gradually, with wonderful views of the ocean to the west. It continues to climb through a softwood forest over wet ledge for 1.1 miles, where it reaches the summit of Bowditch Mountain. At this point, it connects with Median Ridge Trail.

APPENDIX B
OTHER SUNNY- AND RAINY-DAY ACTIVITIES

Acadia National Park offers so much to do, you could spend years there and never run out of possibilities. This appendix lists idea for filling in the spaces between your hiking, bicycling, and paddling trips.

AIRPLANE/GLIDER RIDES
Nothing helps you get the big picture of Acadia better than seeing it from above. There are two options for getting airborne:

- **Acadia Air Tours:** Bar Harbor Airport, 968 Bar Harbor Road (Route 3), Trenton, ME; 207-288-0703; acadiaairtours.com.

- **Scenic Flights of Acadia:** Bar Harbor Airport, 1044 Bar Harbor Road (Route 3), Trenton, ME; 207-667-6527; mainecoastalflight.com.

BOATS AND FERRIES
Seeing the beauty of Acadia from the water provides you with a unique perspective of the park; plus, boat rides are a great way to see seabirds and marine mammals up close. Ferries can take you to some of the outer islands in the area, each of which has its own culture and scenery apart from Mount Desert Island. See Appendix C for a list of ferries and tour companies.

GUIDED TOURS
Let someone else do the driving. Sit back and enjoy the scenery while you listen to the story of the land. If you've never visited the park before, taking a guided tour is a good introduction to Acadia and Mount Desert Island.

- **Oli's Trolley:** 55 West Street, Bar Harbor, ME; 207-288-9899; acadiaislandtours.com. Go on a historical tour and hear tales of a lost era, the cottage days of Bar Harbor. Also find out about the park's flora and fauna.

- **Acadia National Park Tours** (accessible): Testa's Restaurant, 53 Main Street, Bar Harbor, ME; 207-288-0300; acadiatours.com. Learn about the island's history, flora and fauna, geology, and mansions, and see the major sights.

- **Dawnland Tours:** P.O. Box 522, Bar Harbor, ME 04609; 207-404-4113, barharborghosttours.com. Learn about the history of Bar Harbor. Dawnland is a Wabanaki-owned company, and its tours are designed to bring the past together with the present using stories and traditions from a shared history.

- **Red Cloak Haunted History Tours:** 207-380-3806, redcloakhauntedhistory-tours.com. Stroll along Shore Path, learn about the early history of Bar Harbor, and hear some ghostly tales.

GARDENS

Enjoy a peaceful stroll through lovely gardens.

- **Asticou Azalea Garden:** Asticou Way, Route 3/198, Northeast Harbor, ME; 207-276-3727; gardenpreserve.org. This garden was inspired by Japanese garden design and has been adapted to use many of the natural features and native vegetation of coastal Maine. Enjoy some peace and quiet away from the summer crowds. June is the best time to find the azaleas in bloom.
- **Thuya Garden:** Route 3, Northeast Harbor, ME; 207-276-5130; gardenpreserve.org. This garden is open seven days a week, late June through September. It is an English-style garden featuring 80 percent perennials. The best time to catch everything in bloom is August. It also has hiking trails on 260 acres of land.
- **Wild Gardens of Acadia:** Sieur de Monts, on Park Loop Road, 5.7 miles south of the Hulls Cove Visitor Center, Acadia National Park, ME; 207-288-3338; nps.gov/acad/index.htm. These gardens are perfect for those who want to study the local flora of Acadia. The garden is home to a wide variety of the flowers and foliage typically found in the park, and everything is labeled with common and scientific names.

HORSE-DRAWN-CARRIAGE RIDES

Experience the carriage roads as they were originally intended.

- **Wild Iris Farm:** 2 Lakewood Farm Road, Bar Harbor, ME 04609; 207-288-5234; wildirishorsefarm.com.
- **Wildwood Stables:** Park Loop Road, 0.5 mile south of Jordan Pond House, Acadia National Park, ME; 207-276-3622; acadiahorses.com. An accessible carriage is available.

JORDAN POND HOUSE RESTAURANT

- On Park Loop Road, Acadia National Park, ME; 207-276-3316; acadiajordan-pondhouse.com. One of our favorite things to do is stop in at the Jordan Pond House restaurant for afternoon tea and popovers. The food is delicious, and the scenery is spectacular. Make a reservation, or the wait will be very long.

MUSEUMS

A great way to learn about the island (especially on a rainy day). Most museums are seasonal, so be sure to call ahead for hours.

- **Abbe Museum:** 26 Mount Desert Street, Bar Harbor and Sieur de Monts Spring, Acadia National Park, ME; 207-288-3519; abbemuseum.org. This museum celebrates Maine's American Indian heritage through exhibits, craft workshops, and ongoing archaeological research.

- **Bar Harbor Historical Society:** 33 Ledgelawn Avenue, Bar Harbor, ME; 207-288-0000; barharborhistorical.org. Experience the "lost" Bar Harbor and its famous summer colony through this fine collection of early drawings, hotel memorabilia, photographs, sketches, and pictures of the devastating fire of 1947.

- **Islesford Museum:** Little Cranberry island, ME; 207-244-9224; islesfordhistoricalmuseum.info. This historic maritime museum is part of Acadia National Park. The exhibits portray the lives of the hardy seafaring people of the Cranberry Isles. You need to take a ferry (see Appendix C); call Acadia National Park for information: 207-288-3338.

- **Mount Desert Island Historical Society:** Somesville Museum, 2 Oak Hill Rd, Mount Desert; 207-244-5043; mdihistory.org. Explore Mount Desert Island's history through settlement artifacts, including furniture and household items. Learn about the hotels, shipbuilding, and mills of the island's history. Be sure to visit the first town office by walking over the scenic—and highly photographed—decorative bridge.

- **Mount Desert Island Historical Society:** Somes Sound School House, 373 Sound Drive, 207-276-9323; mdihistory.org. Built in 1892, this building survived as a school until 1926. When you visit, check out the genealogy collection, photo archives, and business records.

- **Mount Desert Oceanarium:** 1351 State Road, Route 3, Bar Harbor, ME; 207-288-5005; theoceanarium.com. The Oceanarium offers everything you want to know about lobsters, including a museum, a lobster hatchery, and educational programs about lobsters, lobster fishing, and harbor seals that eat lobsters. The touch tank is fantastic, and the staff is very knowledgeable.

- **Wendell Gilley Museum:** 4 Herrick Road, Southwest Harbor, ME; 207-244-7555; wendellgilleymuseum.org. This museum features wooden bird carvings made by Wendell Gilley, a famous native Maine carver. It also has wildlife art exhibits and natural-history video programs.

NATURE TOURS

- **Down East Nature Tours:** 150 Knox Road, Bar Harbor, ME; 207-288-8128; downeastnaturetours.com. Explore the natural beauty of the park with qualified naturalists and biologists. Get a personalized, one-on-one tour led by a guide. Down East's specialty is native birds. Call in advance to make reservations.

PHOTOGRAPHY

Of course you can aim your camera practically anywhere and get a nice photo, but for some special tips and free advice, contact the National Park Service and hook up with their photography tours, 207-288-8832. Always a good resource, if we do say so ourselves: *AMC Guide to Outdoor Digital Photography* (AMC Books, 2011; amcstore.outdoors.org).

PICNICS

Places to picnic are limited only by your imagination. If you like traditional sites, complete with tables and restrooms, try these:

- **Bear Brook:** Park Loop Road between the visitor center and Champlain Mountain (accessible).
- **Fabbri:** Park Loop Road just after Otter Cliffs (accessible).
- **Frazer Point:** Schoodic Peninsula.
- **Pretty Marsh:** On Route 102 between Pretty Marsh and Seal Cove.
- **Seawall:** Across Route 102A from the Seawall Campground (accessible).
- **Thompson Island:** Route 3 just before Mount Desert Island (accessible).

RANGER PROGRAMS

The National Park Service has programs on just about everything. There are ranger programs for hikers, as well as programs conducted on boats, on buses, and in the campground amphitheaters and other special areas, such as peregrine watching at the base of Champlain Mountain. Ask at the visitor center for a complete list of programs available during your stay, call 207-288-3338, or search at nps.gov/acad.

ROCK CLIMBING

While Acadia is not one of the East's premier rock-climbing destinations, the glaciers did leave behind some wonderful climbing at Otter Cliffs, Champlain Mountain, and South Bubble. For information about climbing routes or to explore these climbs safely by hiring a guide, contact:

- **Acadia Mountain Guides Climbing School:** 228 Main Street, Bar Harbor, ME; 207-288-8186; acadiamountainguides.com.

- **Atlantic Climbing School:** 67 Main Street, 2nd Floor, Bar Harbor, ME; 207-288-2521; climbacadia.com.

SNOWSHOEING OR CROSS-COUNTRY SKIING/WINTER HIKING

On those rare occasions when the coast gets hit with a big snow, the carriage roads are a fantastic place to get into the backcountry. Use this book's biking chapter (Section 2) as a guide for snowshoeing or cross-country skiing.

Only experienced winter hikers should try to use the hiking trails in winter, since the steep routes often require crampon use. When planning a hike, remember Park Loop Road is closed in winter, except for the Ocean Drive portion and the access to Jordan Pond from Seal Harbor.

SWIMMING

On a hot summer day, nothing will cool you off faster than jumping into refreshing Maine waters. There are only two places to swim in Acadia: Echo Lake Beach and Sand Beach. By July, the water at Echo Lake Beach, at the south end of Echo Lake, is considerably warmer than the cold waters of the Atlantic, which rarely get warmer than 55 degrees. Most of the lakes and ponds on Mount Desert Island are used as public water supplies, so please respect the no-swimming rules.

THEATERS

- **Acadia Repertory Theatre:** Take in live, professional theater. 1154 Main Street, Mount Desert, ME; 207-244-7260; acadiarep.com.

- **Criterion Theatre and Arts Center:** Catch films and live events. 35 Cottage Street, Bar Harbor, ME; 207-288-3441; criteriontheatre.org.

- **Reel Pizza:** Enjoy a pizza while you watch the movie. Top of Rodick Street, Bar Harbor, ME; 207-288-3811; reelpizza.net.

WHALE WATCHING

If you have never gone on a whale watch before, Acadia is a fantastic place to give it a try. Sighting whales is so common that all of the tour operators guarantee you will see at least one—or your money back or a free ride on another trip. See Appendix C for a list of whale-watch tours.

APPENDIX C
BOAT TRIPS

Bar Harbor Whale Watch Co.
Nature and sightseeing, whale and seal watching, lighthouse tours, lobster fishing
207-288-2386, barharborwhales.com
Leaves from: 1 West Street, Bar Harbor

Bass Harbor Island Cruises
Frenchboro, Bass Harbor Head Light, and sailboat tours
207-244-5785, bassharborcruises.com
Leaves from: Bass Harbor

Beal & Bunker Mail Boat Ferry
Ferry to the Cranberry Isles
207-244-3575, cranberryisles.com
Leaves from: Northeast Harbor. Runs all year.

Cranberry Cove Boating Co.
Ferry to the Cranberry Isles
207-244-5882, cranberryisles.com
Leaves from: Southwest Harbor

Delight Water Taxi
Custom rides and tours
207-244-5724, cranberryisles.com
Leaves from: College of the Atlantic, 105 Eden Street, Bar Harbor

Diver Ed Dive-in Theater
Frenchman Bay, with a video tour of the ocean floor in real time
207-288-DIVE, divered.com
Leaves from: College of the Atlantic, 105 Eden Street, Bar Harbor

Down East Friendship Sloop Charters
Lobster boat and sailing cruises
207-266-5210, sailacadia.com
Leaves from: Southwest Harbor and Northeast Harbor

Down East Sailing Adventures
Sailing, lobster fishing, and custom tours
207-288-2216, downeastsail.com
Leaves from: Southwest Harbor

Down East Windjammer

Windjammer cruises on the Margaret Todd and Bailey Louise Todd, Lobster Sloop, Winter Harbor Ferry, Cranberry Cove Ferry
207-288-4585, downeastwindjammer.com
Leaves from: Bar Harbor Pier

Frenchman Bay Research Boating

Ferry to Schoodic, Winter Harbor
207-801-9444, frenchmanbayresearchboating.org
Leaves from: College of the Atlantic, 105 Eden Street, Bar Harbor

Isle Au Haut Co.

Ferry to Isle Au Haut, lighthouse tours, puffin tours, lobster fishing tours
207-367-5193, isleauhaut.com
Leaves from: Stonington. Runs all year.

LuLu Lobster Boat Ride

Lobster fishing, seal watching, and sightseeing
207-963-2341, lululobsterboat.com
Leaves from: 55 West Street, Bar Harbor

Sea Princess Cruises

Scenic nature cruises with a National Park Service naturalist
207-276-5352, barharborcruises.com
Leaves from: Northeast Harbor

Sea Venture Custom Boat Tours

Custom rides and tours
207-288-3355, svboattours.com
Leaves from: Atlantic Oceanside Hotel, 119 Eden Street, Bar Harbor

Swan's Island Ferry

Year-round crossing between Bass Harbor and Swan's Island
207-244-3254, maine.gov/mdot/ferry/swansisland/
Leaves from: Bass Harbor. Runs all year.

APPENDIX D

OUTFITTERS

Name, address	Website, phone	Season
Acadia Bike 48 Cottage Street, Bar Harbor	acadiabike.com 800-526-8615	May–Oct
Acadia 1 Watersports 1564 Shore Road, Lamoine	barharborguideservice .bravehost.com/ 888-786-0676	June–Sept
Acadia Outfitters 106 Cottage Street, Bar Harbor	acadiaoutfitters.com 207-288-8118	June–Oct
Acadia Stand Up Paddleboarding 200 Main Street, Bar Harbor	acadiasup.com 207-610-2970	June–Oct
Aquaterra Adventures 1 West Street, Bar Harbor	aquaterra-adventures.com 877-386-4124	May–Sept
Bar Harbor Bicycle Shop 141 Cottage Street, Bar Harbor	barharborbike.com 207-288-3886	Year-round
Cadillac Mountain Sports 26 Cottage Street, Bar Harbor	cadillacsports.com 207-288-4532	Year-round
Coastal Kayaking Tours 48 Cottage Street, Bar Harbor	acadiafun.com 207-288-9605	Year-round
Maine State Sea Kayak 254 Main Street, Southwest Harbor	mainestateseakayak.com 207-244-9500	May–Sept
National Park Canoe & Kayak 145 Pretty Marsh Road, Mount Desert Island	nationalparkcanoerental.com 207-244-5854	May–Oct
National Park Sea Kayak Tours 39 Cottage Street, Bar Harbor	acadiakayak.com 800-347-0940	May–Sept
Seascape Kayak & Bike 8 Duck Pond Road, Winter Harbor	seascapekayaking.com 207-963-5806	May–Sept
Southwest Cycle 370 Main Street, Southwest Harbor	southwestcycle.com 207-244-5856	Year-round

Bicycle rentals	Bicycle tours	Kayak rentals	Kayak tours	Canoe rentals	Other
🚲	🚲				
		🛶			
🚲		🛶	🛶		Scooters
					Stand-up paddleboards
			🛶		
🚲					
					Bike and kayak rentals out of Ellsworth
		🛶	🛶		
			🛶		
		🛶		🛶	
			🛶		
🚲		🛶			
🚲					

APPENDIX E
CONSERVATION AND RECREATION ORGANIZATIONS

American Oceans Campaign: 202-833-3900; oceana.org

Appalachian Mountain Club: 617-523-0655; outdoors.org

Frenchman Bay Conservancy: 207-422-2328; frenchmanbay.org

Friends of Acadia: 207-288-3340; friendsofacadia.org

Island Institute: 207-594-9209; islandinstitute.org

Leave No Trace: 303-442-8222; lnt.org

Maine Audubon Society: 207-781-2330; maineaudubon.org

Maine Coast Heritage Trust: 207-729-7366; mcht.org

Maine Island Trail Association: 207-761-8225; mita.org

National Park Conservation Association: 800-628-7275, npca.org

Natural Resources Council of Maine: 800-287-2345; nrcm.org

The Nature Conservancy: 207-729-5182; nature.org

Sierra Club, Maine Chapter: 207-761-5616; maine.sierraclub.org

The Trust for Public Land: 207-772-7424; tpl.org

APPENDIX F
RECOMMENDED READING

Appalachian Mountain Club. *Maine Mountain Guide, 9th edition.* Boston: AMC Books, 2005.

Blagden, Thomas. *First Light.* Boulder, Colo.: Westcliffe Publishing, 2003.

Daugherty, Michael. *AMC's Best Sea Kayaking in New England.* Boston: AMC Books, 2016.

Grierson, Ruth Gortner. *Wildlife Watcher's Guide: Acadia National Park.* Boulder, Colo.: NorthWord Press, 1995.

Hill, Ruth Ann. *Discovering Old Bar Harbor and Acadia National Park.* Camden, Maine: Down East Books, 1996.

Kish, Carey. *Maine Mountain Guide, Tenth Edition.* Boston: AMC Books, 2012.

Monkman, Jerry, and Marcy Monkman. *A Photographer's Guide to Acadia National Park.* Woodstock, Vt.: Countryman Press, 2010.

Monkman, Jerry. *AMC Guide to Outdoor Digital Photography.* Boston: AMC Books, 2011.

Monkman, Jerry, and Marcy Monkman. *Wild Acadia.* Lebanon, N.H.: University Press of New England, 2007.

Paigen, Jennifer Alisa. *The Sea Kayaker's Guide to Mount Desert Island.* Camden, Maine: Down East Books, 1997.

Roberts, Ann Rockefeller. *Mr. Rockefeller's Roads: The Untold Story of Acadia's Carriage Roads & Their Creator.* Camden, Maine: Down East Books, 1990.

St. Germain, Tom, and Jay Saunders. *Trails of History: The Story of Mount Desert Island's Paths from Norumbega to Acadia.* Bar Harbor, Maine: Parkman Publications, 1993.

Thayer, Robert A. *The Park Loop Road: A Guide to Acadia National Park's Scenic Byway.* Bar Harbor, Maine: Down East Books, 1999.

Wilson, Alex, and John Hayes. *Quiet Water: Maine, Third Edition.* Boston: AMC Books, 2017

INDEX

P

paddling trips. *See quietwater paddling; sea kayaking trips*
    canoe/kayak rentals, 256–257
Paradise Hill, xii–xiii, 81–83
Park Loop Road, 124
Parkman Mountain, x–xii, 49–51
Parkman Mountain Trail, 50, 225
peat bogs, 80
Pemetic East Cliff Trail, 38, 216
Pemetic Mountain, x–xi, xii–xiii, 37–39, 62–65
    trails close to, 215–219
Pemetic North Ridge Trail, 37–38, 63–65, 216
Pemetic Northwest Trail, 38, 217
Pemetic South Ridge Trail, 38, 65, 216
Penobscot Mountain, x–xi, 43–45
    trails close to, 219–225
Penobscot Mountain Trail, 44–45, 220
peregrine falcons, 36
Perpendicular Trail, 46–48, 236
picnics, recommended locations, 252
pitch pines, 58
Porcupine Islands, xiv–xv, 165–168
porpoises, 163–164
Precipice Trail, 33–34, 194
Pretty Marsh, xiv–xv, 178–180
public transportation
    biking trips accessible by, 76–77, 90–92, 93–95, 96–97, 98–100, 103–104, 107–109,
        115–117, 118–121, 122–124
    hikes accessible by, 6–7, 10–12, 13–15, 17–19, 20–22, 23–25, 30–32, 37–39, 40–42,
        43–45, 49–51, 52–54, 56–58, 59–61, 62–65, 66–69
    See also Island Explorer Bus System

Q

quietwater paddling, 127–155
    canoe rental, 153, 256–257
    easy trips, 130–131, 134–135, 137–138, 139–141, 142–143
    moderate trips, 146–148, 149–150
    safety and etiquette, 127–129
    strenuous trips, 153–154
    trip planning, xiv–xv, 127–129

R

ranger programs, 252
Razorback Trail, 238
recommended reading, 259

ABOUT THE AUTHORS

Known for their conservation work in New England's wild places, Jerry and Marcy Monkman have spent the last twenty years artfully documenting the mountains, forests, and coastlines that define the region. The authors of ten books, including four AMC guides, their work has appeared in publications worldwide, and their client list includes *National Geographic Adventure, Audubon, Men's Journal, Outdoor Photographer*, L.L. Bean, The Trust for Public Land, and The Nature Conservancy. Jerry's book *AMC Guide to Outdoor Digital Photography* received a 2012 National Outdoor Book Award. Jerry and Marcy live in Portsmouth, New Hampshire, with their daughter, Acadia, and their son, Quinn.

AMC IN MAINE

AMC's Maine Chapter offers a wide variety of hiking, backpacking, climbing, paddling, and skiing trips each year, as well as social and young member programs and instructional workshops. The chapter also offers trail volunteer opportunities. To view a list AMC activities in Maine and other parts of the Northeast, visit activities.outdoors.org.

AMC also is engaged in the Maine Woods Initiative, a conservation effort with a goal of protecting 100,000 acres of forestland in the 100-Mile Wilderness region. The initiative is an innovative approach to conservation that combines outdoor recreation, resource protection, sustainable forestry, and community partnerships. The strategy represents the most significant investment in conservation and recreation in AMC's history. The public is welcome to hike paddle, snowshoe, and ski on AMC's 66,000 acres of conservation and recreation land, which includes a growing trail network and AMC's Maine Wilderness Lodges. For more information about this effort and how to support it, visit outdoors.org/mwi.

AMC BOOK UPDATES

AMC Books strives to keep our guidebooks as up-to-date as possible to help you plan safe and enjoyable adventures. If, after publishing a book, we learn trails have been relocated or route or contact information has changed, we will post the updated information online. Before you hit the trail, check for updates at outdoors. org/publications/books/updates. If you notice discrepancies in the descriptions or maps while hiking or paddling, or if you find other errors in the book, please let us know by submitting them to amcbookupdates@outdoors.org or in writing to Books Editor, c/o AMC, 5 Joy Street, Boston, MA 02108. We will verify all submissions and post key updates each month. AMC Books is dedicated to being a recognized leader in outdoor publishing.

Thank you for your participation.

APPALACHIAN MOUNTAIN CLUB

At AMC, connecting you to the freedom and exhilaration of the outdoors is our calling. We help people of all ages and abilities to explore and develop a deep appreciation of the natural world.

AMC helps you get outdoors on your own, with family and friends, and through activities close to home and beyond. With chapters from Maine to Washington, D.C., including groups in Boston, New York City, and Philadelphia, you can enjoy activities like hiking, paddling, cycling, and skiing, and learn new outdoor skills. We offer advice, guidebooks, maps, and unique lodges and huts to inspire your next outing. You will also have the opportunity to support conservation advocacy and research, youth programming, and caring for 1,800 miles of trails.

We invite you to join us in the outdoors.

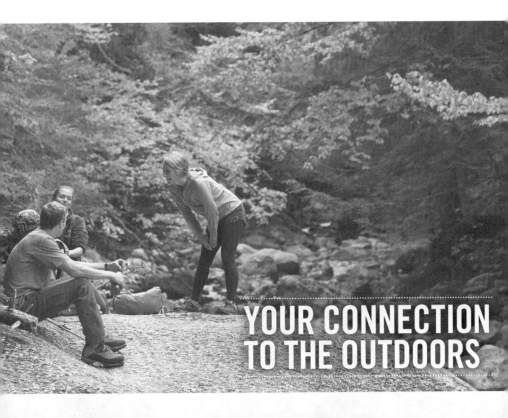

YOUR CONNECTION TO THE OUTDOORS